'temples ... worthy
of His presence':
the early publications of the
Cambridge Camden
Society

The Ecclesiological Society is the society for those who love churches. It was founded in 1879 and today has a growing membership, and is active in organizing visits, lectures and conferences. It publishes a periodical three times a year, and monographs on particular aspects of churches and their use.

The emphasis is on scholarship, discussion and informed debate. There is no party view. Membership is open to all with an interest in churches and their use, whether expert or beginner. The Society can be contacted at www.ecclsoc.org or at the address on the reverse of the title page.

"'temples ... worthy of His presence'": the early publications of the Cambridge Camden Society

the complete texts of eight important pamphlets published between 1839 and 1843 with a critical analysis

Edited by

Christopher Webster

Spire Books Ltd
in association with the
Ecclesiological Society

Published by
Spire Books Ltd
PO Box 2336
Reading RG4 5WJ
www.spirebooks.com

in association with

The Ecclesiological Society
c/o Society of Antiquaries
Burlington House
Piccadilly, London W1V 0HS
www.ecclsoc.org

CIP data:
A catalogue record for this book is available
from the British Library
ISBN 0 9543615 2 0

Designed and produced by John Elliott
Text set in Adobe Bembo

Printed by Alden Group Ltd
Osney Mead
Oxford OX2 0EF

Cover photograph:
E. M. Leach, 'Church Interior', 1906. Watercolour painting of the chancel of an unidentified church, showing what would have been regarded as an ideal Camdenian-inspired arrangement and decorative scheme.

Back:
St Mary, Whitby, North Yorkshire. The interior is the result of various late-Georgian alterations, and is a rare survival of a church interior untouched by Camdenian innovations (*Courtesy of the rector and churchwardens of St Mary's, Whitby*).

Somers Town Chapel, London, W. and H. Inwood, 1824-7. This clearly illustrates the gulf that had arisen by the late-Georgian period between medieval and modern Gothic. Despite the architects' use of obviously Gothic motifs such as pointed arches or buttresses, the building could never be mistaken for the product of the Middle Ages. Its main facade clearly bears no relationship to the roof-line behind it and this, together with the arrangement of the three doors, suggests a 'Commissioners' preaching box'. For the Camdenians, it was not enough for a church to be nominally Gothic, but its style, plan, details and internal arrangements had to be in accord with those of the pre-Reformation period.

For Susan
Like Pugin, the editor also has
'got a first-rate Gothic woman at last'.

Contents

1. All Saints, Margaret Street, London, William Butterfield, 1849–59. The engraving appeared in the *Builder* of 4 June 1859. In many ways, this was the Ecclesiologists' model church and is in obvious contrast to the probably fictitious building shown in plate 2.

Foreword

J. M. Crook has claimed that '[by 1867] the triumph of ecclesiology was incontestable … a group of Cambridge undergraduates had succeeded in transforming the appearance of *every Anglican church in the world*.'[1] (editor's italics). It might be argued that the 'triumph' should be given a somewhat later date, but few would disagree with the substance of Crook's point: a world-wide revolution in the way in which an Anglican church was conceived had been achieved. However, it was not just the extent of the changes in church planning and liturgical thinking that was of almost staggering proportions, but the means by which

2. Circle of Thomas Rowlandson, 'A Church Service', *c.*1800. The lithograph illustrates many of the features of churches and services that the Cambridge Camden Society wished to change: the absence of any obvious orientation of the church towards the altar and chancel; the large three-decker pulpit; galleries and private pews; the poor having to sit on crude benches or stand; an apparently anarchic choir and band; an atmosphere for the service lacking piety.

3. All Saints, Dewsbury, West Yorkshire, from a mid-nineteenth century lithograph. Fragments of the Anglo-Saxon minster survive in a fabric rebuilt to form what must have been an impressive medieval church. However, like most pre-Reformation structures, it was altered in the eighteenth and early nineteenth centuries including the introduction of galleries and box pews, an immense pulpit and sounding board, debased window tracery to replace the decayed original, a Baroque reredos, hatchments and monuments. The result is a typical example of a medieval fabric adapted, piecemeal, for Georgian worship and, subsequently, one deemed ripe for a Camdenian 'restoration'.

the revolution had been brought about was also remarkable. The new ideas were developed, circulated and debated via a series of pamphlets that were printed cheaply, sold for only 3d or 6d and circulated widely.[2] Some were intended for those with wealth and obvious influence, but equally important were those aimed at the ordinary 'man in the pew'. It was through these modest documents – here reprinted for the first time – that the appropriate setting for an Anglican service was re-defined. And despite various subsequent initiatives concerning liturgical re-assessment, for many at the beginning of the 21st century, the concept of 'a church such as it ought to be',[3] conforms precisely with the model conceived by the Cambridge Camden Society more than a century and a half ago: Gothic in style;

4. St Philip, Birmingham (now the Cathedral), Thomas Archer, 1710-15, from a lithograph of c.1820. There is much here for Camdenian censure beyond the obvious classical - 'pagan' - style: the pulpit is placed directly in front of the altar, the free seats are tightly packed down the central aisle and extra benches are provided for the poor - seen here in the foreground - where they cannot see, and probably cannot hear, the service. In 1883-4, a chancel was added by J. A. Chatwin indicating, arguably, that no church, no matter how far removed it was originally from the Camdenian ideal, was beyond the Society's reforming zeal.

a long chancel with the altar raised on steps; stained glass windows; a surpliced choir placed in the chancel; the congregation occupying uniform, east-facing benches. The writers of these pamphlets claimed historical precedent for these initiatives, but the model they sought to promote was, in many ways, an early-Victorian invention.

Although often quoted in works dealing with architectural or ecclesiastical history, original copies of the Cambridge Camden Society's publications are almost impossible to purchase, and are available for consultation in only a very small number of specialist libraries. They have never been reproduced, although the material they contain is central to any comprehensive understanding of the period's religious and architectural attitudes.

The present collection makes available in full a selection of the Society's early publications, chosen to present a set of documents that reveal both the scope of its interests, opinions and ambitions, and at the same time allow the reader to savour the language and tone of its proselytizing.

The book also brings together a number of images to illustrate the now largely forgotton world – 'forgotten', to a considerable extent, as a result of Camdenian successes – of the Georgian service and church interior.

Christopher Webster
Barwick in Elmet, Leeds
October 2002

Notes

[1] J. M. Crook, *The Dilemma of Style* (John Murray, London, 1987), p. 63.
[2] The *Ecclesiologist* reinforced some of this material, but while this journal was distributed to members, a relatively small group and one already committed to the Camdenian cause, the significance of the documents reprinted here is that they reached a much wider audience.
[3] Cambridge Camden Society, *A Few Words to Church Builders* (University Press, Cambridge, 1841), p. 4.

Introduction

The Cambridge Camden Society came into existence, inauspiciously, in 1839, as an earnest undergraduate club for members of the University. In an age when the architecture of the Middle Ages was becoming an increasingly popular subject for both academic study and popular enjoyment, the Society's object – 'to promote the study of Ecclesiastical Architecture and Antiquities, and the restoration of mutilated Architectural remains'[1] – seemed innocent and unremarkable. However, as soon became clear, there was a much more subversive High Church agenda to be followed. If the doctrines of the Oxford Movement were to be fully implemented, its supporters needed to look beyond theology: a new approach to the liturgy and the design of churches as a necessary concomitant. The Camdenian response, according to Chris Brooks, 'was a compound of dogmatic theology gleaned from the Tractarians and dogmatic architectural theory gleaned from

5. Rievaulx Abbey, North Yorkshire, engraving by H. Warren, *c.*1840. The print successfully captures the picturesque qualities to be found in medieval ruins in the mid-nineteenth century, and the growing interest in their exploration.

Pugin.'[2] In practical terms, this meant a return to the style, plan and arrangement of pre- and immediately post-Reformation churches. Thus, surviving medieval ones needed to be cared for sympathetically and new ones needed to be built on the same principles. Fundamental to this prescription was that there was no place for the architectural and liturgical innovations of the previous three centuries, epitomised in the Camdenian manifesto by the despised Georgian preaching box. Under the pervasive influence of the Society, words such as 'contemptible'[3], 'wretched'[4], 'depraved'[5] and 'abominable'[6] soon became the common epithets in any discussion of a church, or addition to a church, dating from the Georgian period.

The principal weapon in the crusade was the printed word and, within months of its inception, the Society was prolific in its production of pamphlets, reports and, most famously, its polemical journal, the *Ecclesiologist*, which first appeared in 1841.

The various published accounts of the Gothic Revival have, rightly, examined in detail the crucial role played by writers – in addition to architects – as the movement repositioned itself in the 120 years from *c.*1750, moving slowly from the stylistic periphery to the centre.[7] There was, then, nothing remarkable about the Society promoting its ideas about medieval architecture through print; what was unprecedented was the approach it took to the subject.

For a subject constantly in the shadow of its more prestigious – and much more thoroughly researched – relative, the Classical tradition in architecture, there was much ground to make up.[8] There were important gaps – some quite basic – to be filled and late-Georgian books about Gothic approached the subject from a number of standpoints. Some, like the numerous works published by John Britton, were essentially topographical and historical, for instance his *Architectural Antiquities of Great Britain*, which appeared in five volumes between 1807 and 1826. Britton's books were noted for their high-quality illustrations of medieval buildings including perspective views, plans and elevations. More contentious were the writers who attempted to provide an appropriate nomenclature for the various phases of the 'pointed' style: for instance, Rev. John Milner in his *A Treatise on the Ecclesiastical Architecture of England During the Middle Ages,* of 1811; Thomas Kerrick in

6. Peterborough Cathedral, view across the south transept, looking south-east. From John Britton, *The History and Antiquities of the Abbey, and Cathedral Church of Peterborough* (1828).

his 'Some Observations on the Gothic Buildings abroad, particularly those of Italy, and on Gothic Architecture in General', which appeared in the journal *Archaeologia* in 1809; and, most enduringly, Thomas Rickman's *Attempt to Discriminate the Styles of English Architecture, from the Conquest to the Reformation; Preceded by a sketch of the Grecian and Roman Orders, with Notices of Nearly Five Hundred Buildings,* first published in 1817.

Theories about the origin of the Gothic style and its location also generated much printed material. Although there had earlier been support for the idea that Gothic had originated in England, by the beginning of the 19th century this chauvinism was giving way to the more accurate conclusion of Continental origin, for instance in the Rev. G. D. Whittington's *An Historical Survey of the Ecclesiastical Antiquities of France with a view to illustrate the Rise and Progress of Gothic Architecture in Europe,* of 1809; Milner's *Treatise…*(already quoted); or Thomas Hope's *An Historical Essay on Architecture,* published posthumously in 1835.[9] The pages of *Archaeologia* carried a succession of scholarly articles in which Gothic was examined with scientific exactitude and this tradition of impeccable archaeological scholarship was carried on by two Cambridge academics, William Whewell in his *Architectural Notes on German Churches, with Remarks on the Origin of Gothic Architecture,* of 1830, and Robert Willis in his *Remarks on the Architecture of the Middle Ages, especially of Italy,* published in 1835, and especially in his remarkable 'On the Construction of the Vaults of the Middle Ages', first published in 1842,[10] and most generously praised by Pevsner.[11] At the other end of the academic spectrum were volumes like Walter Scott's *The Border Antiquities of England and Scotland Comprising*

Opposite: 7. 'Turret', plate 89 from J. H. Parker, *A Glossary of Terms used in Grecian, Roman, Italian and Gothic Architecture* (third edition, 1840).

TEWKESBURY CHURCH, c. 1150

GLASTONBURY ABBEY, c. 1200

CHAPEL (OF ST. NICHOLAS?) GLASTONBURY,
c. 1250

ST. MARY'S CHURCH, BEVERLEY
c. 1440

Specimens of Architecture and Sculpture and other Vestiges of Former Ages Accompanied by Descriptions, Together with Illustrations of Remarkable Incidents in Border History and Traditions, and Original Poetry, which appeared in 1814. The two halves of the title appropriately suggest Scott's idiosyncratic, but highly popular, Romantic blend of archaeology, folklore and the historical novel. A. W. N. Pugin developed an original and highly persuasive *genre* that assessed architectural worth not from an aesthetic but a moral standpoint, exemplified by *Contrasts* of 1836.

For the professional architect, eager to find reliable illustrations of the 'new' and increasingly fashionable style, Britton's works were indispensable, and later on J. H. Parker's *A Glossary of Terms used in Grecian, Roman, Italian and Gothic Architecture,* first published in 1836 with 700 illustrations, almost all of which show Gothic details, or Matthew H. Bloxam's *The Principles of Gothic Ecclesiastical Architecture,* the first edition of which is dated 1829, with over 220 fine woodcut illustrations, did much to supplement what was likely to have been a basically Classical architectural education if, indeed, there had been any sort of systematic education at all.

Despite this earlier range of methodological approaches, in one very important respect the early publications of the Cambridge Camden Society took the available literature of the Gothic Revival in new directions: the study of Gothic architecture was no longer to be approached largely from an academic, antiquarian or architectural standpoint but from those of worship and liturgy. This distinction led to several subsidiary methodological innovations and underpinning the message of the Society's publications were three beliefs. Firstly, that Gothic was an essential aspect of Anglicanism's Catholic heritage. Secondly, that the study of the medieval Gothic heritage was not only necessary for those wishing to design new churches, restore old ones or maintain existing

8. The Chapel of the Philanthropic Society, Southwark, London, from Rudolph Ackermann's *The Microcosm of London* (Ackermann, London, 1808-10). Prints such as this offer a fascinating record of late-Georgian services in progress. Despite the Gothic style of the building, designed by James Peacock and erected in 1803-6, its form is quite unlike a medieval church. Indeed, according to Camdenian orthodoxy, such buildings did not warrant the title 'church' at all, but were dismissed as merely 'preaching rooms or meeting houses'.

ones, but that those undertaking such study – at no matter how rudimentary a level – could not fail to be moved by it to a point where conversion to the Camdenian viewpoint would become axiomatic. Thirdly, the campaign was open to all; while education in, and the study of the Gothic past had, it is true, been moving in a more populist direction for some time, the Society was instrumental in promoting an understanding of the principles and ingredients of ecclesiastical Gothic, complete with all its liturgical significance, not simply to a less academic readership but even to the level of the humble building labourer or sexton.

Undoubtedly, the most well known aspect of the Society's numerous publicising initiatives was its journal, the *Ecclesiologist*. This was intended for distribution to its members, predominantly graduates of Cambridge

University, and its tone reflects the academic and theological interests of this constituency. Discussion of it forms an almost obligatory milestone in published histories of the Gothic Revival; Georg Germann goes so far as to refer to it as 'one of the most important organs of the new "Gothic movement"'.[12] Perhaps somewhat surprisingly then, much less attention has been paid by these writers to the Society's other publishing activities, a significant selection of which are included here. Their neglect may be explained by their scarcity.

The present volume opens with the Society's *Rules* and the first *Annual Report,* which outline the society's aims and early days, and which may be seen as 'introductory material'. As such, they are essential components for a compendium such as this. The rest of the material in this volume is linked by the common theme of advice for those engaged in the building, restoration or maintenance of churches. But this advice, termed somewhat disarmingly 'hints' or 'a few words' – 'commandments'[13] might have been a more appropriate noun given the writers' uncompromising opinions – is not simply practical assistance of an objective kind. Ubiquitously and, to the early-21st century mind at least, without much subtlety, is to be found the Camdenian mantra that Gothic is not simply a topic for historical enquiry, but is a living subject of central importance to every practising member of the Church of England. It is a mark of the Society's well-orchestrated war machine that it was comprehensive in the fronts on which it sought to generate support; when the pamphlets reprinted in this volume are seen together with the material that appeared in the *Ecclesiologist*, the Society was providing something for everyone, from Archbishops to humble sextons. As Archdeacon Thorp points out in his first *Address,*[14] 'restoration' for Anglicans should have both physical and spiritual resonance. Similarly, when the

Ecclesiologist stated that 'A thorough Catholic restoration' is a duty to be fulfilled 'fearlessly',[15] the wording was both ambiguous and comprehensive. Everyone had a part to play. Those with wealth and influence were encouraged to help fund restoration or new building in the approved way – 'the noblest [work] perhaps in which man can engage'[16] – but even those charged with keeping churches and church yards tidy – those near the bottom of the social ladder – had their part to play, for how could congregations be receptive to the 'new' spirituality inherent in Tractarian thinking if they failed to treat God's house with respect and keep it decently?

The items in this volume are not explicitly concerned

9. 'The Altar Decorated', a Victorian caricature of an unrestored and unrevitalised church, highlighting the lack of reverence shown to the chancel. Note the hat and umbrella casually laid on the altar, the sweeping brush left in the corner, the stove and extensive pipe placed without thought for the ancient fabric, the clumsy modern glazing in the east window. *(Geoff Brandwood collection)*

with liturgical or theological reform – although there are occasional nods in that direction – but with the much more modest aim of setting out and encouraging basic principles which those charged with the building, repair or cleaning of churches should follow. Perhaps the absence of erudite theological debate is to be expected; as the *Laws* make clear, the Society's stated aim is merely antiquarian. Although the Society was to be charged with seeking to move the Church of England in a more 'Roman' direction, it was always careful to avoid any public statements which its critics could use against it. Anyway, members of the Oxford

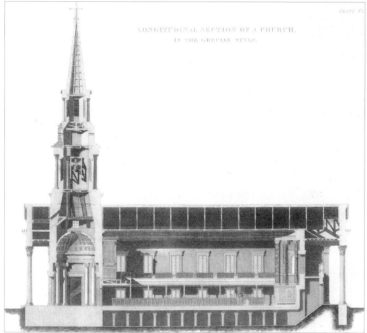

10, 11 & 12. Above & opposite: 'A Church in the Grecian Style', plates 16, 17 and 20 from P. Nicholson, *The New Practical Builder and Workman's Companion*, (1823-5). Designs such as this are typical of many of the urban churches erected in middle class districts in the early nineteenth century. The tightly-packed free seats arranged down the central aisle are flanked by the more generously spaced private pews. There is no chancel; the altar is placed in an apse, and the whole building uses the then fashionable Grecian style, later to be dismissed by Pugin and the Camdenians as 'pagan'. The capacious cellar was intended for private burial vaults.

Movement were already busy fighting on that front and, quite clearly, were frequently in trouble for those ambitions. It suited the Camdenians to leave this aspect of the High Church revival to the Oxford men and concentrate their own energies on the issues of the physical setting for worship, an area of debate in which the Oxford Movement stated it had little interest.[17] Conversely, for the Camdenians, the setting for worship was a fundamental aspect of the desired reform. How could the longed-for return to the pre-, or immediately post-Reformation service be accommodated in buildings either designed specifically for the Georgian service, or in medieval ones adapted over the following 300 years to accommodate the post-Reformation liturgical innovations?

In the pamphlets reproduced here, much attention is devoted to essentially practical matters, prosaic to the extent that the modern reader may feel they hardly needed stating, for instance, that dogs should be kept out of churches or that parishioners should be discouraged from hanging

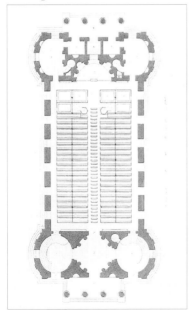 

13. Arundel Church, Sussex, lithotint by J. D. Harding, published in 1844. The print satirizes irreverent workmen, the general neglect of this important medieval structure, and the practise of intra-mural burial. Prominent in the foreground is part of a broken tomb stone with the word 'sacred' clearly shown, idly tossed aside with what could be a human bone beside it. One workman has left his hat on the tomb chest. Large hatchments are placed around the walls, showing both a secularisation of the building and a disregard for its historical importance. The flat, plaster ceiling would have been a relatively recent addition and elsewhere there is evidence of general neglect and decay. *(Geoff Brandwood collection)*

washing in the graveyard; the fact that such things clearly *did* need stating should be noted. Then there are the warnings about the dangers of blocked gutters and damp caused by earth piled up against the church's walls. On the one hand, it is all predictable, uncontentious stuff, but it was a clearly-needed reminder that a church is the house of God, and His house, above all others, required thorough care and veneration. It was an essential ingredient in the acceptance of the concept that a church was fundamentally different from all other types of building. In an age when many churches remained divided – part place of worship, part schoolroom or village hall – it is not surprising that the distinction between secular and religious usage was not always clear-cut. Similarly, churches built in the Georgian era were often scarcely distinguishable from contemporary secular buildings, for instance assembly rooms or town halls; they were often about the same size and used the same fashionable architectural vocabulary. It is instructive to glance through the plates of Ackermann's *The Microcosm of London* with its illustrations by Thomas Rowlandson and Augustus Pugin, showing the interiors of many of the major public buildings of the city in characteristic use. It was published in 1808-10, just a generation before the formation of the Society. The modern reader is likely to experience some difficulty in differentiating between the buildings in which Anglican worship is taking place and those which house debating societies, courts of law or even auction houses. Neale makes the same point in *A Few Words to Churchwardens [of] Town … Parishes*: 'Some churches, – or rather sermon houses, for they are not fit for prayer, – remind one of auction or assembly-rooms'.[18]

The four *A Few Words* …pamphlets reprinted here and *Church Enlargement* …, all from the pen of J. M. Neale, are aimed at the full range of those engaged in the care, maintenance or building of churches, although each is skilfully and thoughtfully written with its intended readership in mind. And despite the latter's diversity, there are a number of common themes, which will be dealt with shortly. At the bottom of the social scale were the sextons and parish clerks. Their pamphlet is written in clear, straight-forward language which successfully avoids seeming to patronise, and what were likely to be unfamiliar terms are avoided. Thus when discussing the stalls found in 'some old churches … where the bottom lifts up or shuts down',[19] Neale eschews the word 'misericord'. However, he does say much about the importance of keeping churches clean and free from damp, and about sextons and clerks going about their duties with an appropriate air of reverence. And while Neale acknowledges that sextons have no real authority in the parish and 'can not have things their

14. Above & next page: Great Bowden, Leicestershire, before and after views of the restoration of 1886-7. In the later photograph, the big pulpit, the west gallery and box pews, some of which run into the chancel, have all been removed and replaced by more 'appropriate' alternatives. In the earlier one, note the insensitively places stove-pipe. *(Geoff Brandwood collection)*

own way', he never misses an opportunity to bang the Camdenian drum: you must take just as much care of 'the old-fashioned open seats where the poor people sit … carved of hearty four-inch old English oak, not built of miserable half-inch deal, [which] are a great deal worthier of your care than the … ugly and wicked things called pues', with which your church is likely to be 'infested'.[20] *A Few Words to Churchwardens* … also avoids conspicuous erudition, and Neale referred to the 'homely English'[21] that he had adopted in the pamphlet destined for the country parishes. *A Few Words to Church Builders* is addressed to those 'whom God has given, not only the means, but the will, to undertake … the building of a House in some degree worthy of His majesty',[22] while *Church Enlargement and Church Arrangement* was intended to 'be useful to such clergymen as find themselves, without any previous

15. Great Bowden, Leicestershire, after the restoration of 1886-7. *(Geoff Brandwood collection)*

knowledge of church architecture, compelled … to increase the size of their church … as well as those [who wish] to take steps towards its restoration to its original beauty.'[23] The latter two pamphlets are clearly aimed at a more educated audience, and employ what was, no doubt, Neale's more usual vocabulary.

Despite the breadth of readership encompassed by these

16. St Stephen, Fylingdales, North Yorkshire, 1821. Placing the pulpit in the centre of the north or south wall – with seating arranged to focus on it rather than the altar – was a popular alternative to east-facing pews. Plate 30 on p. 129 of Hunslet Chapel, Leeds illustrates the plan of a similar arrangement. *(RCHME Crown copyright)*

pamphlets, the key themes of the Camdenian agenda can be identified in each of them, although there are shifts of emphasis. Firstly, the Society was concerned to bring about liturgical reform. It wished to revive the forms and

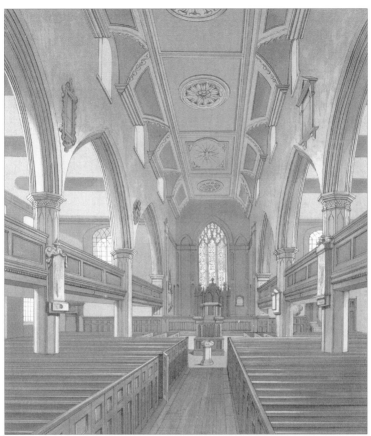

17. St Martin, Birmingham, prior to rebuilding of 1873-5. From J. T. Buncespake, *History of the Old St Martin's, Birmingham* (Cornish Bros, and Hall and English, Birmingham, 1875). The author – clearly a Camdenian convert – is predictably critical of the alterations to the medieval fabric that took place in the eighteenth century. 'What [the church] became in its latter days, was too plainly open to view, by anybody who chose to … survey the dismal spectacle. He would see nothing but hideous tasteless brickwork, dull and weather stained without ; and plaster and whitewash, still more hideous and tasteless within. The old fabric was there, buried in an ugly tomb, literally bricked up as if like unhappy Constancé in "Marmion" it has committed an inexpiated sin, and had received sentence of living death. By those who had forgotten it, … the appearance of interior may be judged by turning to [this plate showing, among other things] the heavy galleries by which the old Church was well-nigh choked … How this came about is explicable in one word – churchwardens … [and] … that incarnation of tasteless mischief, the vestry, plagued with the perpetual itching to be meddling with their parish Church.' (pp. 18-21). *(Geoff Brandwood collection)*

ceremonials of the immediately post-Reformation services – especially the communion service – that were still close to their pre-Reformation counterparts. As stated above, these pamphlets avoid any explicit statements on this subject, but much that Neale has to say about apparently architectural matters were all necessary concomitants to the liturgical reforms he desired. Secondly, and closely linked to the previous point, the Society desired to see the creation – or in the case of medieval churches, the 'restoration' – of interiors which followed the arrangements of pre-Reformation churches, mediated by the Elizabethan Settlement. These would not only facilitate liturgical reform, but their inherent symbolism would reinforce devotion and piety. In this context, Neale has much to say about the propriety of long, pew-less chancels, complete with sedilia and piscina, altars raised on steps, congregational seating facing east and the removal of centrally sited, three-decker pulpits, for instance. Sextons and churchwardens might not be in a position unilaterally to re-plan their chancels, but Neale still reminds them to take care of their piscinas, dealt with in the context of general maintenance. Fonts, often moved since the Reformation, were to be returned to their rightful position near to the main entrance. Post-Reformation examples, especially if Classical in style, should be banished, and if the whereabouts of the 'old' i.e. medieval font was known, it should be brought back to the church.[24] For Neale, like the rest of the Society, the concept of a 'proper' church as anything other than Gothic in style was so unthinkable that nowhere is it actually stated.

Thirdly, the Society wished to see a modification of the attitudes of congregations and lay-appointees. This encompassed the encouragement of a greater reverence for the church as a building and for the consecrated ground on which it stands. Thus, wardens were encouraged to keep

18 & 19. All Saints, Skelton, North Yorkshire, 1785. Each pew was privately owned and had a lockable door. The name of the owner, or in this case the joint owners, is painted on a board in each pew.

their churches not just in good order but reverently; sextons were reminded not to talk loudly or profanely, especially when cleaning the chancel. The Society also sought a more pious attitude on the part of worshippers. This is best demonstrated by the Camdenian dictat that all members of the congregations should face east, whereby they could offer their prayers to God, rather than each other, and that they should be accommodated on uniform, free benches. Big, ostentatious private pues, 'fitted up like a drawing room',[25] were the most detested, but even quite modest ones, providing they had a door and were rented, were unacceptable. They encouraged pride and self-satisfaction, as well as being wasteful of space that could be used more economically if fitted with benches thus allowing more space for the poor. There was, in short, no place for private space in the house of the Lord.

It has often been stated by writers active after *c.*1850 that the Georgians neglected their churches to the point of imminent, if not actual, collapse. However, while the Camdenians may not have liked the form and appearance of the churches that Victoria's reign inherited, there is little in any of these pamphlets to reinforce this stereotype.

Geoff Brandwood has chronicled the extent and speed of the Society's remarkable growth and, by implication,

20. St Martin in the Fields, London, James Gibbs 1722-6, from Rudolph Ackermann's *The Microcosm of London* (Ackermann, London, 1808-10). By the early part of the nineteenth century, the parish enjoyed only moderate social status, but clearly there was no shortage of willing tenants for the private pews which line the nave and galleries; the poor were left to sit on benches or stand in the central aisle. The illustration makes clear how the interior seating arrangements and form of pulpit in churches such as this had been perfected for the type of service referred to dismissively by the Camdenians as that of the 'preaching room'. It was an arrangement common in new churches of the Georgian era, but one that Camdenian-inspired schemes almost totally replaced. In this instance, the immense pulpit is placed to the side of the altar instead of in front of it, as was so often the case in this period (see plates 4 and 17), but the altar still remains partially obscured, here by a huge heating stove.

support.[26] It had started, let us not forget, as merely an undergraduate club; John Mason Neale and Benjamin Webb, the two most important founder-members, were only 21 and 20 respectively when it was formed. Yet within only two years, it had secured the patronage of the primates of England and Ireland, as well as that of 12 other bishops. Two years later, in 1843, the number of bishops had risen to 16 and it could boast 31 peers and M.Ps, 7 deans and diocesan chancellors and 21 archdeacons and rural deans.[27]

Membership peaked at around 870 in 1845. However, it would be a mistake to assume that the Society's initiatives were universally welcomed. Indeed, it generated antagonism from both the Evangelical and the 'High and Dry' wings of the Church of England. Opposition was most strident, predictably, from the former group who saw in every pointed arch or pinnacle, subversive plots intending to secure papal domination, perhaps best exemplified by the oft-quoted pamphlet by the Rev. Francis Close, *The 'Restoration of Churches' is the Restoration of Popery.*[28] However, the Society was always most careful to maintain a dignified distance from those who eventually ceded to Rome. It may have been 'guilty' of pushing Anglicanism in a Roman direction, but there was a clear boundary, which it would not cross. Thus, in setting out its ideals for new churches, the Society urged that they should be built 'in accordance with Catholicity and antiquity' adding significantly, 'and the voice of the Anglican Church'.[29]

There was also opposition from within the architectural profession, a group whose support was essential if the Camdenian ideals were to be implemented. Although Neale and Webb had much to say on architectural matters, one only needs to read *A Few Words to Church-Builders* or *Church Enlargement and Church Extension* to conclude that their understanding of the practicalities of architectural matters was woefully inadequate to bring about the physical changes in churches which they sought without professional assistance. To take just one example, in *Church Enlargement ...,*[30] they argue that building a gallery can actually *reduce* accommodation rather than increasing it; clearly ideology and mathematics were not comfortable bedfellows! R. D. Chantrell, initially in practice in Leeds, but after 1846 in semi-retirement in London, was clearly not prepared to maintain a dignified silence when he identified nonsense. 'As the list of members contains the names of some practical men [i.e. architects], it is extraordinary that those who·pen the articles for publication, should not from those practical men seek the information of which they stand so much in need.'[31] Yet despite the obvious indispensability of architects who were both professionally skilled and suitably biddable, the Society was uncompromising in its criticism of those members of the 'profession' who seemed not to follow the Camdenian principles. 'This is one of those cases in which no mercy ought to be shown to the architect', began one, not untypical, vituperative assessment.[32] The pages of the *Ecclesiologist* provide ample evidence that no architectural solecisms, no matter how distinguished their perpetrator, would escape censure as, for example, its comments on Christ Church, Hoxton, London, by Edward Blore, of 1839 show. Although now rather marginalised in the pantheon of architects, at the time of the article Blore was one of the country's most distinguished practitioners, and among his huge portfolio of commissions he was currently working at Buckingham Palace and Windsor Castle, as well as holding the post of Surveyor to Westminster Abbey. '[This church] has often been mentioned on our pages as one of the most contemptible designs of Mr. Blore. It is a building which has not a shadow, in any one point of view, of a redeeming quality'.[33] Then there was the infamous list of 'Architects Condemned' which appeared in the *Ecclesiologist* in 1843, as a complement to the list of 'Architects Approved'.[34] Even L. N. Cottingham, elsewhere described by the Camdenians as 'the most eminent ecclesiastical architect of the day',[35] appeared in the 'condemned' list. In trying to assess the true response of the profession to the Society's dicta, one has to remember that all but the most naïve practitioner must have realised the potential for lucrative employment that could flow for those prepared to 'sing from the Camdenian hymn sheet': criticism was inevitably muted. Nevertheless,

21. Above: design for a 'Protestant Cathedral', plate 60 from George Wightwick, *The Palace of Architecture* (1840).

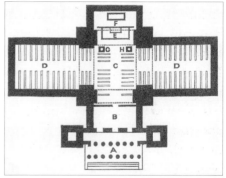

22. Right: plan of a 'Protestant Cathedral', un-numbered illustration on page 185 from George Wightwick, *The Palace of Architecture* (1840).

resistance to doctrinaire Camdenian arrogance is not impossible to find. George Wightwick, practising in Plymouth, designed a series of West Country churches in the 1840s, all of which showed a dogged determination not to capitulate to the Camdenian principles of design that he saw as 'a contradiction, a denial of contemporary requirements and a vain harking back to the past.'[36] In an article entitled 'Modern English Gothic Architecture (continued)', Wightwick described his earlier article on the subject as being 'in opposition to the proclaimed view of

23. St Philip, Leeds, R.D. Chantrell, 1845-7. Despite much nit-picking criticism, 'on the whole ... there is no actual fault we can find with the church', the *Ecclesiologist* grudgingly acknowledged.

the Camden Society', adding that, in his opinion, the Society was quite unable to consider architecture in any other light than as an historical language which was relevant only to preceding ages. He advocated that, after the demise of the present Society, which he considered to be a distinct possibility, another such should be formed more relevant to contemporary needs. He added that 'a slavish obedience to *past* periods has tended to extinguish the chance of that respect which we should desire *future* periods to have for us'.[37] Perhaps his ultimate insult to Camdenian sensibilities was his design for a 'Protestant Cathedral', with a drum and dome unmistakably based on 'the matchless beauty and majesty of St Paul's', a decastyle Roman Corinthian portico, and an innovative plan with almost no chancel or nave, but huge transepts.[38] Chantrell was even more explicit. Responding to a nit-picking review of his recently completed St Philip's, Leeds – which the *Ecclesiologist* thought was by Scott – he complained to the *Builder*, '"The Ecclesiologist", if not so acknowledged by practical men, considers itself the oracle of ecclesiastical matters, but it is indispensable for its notices of new churches or restorations of old ones, a personal inspection by a competent judge' should be made. He proceeds to complain that the article includes 'a few *oracular* absurdities, by advocating the most arrant quackery.'[39] Elsewhere, he described the journal as 'a mischievous tissue of imbecility and fanaticism.'[40]

Following the assertion of C. L. Eastlake, who, writing in 1870, or slightly earlier,[41] felt able to proclaim the triumph of Gothic, there has been a tendency for later commentators to see the rise of the style through the first half of Victoria's reign as both comprehensive and, indeed, almost inevitable. However, in the middle years of the 19th century, the architectural establishment – overwhelmingly Classical by training, and largely Classical in inclination – certainly saw things differently. It is a further mark of the Society's long-term success that this rearguard action to maintain the dominance of the Classical tradition was, for the time being, comprehensively marginalised. For evidence of the attitude of what we might term the mainstream of the profession, we could turn to Joseph Gwilt's hugely popular *Encyclopaedia of Architecture,* first published in 1842, 'the continued demand [for which] by the public, and by the profession for which it was specially prepared'[42] led eventually to a sixth edition in 1889. It is instructive to read its comments on 'The Practise of Architecture: Churches' in the fourth edition of 1867, just the year before the Society ceased its operations, claiming 'the satisfaction of retiring from the field as victors.'[43] The section begins: 'The churches whereof we propose speaking are not such as the present commissioners for building churches in this country sanction, but true good churches, such as appeared here under the reign of Queen Anne [i.e. the Baroque designs of Hawksmoor and Archer]; true honest churches, one whereof is better than a host of the brick Cockney-Gothic things that are at present patronised.'[44] No mention here of the 'greatest glory which Christian architecture … attained … in the early part of the Decorated Style'.[45] Perhaps the Camdenian 'victory' was not immediately so convincing! And Eastlake himself had to acknowledge that 'by many outsiders [ecclesiological principles] were regarded with suspicion and positive dislike.'[46]

There were also sustained attacks on the Society's literature from the antiquarian establishment, which objected to the conflation of archaeology and High Church proselytising. Few would disagree with Tina Bizzaro when she claims that, 'From about 1740 through the early decades of the nineteenth century in England, Cambridge University was the centre for the study of medieval architecture.' However, her next sentence is more contentious: 'The work by members of the Cambridge Camden Society was the high point of this development.'[47] Indeed, many in the mid-19th century would have taken serious exception to this claim. The factors which made the Society's approach to the study of the Gothic past unique were precisely the reasons for the opposition. For the Camdenians, the study of Gothic was no longer primarily antiquarian, as it had hitherto been, but was a fundamental part of ecclesiology. Just as the study of Gothic reached a level of maturity when it could claim to parallel Classical scholarship in quality, respectability and status, what was perceived by many in the field as the Camdenians' attempt to hijack the subject for decidedly non-archaeological ends was by no means universally endorsed. Perhaps a more obvious recipient of Bizzarro's palm would have been Robert Willis whose writings on Gothic encompass almost precisely the same time-span as the existence of the Society, and who has been nominated by David Watkin as, 'probably the greatest architectural historian England has ever produced.' Quoting Pevsner, he records that one of Willis's papers, 'On the Construction of Vaults in the Middle Ages',[48] 'established a standard of insight and meticulous accuracy which has never since … been surpassed.' Watkin later explains, 'in a polemical age, [Willis] probably wished to keep religion out of architecture.'[49] This seems a perfectly reasonable conclusion to draw as Willis actually wrote that it was 'in the highest degree improper' to 'convert the [Cambridge Camden] Society into an engine of polemical theology instead of an instrument for promoting the study and practise of Ecclesiastical Architecture.'[50]

Willis was not alone in his criticism of the Society's approach to historical research. John Weale, the important mid-19th century architectural publisher, went further claiming 'An eleventh commandment seems to have issued from heaven itself, declaring "thou shalt not worship [the architecture] of Egypt … Greece … Rome, nor … of Italy – but thou shalt worship only GOTHICISM!"'[51] This he blamed on 'the diocesan architectural societies', following the lead of the Cambridge Camden Society. 'Impotent incipiency of a bastard superstition! … under the banner of architecture [they seek] to revive … the power of Popery'.[52] 'Ere another fifty years have elapsed … Camdenism will have gone the way of all other

24. St George's, Doncaster, G. G. Scott, 1854-8, much admired by the Ecclesiologists.

Oldwomanisms.'[53] E. A. Freeman's objections to the Society, as set out in his *A History of Architecture* of 1849, take a slightly different form. While he claimed that 'painting and sculpture had never lost their character of arts', the study of architecture had been 'reduced to matters of antiquarian or ecclesiological research.'[54] Although Freemen referred to himself as 'an ecclesiologist',[55] he nevertheless criticised the ecclesiological movement for its 'narrowness and prejudice', claiming that for its adherents, architecture was 'only an incidental feature of their pursuits'.[56]

Despite the controversy and the hostility generated by those who objected to the ecclesiologists' pronouncements from religious, theological or archaeological standpoints, the Society's success was undeniable. With the passage of time, its research interests broadened, and the character of its argument became, on the one hand more confident and less strident, and on the other, more sophisticated. It could, with

25. St Barnabas, Pimlico, London, Thomas Cundy II, perhaps with assistance from William Butterfield, 1846-50. The church illustrated the growing strength of High-Church Anglicanism prompted, in part, by groups such as the Camden Society.

a degree of conviction, claim 'the satisfaction of retiring from the field as victors',[57] when the *Ecclesiologist* ceased publication in 1868. Although this remark referred, no doubt, to liturgical and architectural victories, the Society might, with equal validity, have claimed success in the fields of the care, maintenance and veneration for churches, the topics covered in this set of documents. Conceivably, some aspects of these first fruits of the Society's youthful enthusiasm were a source of mild embarrassment to their writers thirty years later. However, it is undeniably a mark of the effectiveness with which the Society had promoted its views that, in 1868, it would have seemed unthinkable that only a generation earlier it had been necessary to point out the exigency of preventing dogs from entering churches or keeping altar tables free from hats and coats. Perhaps most importantly, it had succeeded in cementing in the mind of the 'man in the pew', the importance of respecting and treasuring Anglicanism's Gothic heritage.

Notes

1 *Laws etc. of the Cambridge Camden Society* (University Press, Cambridge, 1839), p. 1.

2 C. Brooks, *The Gothic Revival* (Phaidon Press, London, 1999), p. 246.

3 *Ecclesiologist,* 7 (1847), p. 117.

4 Cambridge Camden Society, *Church Enlargement and Church Arrangement* (University Press, Cambridge, 1843), p. 7.

5 Rev. William Keane, Vicar of St Mary, Whitby, describing his own church, quoted in A. White, *The Buildings of Georgian Whitby* (Keele University Press, Keele, 1995), p. 38-9.

6 F. T. Mott, *Charnwood Forest* (Leicester, 1868), p. 70, quoted in G. K. Brandwood, *Bringing them to their Knees: Church-Building and Restoration in Leicestershire and Rutland 1800-1914* (Leicestershire Archaeological and Historical Society, Leicester, 2002), p. 2.

7 For example, C. L. Eastlake, *A History of the Gothic Revival* (London, 1872), reprint (Leicester U. P., Leicester, 1978); K. Clark, *The Gothic Revival* (Constable, London, 1928); C. Brooks, [note 2].

8 J. M. Crook, *The Greek Revival* (RIBA, London, 1968), p. 1.

9 See especially Chapter 27, 'An inquiry into the claims of England to the invention of pointed architecture', pp. 354-63 of the 1840 edition. The date of Hope's manuscript is discussed in D. Watkin, *The Rise of Architectural History* (Architectural Press, London, 1983), pp. 61-3.

10 It was reprinted by the RIBA, London, 1910, where it is stated that it was originally published in the *Transactions of the Royal Institute of British Architects*, 1, part 2 (1842).

11 D. Watkin [note 9], pp. 65-6.

12 G. Germann, *Gothic Revival in Europe and Britain* (Lund Humphries, London, 1972), p. 99.

13 Although it must be acknowledged that the tone of these pamphlets is much more benign and less strident than the contemporary volumes of the *Ecclesiologist*. The difference can, no doubt, be explained by the fact that these pamphlets were aimed at an audience perhaps not

unsympathetic, but still to be formally enlisted in the Camdenian cause; the *Ecclesiologist* was for the consumption of the converts.

[14] Cambridge Camden Society, *Address Delivered at the First Evening Meeting of the Cambridge Camden Society ... by the President* (University Press, Cambridge, 1840), p. 12.

[15] *Ecclesiologist,* 2 (1842), p. 59.

[16] Cambridge Camden Society, *A Few Words to Church Builders* (University Press, Cambridge, 1841), p. 3.

[17] J. M. Crook, *The Dilemma of Style,* (John Murray, London, 1987), pp. 58-9, offers several useful quotations about the opinions of Keble, Pusey and Newman on this subject.

[18] Third edition, (University Press, Cambridge, 1841), p. 5.

[19] Cambridge Camden Society, *A Few Words to the Parish Clerks and Sextons ...* (University Press, Cambridge, 1843), p. 5.

[20] Ibid.

[21] Cambridge Camden Society, *A Few Words to Churchwardens ... No. II (second edition, University Press, Cambridge, 1841)*, p. 3.

[22] *A Few Words to Church Builders* [note 16], p. 3.

[23] First edition (University Press, Cambridge, 1843), p. 3.

[24] Brandwood quotes cases of venerable fonts being used as horse-troughs or rainwater butts. Brandwood [note 6], p. 10.

[25] *A Few Words to Churchwardens ...No. II* [note 21], p. 6.

[26] G. K. Brandwood, 'Fond of Church Architecture', in C. Webster and J. Elliott (eds), *'A Church as it should be': The Cambridge Camden Society and its Influence* (Shaun Tyas, Donington, 2000), pp. 45-61.

[27] E. J. Boyce, *Memorial of the Cambridge Camden Society, Instituted May, 1839, and the Ecclesiological (late Cambridge Camden) Society, May, 1846* (London, 1888), p. 10, quoted in Brandwood [note 26], p. 56.

[28] Published London, 1844, quoted in C. Brooks [note 2], p. 256.

[29] *A Few Words to Church Builders* [note 16], p. 3.

[30] *Church Enlargement* [note 4], p. 7.

[31] *Builder,* 5 (1847), p. 485.

[32] *Ecclesiologist,* 4 (1845), p. 185. The article is a review of George Wightwick's church at Treslothan, Cornwall.

[33] *Ecclesiologist,* 7 (1847), p. 117.

[34] *Ecclesiologist,* 3 (1843), index page (not numbered). It should be pointed out that 'approved' or 'condemned' is not a comprehensive assessment of an architect's output, but rather refers only to a specific project, reviewed in that journal.

[35] Quoted in J. Myles, *L. N. Cottingham: Architect of the Gothic Revival* (Lund Humphries, London, 1996), p. 39.

36 R. Reid, 'George Wightwick: a Thorn in the Side of the Ecclesiologists', in C. Webster and J. Elliott (eds) [note 26], p. 255.

37 G. Wightwick, 'Modern English Gothic Architecture (continued)' in *Weale's Quarterly Papers on Architecture,* 4 (1845), p. 6.

38 It is illustrated and described in Wightwick's *The Palace of Architecture* (James Fraser, London, 1840), pp. 183-90.

39 *Builder,* 5 (1847), p. 485.

40 Quoted in B. F. L. Clarke, *Church Builders of the Nineteenth Century* (S.P.C.K., London, 1938), reprint (David & Charles, Newton Abbot, 1969), p. 100.

41 C. L. Eastlake [note 7]. In the introduction to the 1978 edition, J. M. Crook tells us it 'was finished in 1870 and published in 1872, at the zenith of the revivalist movement', p. <13>.

42 J. Gwilt, *Encyclopaedia of Architecture* (third edition, Longmans, London, 1867), p. xi.

43 *Ecclesiologist*, 29 (1868), pp. 315-6.

44 Gwilt, *Encyclopaedia* [note 42], p. 1026.

45 *A Few Words to Church Builders* [note 16], 1844, p. 6.

46 C. L. Eastlake [note 7], p. 109.

47 T. W. Bizzarro, *Romanesque Architectural Criticism: a prehistory* (University Press, Cambridge, 1992), p. 76. This is a remarkable statement when one considers the concurrent work of Willis.

48 See note 10.

49 D. Watkin [note 9], pp. 65-66.

50 Quoted in N. Pevsner, *Some Architectural Writers of the Nineteenth Century* (Oxford U. P., London, 1972), p. 124.

51 Anon., but presumably by Weale, 'On the Present Condition of and Prospects of Architecture in England', in *Weale's Quarterly Papers on Architecture,* 2, (1844), p.2. (Note, the page numbering in these *Papers* does not run in sequence through the volume, but each article begins with p. 1.)

52 Ibid.

53 Ibid., p. 16.

54 E. A. Freeman, *A History of Architecture* (Joseph Masters, London, 1849), pp. xi-xii.

55 Ibid., p. xii.

56 Ibid., p. xiv.

57 *Ecclesiologist* 29 (1868), pp. 315-6.

The Society's *Laws*

The Society's *Laws* were first published in 1839, and subsequently reprinted several times. The 1841 edition is reproduced here.

Although there are in total seventeen laws, sixteen of them concern procedural or management matters. Only the first, 'The object of the Society shall be, to promote the study of Ecclesiastical Architecture and Antiquities, and the restoration of mutilated Architectural remains', is of interest to those seeking to identify the Society's aims and ambitions. As such, it is, perhaps, more illuminating for what it doesn't say, rather than for what it does. There is not even a hint of concern for liturgical reform, for the supremacy of Gothic as a style and certainly nothing to suggest 'Roman' sympathies. Such omissions were, of course, no accident; despite the Society's leaders' youthful zeal, they were astute enough to understand the exigency of not providing their opponents with ammunition.

When concern about the Society's suspected ideals began to surface, members could hold up their hands in innocence, pointing to their *Laws* for corroboration. In a similar vein, as Geoff Brandwood has identified,[1] the first volume of the *Ecclesiologist* carried an 'Address' pointing out that the intended appeal of the new journal was 'to all connected with, or in any way engaged in church-building, or in the study of ecclesiastical architecture and antiquities' – no mention of the theory and conduct of worship. 'It is earnestly hoped,' it added with a sense of foreboding, 'that the motive for this little publication, liable as it is to misconstruction, will not be mistaken.' But, as James White crisply noted, 'the Society had a very distinct theological position.'[2]

Notes

[1] The rest of this paragraph comes from: G. K. Brandwood, 'Mummeries of Popish Character', in C. Webster and J. Elliott (eds), *'A Church as it should be': The Cambridge Camden Society and its Influence* (Shaun Tyas, Donington, 2000), p. 69.

[2] J. F. White, *The Cambridge Movement* (University Press, Cambridge, 1962), p. 131.

L A W S.

I. The object of the Society shall be, to promote the study of Ecclesiastical Architecture and Antiquities, and the restoration of mutilated Architectural remains.

II. The Society shall consist of a President, Vice-Presidents, and Ordinary Members, who are or have been members of the University.

III. The names of Candidates shall be proposed in the form following:—

> I, the undersigned, do hereby recommend ———,
> of ——— College, to be a Member of the *Cambridge Camden Society*, believing him to be disposed to aid its designs.
>
> (Signed) ————
>
> ——— College.

and shall be suspended (for at least a week) in the Society's Rooms; and the Candidates so proposed shall be balloted for at the next General Meeting. One black ball in five to exclude.

IV. Other Ordinary Members, as also Honorary Members, may be elected in the same manner, having been first recommended by the Committee.

V. The Chancellor of the University, the High Steward, and such of their Lordships the Bishops, and of the Heads of Houses, as shall signify their pleasure to become Members of the Society, shall be admitted as Patrons without ballot.

VI. Each Member shall pay Ten shillings on admission, and Seven shillings a Term for nine Terms, to be paid on or before the Division of each Term.—It shall be competent to any Member to compound for all future Subscriptions, by one payment of Three Guineas.

VII. If any Member continue in arrear for two Terms, he shall cease to be a Member of the Society.

VIII. The affairs of the Society shall be conducted by a Committee, composed of the President, Vice-Presidents, and six Ordinary Members, who shall be elected at the Anniversary Meeting in the Easter Term of each year, and of whom three at least shall have been Members of the Committee of the preceding year.

IX. The Committee shall elect out of their own body, so appointed, a Chairman, Treasurer, and two Secretaries :— and may subsequently add to their number.

X. Two Ordinary Members, not being members of the Committee, shall be chosen annually by the Society at the same time with the Committee, to audit the Society's Accounts.

XI. The Society shall meet twice a Term: the days of meeting to be appointed, at the beginning of each Term by the Committee.

XII. The chair shall be taken at half-past seven by the President, or in his absence by one of the Vice-Presidents, or other officers of the Society ; and the Meeting shall adjourn not later than a quarter to ten.

XIII. The day of meeting may be changed, or a special meeting called by the Committee, due notice being given.

XIV. The officer in the chair shall be sole interpreter of the laws, and shall have unlimited authority on every question of order.

XV. The Secretaries shall have charge of the records of the Society, and shall keep a minute-book containing the reports of the Meetings, and particulars relative to all matters of interest to the Society.

XVI. No motion or communication shall be laid before the Society until it has been approved by the Committee.

XVII. The Society invites its Members to examine every church in their power, to furnish reports and drawings thereof to the Secretaries, and to contribute original papers on any subject connected with its designs.

The Society trusts that its Members, while pursuing their antiquarian researches, will never forget the respect due to the sacred character of the edifices which they visit.

First Annual Report of the Committee of the Cambridge Camden Society, May 9, 1840, published in 1840

The first *Report* provides a useful insight into the Society's early activities and ambitions. It reflects the committee's earnest enthusiasm but at the same time, its confidence and determination, and conveys the justifiable self-satisfaction at the completion of the first, and very successful, year's existence, in which membership rose from just eight to 'upwards of a hundred and eighty' (p. 13). While much of the document is devoted to the Society's stated objective of 'the study of Ecclesiastical Architecture and Antiquities', (p. 14) already there are ominous references to its 'difficulties' and its 'delicate position.' (p. 13). This is amplified further on in the document where it notes that the Society's pursuits are 'running counter to the spirit of the times', (p. 20) although this probably refers to nothing more controversial than the age's indifference to history and antiquity, and its devotion to financial profit. However, it proceeds to state that the Society opposes 'the well-meaning objections of those who, from ignorance of the subject of our researches, or a want of the reverence due to antiquity, regard with a jealous eye every attempt to restore our temples to their primitive state of dignity and beauty, with whom restoration is superstition, and symbolical representation, idolatry.' (p. 20).

Here we encounter, at the very beginning of the Society's existence, the doctrinal controversies that were to accompany the remainder of its life. But the greater part of the document is devoted to less controversial matters: the Society's stated interest in church architecture. Here four courses of action were determined upon: the funding of restoration projects, so far as its limited resources allowed;

the further circulation and completion of 'the church schemes' (reprinted here in the next document *A Few Hints …Ecclesiastical Antiquities*); the formation of a collection of drawings, either of views of churches or details of them; the 'lay[ing of] the foundation of a collection of brasses'. (p. 17). In order that these objectives could be achieved, there is a call for funds, for 'labour', i.e. for people to carry out investigations of old churches, and for time: 'In the service of our beloved Church you [should attempt, in any way you can, to] minister to the outward beauty of her temples, or preserve the esoteric meaning of her symbols from forgetfulness and neglect.' (p. 21).

The *First …Report* was published in 1840, accompanied by the *Address* given by the president at the First Evening Meeting. This *Address* occupied pages 1-12 of the present document and has not been reprinted here.

26. St Philip, Stepney, London, J. Walters and F. Goodwin, 1818-9. The design was based loosely on the chapel of King's College, Cambridge, a popular model for new churches in the period. St Philip's was assessed by the early-nineteenth century architectural critic James Elmes as 'one of the best designs in the later pointed style of English architecture that has been recently erected ...The whole composition has a very striking and ecclesiastical character.' Certainly, it was a more convincing Gothic design than the contemporary Somers Town Chapel (frontispiece). However, the absence of a substantial chancel and the presence of galleries and private pews made it unacceptable to Camdenian sensibilities.

REPORT OF THE COMMITTEE

OF THE

Cambridge Camden Society,

MAY 9, 1840.

THE Committee of the CAMBRIDGE CAMDEN SOCIETY, on resigning their office, wish to offer to the Society the following brief account of its proceedings during the year in which they have had the honour of superintending its operations.

They cannot commence more suitably than by congratulating it on the steady and yet rapid increase of its members. Eight names were all that, at the beginning of last May, the Society could boast: at present, it can reckon upwards of a hundred and eighty; and among these it need hardly be said some can be pointed out, which would confer reputation on any literary body in the world.

Great part of this so rapid extension of the Society's sphere must be attributed to the unwearied care, and unceasing vigilance of its President. This it is which has carried it safely through so many difficulties; which has enabled it to steer an unharmed and prosperous course amid the very delicate positions into which its very constitution and designs have repeatedly thrown it, which has so often extended its means, and furthered its influence.

The Committee feel, too, that they have incurred no small debt of gratitude to the **Rev. J. J. Smith, V. P.,** for his constant attendance at their meetings, and for the advantage of his advice and co-operation in their designs.

After it had been resolved at the first meeting of the Society that its objects should be the study of Ecclesiastical Architecture and Antiquities, the question which naturally came next to be discussed was, in what way these objects could be best carried out. It was determined that four courses of action seemed likely to conduce to this end; and on each of these it seems desirable now to offer a few remarks. That nothing has been done which could at all be deemed, from the state of the Society's finances, questionable, the Treasurer's report, leaving a balance of £120. to his successor, amply proves.*

I. The restoration, so far as the funds of the Society would admit, of mutilated architectural remains, was one end to which it seemed desirable that its attention should be directed.

The object to which for some time past the views of your Committee have been more especially bent, is the uncoating of the Saxon tower of St. Benedict's Church. It will be in the recollection of many members now present, that about five months ago a small part of the west end of this building was cleared by their direction of its coating of rough cast, and a very curious arch of construction thereby laid open. The funds of the Society at that time would not allow the design to be carried on; and subsequently difficulties of various kinds have conspired to retard it. The Committee, however, are happy in being able to announce that these obstacles have been at length removed; and that in the course of a very few weeks the tower, from being the eyesore which it now is to the southern entrance of our University, will resume the self-same appearance which it bore in the days of S. Etheldreda, and the Venerable Bede, and S. Alphege.

While on this subject, it may be proper to state that a lithograph of some of the Saxon details of this building

* See Appendix IV.

has been struck off by the Committee; a copy of which may be obtained by any member upon application.

The restoration of Coton Font, and the model which has been taken of it, are subjects so well known that it would be needless to dwell on them. That of the font in S. Patrick's Cathedral, Dublin, is not less interesting. The stained glass in the south aisle or chapel of Coton church has also been put into the best condition that its mutilated remains will allow. The Society has moreover borne its share in the expences of opening and repairing the beautiful Decorated Windows of Sandiacre church, Derbyshire, and the Collegiate church of Howden, Yorkshire.

II. The next method resolved on for carrying out the designs of the Society was the description, by means of printed schemes, of all churches visited by its members. Thus it was, and with justice, conceived that a variety of curious details would be obtained, which could in no other manner be brought to light. The design has proved very fully its own usefulness; though, owing to several accidental circumstances, the number of churches of which full and complete accounts have thus been given is not quite so large as might have been expected; and it is for a moment the more necessary to dwell on the causes of this partial failure, because, if any branch of the Society's operations promises to be useful, it is that which has just been mentioned. This plan can hardly be said to have come into operation till the conclusion of the Summer Vacation. For the octavo schemes issued before that time were too much circumscribed, both as to size and contents, to be fitted for general use; and the plan by which they were to be employed was not generally known. Moreover, they were not issued at all till so very late in the Easter Term, that many members went down unprovided with them. Yet it need hardly be observed, that the Summer Vacation is the very time in which more would have been acccomplished in this

work, than in the whole period since : not only on account of
the comparative liberty then enjoyed by the greater part of
our members, and their dispersion all over the country,
but from the length of the days,—a circumstance of no small
importance in the benefit to be derived from a Church
tour, as they who have tried will readily allow.   And
therefore, under all these disadvantages, and with the
additional consideration of how much time and labour are
required for the accurate description of one church, it is perhaps something to be able to say, that the Society possesses
in its County portfolios one hundred and eighty reports.
The Committee hope that the difficulty of the description of
a church in the manner above described has been lessened
by the little tract which they published in November,
entitled " Hints on the Practical Study of Ecclesiastical
Antiquities."

It is but proper perhaps to notice, that the plan of
describing churches in the way above mentioned, whatever
praise it may be thought to deserve, belongs solely and
entirely to this Society; no other established for the
same, or similar purposes, having issued any papers
calculated to facilitate the correct and minute examination
of a church.   Repeated testimonies to their utility have
been received by the Committee from several of those whose
opinion on such points is decisive.

III. But another class of materials whence the study of
Ecclesiastical architecture may be greatly promoted consists in the collection of drawings, whether of whole
churches, or, which is perhaps more valuable, of details.
In mentioning those which have been received during the
past year,* and may now be seen in the Society's rooms,
the Committee, however anxious they may be not to
instance particular names, where so many are deserving
of gratitude, cannot help expressing their thanks to E. T.

* See Appendix II.

Codd, Esq., and F. Ll. Lloyd, Esq. of St. John's, and to W. H. Oliver, Esq. of Trinity, for their numerous contributions to the portfolio.

Lastly, it has been the object of the Committee to lay the foundation of a collection of brasses, more especially of those of an ecclesiastical character. With respect to these, they find it not easy to speak, for the number possessed by the Society is comparatively small, while those in the possession of individual members amount to many hundreds. The advantages derivable from a study of this branch of the subject, have induced the Committee to undertake the publication of a work, (the first number of which is on the eve of appearing,) to be entitled " Illustrations of the Monumental Brasses of Great Britain." Those which will be contained in the present number, are

Dr. Walter Hewke,	.. ...	1518.
Bishop Goodrich,	... ...	1554.
Bishop Pursglove,	... ...	1579.
Archbishop Harsnett,	...	1631.

THIS, then, is a brief summary of what has been done during the past year. With respect to the future, the Committee cannot but entertain the most sanguine hopes. They feel that the Society has all the materials within itself for accomplishing great things : they need but to be combined and called into action. And with respect to the character which the Society shall eventually take, the ensuing year, the second of its existence, will probably do much towards determining it.

What then is wanted to enable it to carry on its operations during the next twelvemonth ?

Funds are wanted; and if there be any set of men, who beyond all others should be willing to exert themselves to the utmost extent of their means, rather than that a great undertaking should fail, or a large design be cramped, it

C

is surely those, who in the course of their investigations are
called upon to behold such glorious examples of the self-
denying spirit of our ancestors, in the magnificent ecclesiastical edifices with which they have adorned every corner of
our land. Surely we, who can never meet without some new
occasion of admiring the spirit of self-sacrifice which actuated their endeavours, should be the first to contribute
cheerfully in the very cause for which they laboured; and if
we cannot imitate, at least preserve their works: and not
dole out with a niggardly hand, as if to contribute and
to lose were synonymous terms, what we can spare from
ourselves, merely because we know not how else to apply it.
Surely the thousand spires which are crumbling not from
decay, but from neglect; the thousand beautiful windows,
whose elegant tracery is mouldering from damp, or being
destroyed as useless, seem to address us, who make them
our study, in the words, " Is it time for you, O ye, to dwell
in your cieled houses, while the Lord's house lieth waste?"
Well says the pious and witty Bishop Corbet, " The first
way of building churches was by way of benevolence, but
then there needed no petitions: men came in so fast, that
they were commanded to be kept back.   But now repairing
needs petitions.   Some petitions, indeed, there are for pulling down such an aisle, or changing lead for thack.   If to
deny this be persecution, — if to repair churches be innovation and popery, I'll be of that religion too."

But further, we want labour. If you will not be content
to incur some fatigue in the pursuit of your investigations,
how can you expect to derive any advantage from them?
If you cannot make up your minds to many a weary step in
a church tour,—if you are afraid of the labour,—if you are
ashamed to be seen,

> " Non indecoro pulvere sordidi,"

you had far better give up the study at once; for you

will gain nothing by it,—you will contribute nothing to it.
We shall soon be dispersed over the country; and it is
then that the real business of the Society will commence.
It is not in the Committee-room, it is not here, that we
can achieve anything great or useful : it is in the labours
of our true-hearted members, each in his several district,
—it is in their patient investigation of its ecclesiastical
remains,—in their drawings and plans of its churches,—in
their endeavours to prevent future, and to repair past, acts of
barbarism, that our designs are to be efficaciously carried
on.   It is easy enough to be zealous here, while we can
meet weekly to keep up each other's ardour, to discuss and to
communicate our discoveries ; but in the solitude of the
country, without perhaps a friend to participate or to share
our pursuits ; where the study may meet with apathy in
some, with declared opposition in others : then quietly, yet
perseveringly, to pursue the same course ; then never to be
deterred by the common remark, " Oh, there is nothing
whatever in *that* church," from a careful examination of it ;
then to lay up the facts, in order that we may afterwards
communicate the results ;—this indeed deserves all praise.

If such be not the case with any of you, others will indeed labour, (for so good a cause can never want agents),—
but you will not enter into their labours. The merchant-
ship may return with a rich cargo ; but if you have had no
share in the risk and the toil, neither will you have any in
the profit and the honour.

Furthermore, we want time.   Not that such time should
be bestowed on this study as the pressure of academic duties, and the competition for academic honours, may otherwise require.   But hours of relaxation in, and of vacation
from, study, how can they be so pleasantly, how so meetly
employed, as in pursuits which accompany us whither-
soever we may go, at least in any Christian land; which
in their anticipation or recollection at home, as well as in their

c 2

actual enjoyment abroad, are equally delightful, and which are independent on changeable weather and clouded skies?

Again, we stand in need, not of the presence, but of the employment of talent. We stand in need of it, from our running counter to the spirit of the times. Our pursuits are mystery and scorn to an age, which (as it has eloquently been said) "holds nothing useful but what is profitable; with which the present is everything, and the future nothing; which plants the larch where its ancestors sowed the oak; and in which builders of an ancient skill have vainly caught some of the durable conceptions of the clever men of old, being constrained to spend upon mansions, constructed for the luxurious occupations of fifty years, resources which were once devoted to the raising of temples, where generation after generation have prayed and been comforted, and God has been glorified in man's obedience and praise." * We stand in need of it in opposing the well-meaning objections of those who, from ignorance of the subject of our researches, or a want of the reverence due to antiquity, regard with a jealous eye every attempt to restore our temples to their primitive state of dignity and beauty, with whom restoration is superstition, and symbolical representation, idolatry.

Lastly, we stand in need of it in so generalising the inferences we may have drawn from particular observation, as not to bring forward plausible, yet unsound hypotheses on the artistical or religious spirit which animated the efforts of former ages. For nowhere can they be so easily formed; nowhere so speciously defended. Truth, even if contrary to our own views, is what we seek: light, even if it shew us our previous ignorance, is our aim:

$$\dot{\epsilon}\nu \ \delta\dot{\epsilon} \ \phi\acute{a}\epsilon\iota \ \kappa a\grave{\iota} \ \ddot{o}\lambda\epsilon\sigma\sigma o\nu.$$

The task of your Committee is now accomplished. They have hitherto laboured for you,—henceforth they will la-

* Trinity College Commemoration Sermon, 1830.

bour with you ; and that not the less heartily, perhaps not the less effectually, because they have had more experience of the difficulties by which the Society is likely to be met. Go forward then quietly and steadily, yet withal zealously; —go forward temperately, yet mildly; as little regarding the opposition of declared enemies, as the suspicions of mistaken friends. Thus shall you assuredly meet with your own reward : too happy, if in the service of our beloved Church you can in any way minister to the outward beauty of her temples, or preserve the esoteric meaning of her symbols from forgetfulness and neglect. For yourselves, may such be, in some degree at least, your enviable lot: and for her, " peace be within her walls, and plenteousness within her palaces!"

A Few Hints on the Practical Study of Ecclesiastical Antiquities, first published in 1839. The fourth edition of 1843 is reproduced here.

Perhaps nothing illustrates more clearly the Society's wish to popularise 'the science' (p. 20) of ecclesiology than this publication. It is clearly intended to make the subject more accessible for those wishing to engage in field work, but unsure of the procedures. 'It is hoped that the following Hints will prove not altogether useless to those, who, having acquired from books some little knowledge of Ecclesiastical Antiquities, are at a loss how to apply that knowledge to the examination and description of real buildings.' Furthermore, it was intended to 'suffice at least as a directory to the learner, until he shall have made some advancement in the study, and familiarized his eye to those more minute details, which should be seen to be thoroughly understood.' (p. 3). There follows a brief history of the principal phases of ecclesiastical architecture, beginning with Romanesque and proceeding through to the Reformation, at which time England developed 'the vitiated and unhappy taste for Italian architecture' which 'completely corrupted the pure Gothick style.' Feeling that it was 'unnecessary to particularize all the barbarisms which but too frequently occur in churches of the subsequent period' (p. 15) the history terminates.

On one level, it could be claimed that this part of the pamphlet is really just a continuation of the historiographical approach to the subject recently developed by writers such as Bloxam, and that this text is merely a précis of his *Principles*. However, such a conclusion

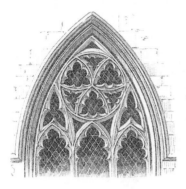

Merton College Chapel, Oxford

Sandiacre, Derbyshire.

St. Mary's, Oxford

Tysoe, Warwickshire.

Oxford Cathedral.

Warmington, Warwickshire.

A Few Hints on the Practical Study of Ecclesiastical Antiquities

would be to misrepresent the real importance of the pamphlet for two reasons. Firstly, because the Society's publication cost only a fraction of the price – 1s. 6d. in 1840 – of a bound book such as Bloxam's, it was destined to reach a hugely expanded readership. Secondly, and this was the real novelty of the Society's approach, it proceeded from the purely historical and theoretical study of the subject to its practical implementation. This it did by the 'Church Scheme' which formed the second part of the pamphlet. Indeed, the Society itself was quick to identify the innovation when it claimed that in the Church Schemes 'our great and original strength may be considered to lie.'[1] Here, in a step-by-step sequence, the reader is led through the process of studying a chosen church and recording his or her findings in a uniform manner. Researchers are encouraged to transcribe these results and transmit them to the Society for its records, thus giving even the most junior of amateur archaeologists a feeling of making a real, if modest, contribution to scholarship, and, no doubt, prompting the researcher to proceed to ever more serious study. The pamphlet's 'user friendliness' extends to hints on how a group of like-minded enthusiasts could explore a church as a team by dividing up the tasks, and it helpfully lists the tools needed to complete the exercise, such as 'drawing apparatus … a measuring line of not less than twenty feet … a leaden tape for taking mouldings' (p. 21).

A Few Hints on the Practical Study of Ecclesiastical Antiquities (which always included the Church Scheme) was first published in 1839 at a price of 1s. 6d. A second edition followed in 1840, a third in 1842, and a fourth and final one in 1843. The Church Scheme was always available separately; the first edition was also issued in 1839 and it was the first publication of the new society. Initially copies of it

27. Opposite: 'Windows in the Decorated Style', page 215 of M. H. Bloxam, *The Principles of Gothic Ecclesiastical Architecture* …, (eighth edition, 1846).

were free to members and available to non-members at 6s. 6d. per hundred;[2] clearly it was anticipated that the new constituency of church visitors would be prolific in their recordings! The Church Scheme ran to a sixteenth edition in 1846, each version of which was greater in scope than its predecessor.

Notes

[1] Cambridge Camden Society, *Second Annual Report of the Committee ...1841* (University Press, Cambridge, 1841), p. 35.

[2] By the ninth edition in 1841 they were priced at 2s. 6d. per score.

A

FEW HINTS

ON THE

PRACTICAL STUDY

OF

ECCLESIASTICAL ARCHITECTURE
AND ANTIQUITIES

FOR THE USE OF

The Cambridge Camden Society

FOURTH EDITION.

CAMBRIDGE
AT THE UNIVERSITY PRESS
STEVENSON CAMBRIDGE PARKER OXFORD
RIVINGTONS LONDON
MDCCCXLIII

"Now, generous reader, let me intreate thy furtherance thus farre, that, in thy neighbouring churches, if thou shalt finde any ancient funeral inscriptions, or antique obliterated monuments, thou wouldst be pleased to copie out the one, and to take so much relation of the other as tradition can deliver; as also to take the inscriptions and epitaphs upon tombes and gravestones, which are of those times; and withall to take order that such thy collections, notes, and observations may come safely to my hands; and I shall rest ever obliged to acknowledge thy paines and curtesie."

WEEVER'S *Funeral Monuments.*

A FEW HINTS,

&c.

It is hoped that the following Hints will prove not altogether useless to those, who, having acquired from books some little knowledge of Ecclesiastical Antiquities, are at a loss how to apply that knowledge to the examination and description of real buildings. To facilitate and direct the researches of such, a brief enumeration of the principal features by which the various periods of English Architecture are distinguished, and some explanatory remarks upon certain particulars specified in the Church Schemes, are annexed to the present edition of this manual; and although the limits of such a work will allow only a concise and imperfect sketch of the general principles of Ecclesiology, it is apprehended that it will nevertheless suffice at least as a directory to the learner, until he shall have made some advancement in the study, and familiarized his eye to those more minute details, which should be seen to be thoroughly understood. It is true that mere description is only the first step towards attaining a practical acquaintance with the subject, and that considerable experience is required before a single glance at a church or a monument or a moulding will be sufficient to determine its date and character. The present volume is designed as a *companion to church visitors;* and is intended rather to point out what should be observed, and how to observe it by the rules laid down, than to attempt to supply complete information on any point, which must be looked for in the larger works referred to in page 17, or acquired by more extended observation.

(1.) The ancient Ecclesiastical edifices of this country may be classed under two distinct kinds of architecture, the *Romanesque,* and the *Gothick,* called also the *Round* and the *Pointed;* each of which has its respective modifications, or *orders,* as they perhaps might be appropriately termed.

(2.) The Romanesque is an imperfect imitation, or rather debasement, of Roman Architecture, and may be considered to comprise the Anglo-Saxon and Norman orders; though these are in reality only branches of a widely extended continental style. The former indeed is by some altogether excluded from the Romanesque, properly so called, and by others not recognised as a separate style; while it has been proposed to designate the latter the *late Romanesque.* But whatever opinions may exist on this subject, we may thus for the sake of

1—2

convenience in classification distinguish the two great divisions of Christian architecture.

As the Romanesque originated directly from the Pagan or Classick styles, so it must not be denied that the Gothick, by certain changes and influences which cannot here be explained at length, arose out of the Romanesque, and may therefore be ultimately traced, by regular gradations, to the Grecian. But in the process of transition the Gothick, as if unwilling to acknowledge any obligation to a Pagan origin, worked itself so entirely clear of Pagan forms by diverging into totally opposite principles, and studiously avoiding all recurrence or approximation to its prototype, that it may rightly be regarded as a style in itself independent of all others, the pure offspring of the genius of the Christian religion, and not (as those who gave it the unmeaning though generally received name of *Gothick* seem to have believed) a barbarous departure from and corruption of the Classick styles.

(3.) The Anglo-Saxon style is probably an indigenous invention derived from the edifices erected in the land during its occupation by the Romans. It may be said to have been in use from the time of S. Augustine, A.D. 600, till about the time of William I. A.D. 1066, when it is generally thought that the Norman was introduced from the Continent: although, as it is known to have prevailed there long before that period, and as those English counties in which churches are most frequently mentioned in the Domesday Survey now contain by far the greatest number of Norman remains, it may well be questioned whether some of these be not of a date antecedent to that period. The history of the so-called Saxon, or earliest Christian style, is at present altogether unknown; and too few remaining specimens have as yet been discovered to determine all its distinguishing features with minuteness and certainty. It is clear, however, that it is materially different in construction and details from any Norman work, of which some erroneously consider it to be merely a rude or early kind. From a comparison of the sculpture on some examples, as the Tower of Barnack church, Northamptonshire, with that on ancient Runic Coffins and Crosses, it appears probable that some of the existing specimens (above forty of which have been described) are relics of the early British churches, built before the invasion of the Danes. Evident representations of Anglo-Saxon masonry, corresponding with existing examples, are also to be met with in MSS. and coins of the seventh and eighth centuries. There is strong historical evidence that the church in the Castle of Dover, and that of Brixworth, in Northamptonshire, were erected in the seventh century; and these have some of their principal features in common with others of supposed Saxon foundation. A list of these churches is given by Rickman, Bloxam, and in the Glossary of Architecture. Some others may be added from the researches of the Cambridge Camden Society; Bosham (a magnificent Anglo-Saxon Tower), Bishopstone, and S. Botolph, in Sussex; S. Mary, Bishophill Junior*, York; a doorway on the north side of Somerford Keynes in Wiltshire; the Minster, and perhaps Flixton, near Bungay in Suffolk. It is remarkable that four out of these seven verify the remark of Rickman, that a large proportion of the Saxon remains exist in parishes the names of which begin with the letter *B*. The Belfry arches of Great Dunham church, Norfolk, and Ilketshall, Suffolk, appear also to be of Saxon date.

(4.) The Anglo-Saxon style, (of which the tower of S. Benet's church, Cambridge, is a plain but very perfect and interesting example,) is distinguished by its rude and irregular masonry of ragstone or rubble, sometimes set in the herringbone fashion; its small and few windows, splayed externally as much as internally, and sometimes divided by a clumsy stone baluster; by its triangular-headed, or straight-sided, arches; by vertical or transverse stone ribs, sometimes, as at Barnack church, springing from the crowns of the door or window-arches, and occasionally, as at Earls Barton, crossing and intersecting each other after the manner of timbers, so as to form a kind of stone carpentry. This evident imitation of wood-work is a strong proof of great antiquity. There are neither stairs, buttresses, nor pilasters in Saxon towers; and one remarkable and all but universal feature is the peculiar construction of the angles, consisting of oblong quoins, placed alternately horizontally and vertically, and thence denominated *long and short work*. Although this peculiarity may be regarded as the most certain test in the event of the discovery of more Saxon remains, yet its existence is not, alone, an absolute proof of Saxon work, since it may be found in a few Norman buildings, as in the ruined church of S. Mary, Stourbridge, and in Rochester Castle: and on the other hand there are some Saxon remains without it. Some Saxon churches are built partly of what are generally called, though perhaps in many cases incorrectly, *Roman* bricks; as the Abbey, and S. Michael's church, S. Albans, and the curious church of Brixworth, which, however, recent discoveries have shewn to be in all probability a Roman edifice converted into a Saxon church. Many Saxon remains are, or appear to have been, covered with a coarse plaister, or roughcast, as the tower of S. Benet's, till recently, was. There is therefore great probability that more specimens may yet be brought to light, at present concealed by this covering. Some of these early edifices have been divided by an arch thrown across the Nave midway; this still remains at Brixworth, and there are similar instances at Daglingworth, Gloucestershire, in the curious desecrated church of Yainville, near Jumieges in Normandy, and the ruined church called the Minster, near Bungay. This seems a vestige of the early Basilican arrangement, which is further confirmed by the fact of several Saxon churches having had semicircular apses, as the last-mentioned example; Worth, Sussex; Brixworth, and the very remarkable

---

* See *Ecclesiologist*, Vol. I. pp. 165. 190.

remains still visible to the east of Little Welnetham church, Suffolk. It is worthy of notice that Saxon churches seem to require more minute classification than they have yet received; for while some bear the marks of the remotest antiquity, in others there are evident proofs of incipient Norman conformation.

(5.) The Norman style, borrowed from the Continent, was a great advance beyond its predecessor. In its fully developed form it extended, in this country, (in which it was brought to its greatest perfection in the elaborate richness of its ornaments,) from about the year 1100 till 1160 or 1170. Before 1100, Norman buildings present a very plain, massy, and even clumsy appearance. The piers are low and enormously thick, and the arches square-edged, without any mouldings, as in the Transepts of Ely Cathedral, and S. Sepulchre's church, Cambridge. Later edifices are frequently rich in detail, but usually of a small size, and therefore deficient in effect; though most of our Cathedrals, as those of Ely and Peterborough, have considerable portions of Norman work in them, the great size and solidity of which impart a grandeur and magnificence scarcely surpassed by any of the subsequent styles.

The principal features of Norman, as distinguished from Gothick, Architecture, are so strongly marked, and so unlikely to be mistaken by the most casual observer, that it is hardly necessary to recount them here at length. They consist chiefly in the evident approximation to, or rather vestiges of, classical forms, and in the predominance of horizontal rather than of vertical lines; in the heavy semicircular or horse-shoe arches, the low massy piers, and the large capitals and square abaci surmounting the piers and shafts, which are sometimes, even in very early work, ornamented all over with spiral fluting or other devices, as in the tower of Winchester Cathedral, and in the crypt of Repton church, Derbyshire. We find small and few semicircular-headed windows, usually having a plain shaft in each jamb ; deeply recessed and richly sculptured doorways; a general prevalence of the chevron or zig-zag, with an almost infinite variety, in later times, of ornamental mouldings ; the use of flat and frequently angular-shafted, and sometimes even semicircular, pilasters in place of buttresses ; arcades of intersecting or disengaged arches; low square towers, nearly as broad as they are high ; and extramural corbel-tables running under the parapets, which do not appear ever to have been surmounted by battlements, though an example of shallow embrasure work, apparently coeval with the structure, occurs in the Norman Tower at Bury S. Edmunds.

Norman churches were frequently built in the form of a cross, and had semicircular apses at the East end. Both these however appear to be, properly speaking, continental features. The roofs, where the space between the walls was small, were generally composed of stone groining, either of the waggon-form, or consisting of massive single ribs, often ornamented with the chevron, intersecting each other in the middle nearly at right angles, as in S. Sepulchre's, Cambridge, which is a very early example, and the Chancel of Tickencote church, Rutland, besides many parts of our Cathedrals. The piers are either complex, round, octagonal, or with semi-cylindrical shafts attached to them, as in the triforia of S. Sepulchre's church; which is perhaps the earliest example of an arrangement from which clustered columns were subsequently derived, and which may be traced to the attachment of a single vaulting shaft on the face of a plain pier. The bases of Norman piers generally rest upon a square plinth, raised a little from the level of the floor. The capitals frequently present a studied diversity of design, so that no two opposite ones are alike; an idea supposed to have been derived from constructing edifices in earlier times of ruined Roman buildings, from which capitals of different kinds were taken and used indiscriminately. The most florid and elaborate period of this style was during the reign of King Stephen, whose *Sagittarius* is constantly found in the ornamental sculpture, and is a sure test of the date.

(6.) The general introduction, though not perhaps the earliest use in this country, of the pointed arch, marks the period of transition from Norman to Early English. Of this most important feature of Gothick Architecture neither the date nor the origin has been satisfactorily ascertained, though it seems to have made its appearance in England early in the commencement of the 12th century. It is thought by some to have been suggested by intersecting Norman arches; by others, by the oval form of the mystical *Vesica Piscis*; by others, to have arisen from necessity in the construction of vaults; while others again regard it as of Saracenic origin, since it seems first to occur in the Norman edifices of Sicily, where Saracenic architects were employed. Be this as it may, it was undoubtedly the chief cause of the adoption of vertical instead of horizontal lines, and thereby of converting Romanesque into pure Gothick architecture.

(7.) Transitional Norman may be regarded as a separate style. About the year 1160, or perhaps earlier, the piers began to be built taller and of a more slender form; the capitals to be rounded, floriated, or moulded into fillets; the shafts to be banded midway, as in the Temple church, London, and S. Leonard's Priory, Stamford; the arches to be usually pointed, and ornamented with bold semi-cylindrical mouldings; most of the decorative mouldings so common in the pure Norman style, the chevron excepted, having gradually fallen into disuse. The general character of Ecclesiastical Architecture now assumed a decidedly lighter and more graceful appearance; it is, however, important to remark, that the use of the round arch was very prevalent for a long time afterwards. A great number of churches of this age, which must, for its comparatively brief duration, have been singularly prolific in ecclesiastical edifices, exist in many parts of the kingdom; and Bourn church, and the west

Tower and Wing of Ely Cathedral, may be mentioned as in-stances.

(8.) The Early English style has been generally considered as indigenous to this country; but it is in fact to be met with, under certain modifications, in continental churches. It commenced about the year 1190; and appears, almost immediately after the capability of its principles was felt, to have attained an extraordinary degree of per-fection. One of the richest and most exquisite specimens in existence, the Galilee Porch of Ely Cathedral, is said to have been built as early as 1215. The principle of the pointed arch seems at once to have been carried out to the utmost extent of which it was capable; for we find arches, especially in arcades, so acutely pointed that the imposts are brought almost into contact with each other. The notion of vertical ascendancy thus suggested, and of the *heaven-ward* tendency of vertical lines, led to the introduction and developement of spires, pinnacles, long slender shafts, arches surmounting piers of great height, and lofty roofs and vaulting.

The marks by which Early English may readily be discriminated from other styles are the following. There is a great prevalence of long, slender, and *detached* shafts, which are in most cases formed of Purbeck or Petworth marble. The capitals are of a very peculiar form, almost always circular, though sometimes octagonal, or circular with octagonal abacus, as in the Transepts of Histon church. Not unfrequently the abacus is formed, especially in arcades, by the continuation of a horizontal string round the capitals. In the earliest examples of the style, the abacus of shafts is usually square. The capitals are frequently enriched with a kind of stiff upright foliage, derived, through the Norman, from the Corinthian acanthus, or, as some think, from the palm-leaves of Palestine. This foliage is of a conventional form, and cannot certainly be referred to any particular plant, though some have traced it to the herb *geum*. It is usually worked with remarkable depth and freedom, frequently standing boldly out, and curling downwards again in thick clusters of the most beautiful form, as in the Galilee Porch at Ely, and the Transepts of York Cathedral. The capitals of the larger columns often differ but little from later examples. We find very deep hollow mouldings in the arches, composed of groups of rolls, often beaded or filleted, alternating with cavettos of three quarters of a circle, and presenting beautiful varieties of light and shade; bases hollowed in such a manner as to hold water, which occur in no other style; long and narrow lancet windows, without mullions or tracery, frequently occurring in groups of two, three, five, or even seven, with the central light often elevated above the others. The larger piers generally consist of a central column surrounded by detached shafts, and joined under common bases and capitals; though much plainer forms constantly occur. The dripstones usually have a hollow moulding underneath, and are frequently terminated by a device called a *notch-head*, though this is also found in Decorated work. The roofs and gables (where they remain, as at Bourn, in their original state) are of a very high pitch; the latter are sometimes pierced with circular, triangular, or oval apertures; though these commonly occur in other places to relieve any large surface of plain walling, and especially in spandril spaces, where foliated circles are frequently found. Early English groining is plain but graceful, usually quadripartite, with deeply moulded ribs having floriated bosses at the intersections, and often springing from slender triple shafts or flowery corbels. The larger doorways are divided by a shaft or clustered column, with a quatrefoil, or other ornament over it; and we frequently find plain and somewhat heavy octagonal pinnacle turrets, with ʻpyramidal heads. Trefoliated forms are a great characteristick of the style; trefoil-headed arches, for instance, constantly occur; and in general, combinations of *three,* symbolising the Holy Trinity, may be traced in almost every feature during this period. The moulding called the dog-tooth is likewise one of the most common and certain marks of Early English work; it is chiefly found in hollows, as under dripstones, or in rows between shafts in door or window-jambs. It is doubtful whether battlements were as yet introduced. Arcades, both internal and external; circular, or Catharine-wheel windows; bands or fillets, either in the middle or in several equidistant points of the shafts, often in continuation of string-courses, which seem to bind and gird them fast against the walls; buttresses, (placed when in corners, not diagonally, but at right angles with the walls,) often with pedimental or triangular heads and chamfered edges, and sometimes decreasing upwards in breadth as well as projection at the set-offs; these, with other minor peculiarities, easily attainable by careful study, are distinctive marks of this elegant and truly beautiful style. Examples in the neighbourhood of Cambridge are the Priory church, Barnwell, the Nave and Chancel of S. Andrew's, Cherry-Hinton, and the Choir of Jesus College Chapel.

The general characteristicks of Early English buildings are, beautiful and highly-finished workmanship, very rarely of inferior kind; grace, consummate taste, infinite variety of device and ingenuity of construction, perfect knowledge of effect, and lavish but not excessive decoration of parts. The appearance of lightness combined with strength, of slender yet stable ascendancy, in this style has probably never been surpassed by the architecture of any age or any country in the world. It may be useful to add, that probably all towers of this age were *designed* to carry spires, though these were for the most part of wood covered with lead, as at Bourn, and have long since disappeared, and in some cases were never added.

(9.) About the year 1280 commenced a new style, which has been denominated the Decorated, and which, from its tasteful arrangements, symmetrical proportions, and chaste enrichment, is usually considered as the most perfect description of Gothick Architecture. In truth, in the early or transitional period of this style, the workmanship was so exquisitely fine, and the ornaments so profuse and yet so delicate, that this may justly be regarded as the age in which Christian architecture attained the most consummate beauty. The interior of the larger edifices, as the Chapter-houses of York and Wells, the Choir of Lincoln, some parts of Westminster Abbey, and the Abbey of S. Mary at York, assumed a flowery, appearance, which charms the eye. They seem garlanded with foliage hanging in clusters from the capitals of the piers, the shafts of the triforia, and the corbels of the vaulting shafts. Every point seems to terminate in a living flower. The doorways had rich strings or fillets of the most delicate leaves, worked out so minutely as only to be attached at the sides and to each other. The windows were now much enlarged, divided by mullions, and the heads filled with geometrical tracery, consisting of trefoils, quatrefoils, circles, &c. Of this kind the east window of Trumpington church is a good plain example. A good doorway of about the same date remains on the south side of S. Clement's church, Cambridge. Crockets* and finials were now first introduced. Later in the style, the windowtracery was composed of wavy or flowing lines, generally boldly cusped or feathered, and presenting an endless variety of the most graceful curves and beautiful combinations. It is well to observe that early featherings are usually sharp, while the later are blunt at the points, and that the heads of the lights are very seldom cinquefoiled. The groined vaults were divided into numerous compartments by intricate ramifications, with heads, shields, or bosses, at every intersection; of which the western portion of the Choir of Ely is a peculiarly valuable example, as being strongly contrasted with the Early English portion of the same roof towards the east. The roofs retained the lofty pitch of the preceding style, though but few now remain. A very fine one exists at Liddington, Wilts, and Mr Bloxam has given an engraving of one from Adderbury, Oxon. The ogee form was very prevalent in small arches and in mouldings, in the latter of which the ball-flower, a delicate ornament of four leaves, and strings of rosebuds, often occur. The representation of *particular* foliage seems very characteristick of the styles: thus, the oak-leaf and acorn are *generally* found in the Decorated, as the strawberry and the vine-leaf are in Perpendicular, work. There is a prevalence of pyramidal rather than vertical or horizontal lines; in accordance with which we find abundance of richly crocketed and finialed canopies, which sometimes project or hang forward with an ogee curvature, as in the Chapterhouse at Ely. The equilateral arch is generally used: though for windows we find the ogee, the square-headed, the lancet, and the plain or pointed segmental, with the dripstones vertically returned

---

* Mr Bloxam suggests, that both the name and the form of the ornament may have been taken from the curved head of the Pastoral Staff, or Episcopal *Crook*. This is amply borne out by a representation of an early English canopy in the MS. of the Life of S. Edward the Confessor, in the University Library, where the crockets are all *Crook* heads, some with part of the staff attached to them.

about one third down the jambs, as in the west window of S. Michael's, Cambridge, which, however, is very late in the style. Dripstones were very rarely in this, as they were in the preceding and subsequent styles, returned horizontally, or carried round buttresses. Sometimes the windows, or each of the lights separately, as at Barnack, are surmounted by rich crocketed canopies: and they frequently have external and internal jamb-shafts, but no longer detached from the walls. The doorways were not always furnished with jamb-shafts, but the mouldings were continued from the arch to the ground; of which the west doorway of Trumpington church is a very good instance. Battlements (with horizontal capping only) and pinnacles, were now generally used * ; though the parapets often consist, as in the Nave of Peterborough Cathedral, of open or blocked wavy lines. The piers are now set diamondwise, that is, in the form of a lozenge, very thickly clustered, with peculiar bases and capitals. In small churches the piers often consist of four beaded and engaged shafts, of which there are examples at Trumpington; though this is also an Early English arrangement, as at Cherry Hinton. The buttresses are peculiarly elegant, having variously ornamented weatherings, and triangular crocketed heads, and being enriched with sunken niches. Good plain examples may be seen in Little S. Mary's church, Cambridge. A peculiar moulding, called the scroll-moulding, which is a kind of cylinder with the lower half withdrawn so as to leave a projecting edge, is frequently used in this style, though also found in the preceding. The capitals are occasionally invested with a delicately crumpled foliage, curling *round* rather than *upwards:* but Decorated piers, as well as arches, are frequently very difficult to distinguish in small country churches, as nearly the same forms were used for about three centuries, though a practised eye will generally recognise some peculiarity in the base or capital mouldings. The western portion of the Choir as far as the screen, the Octagon, the detached Chapter-House, now called Trinity church, and Prior Crauden's Chapel, at Ely Cathedral, are very pure and exquisite examples of this style.

The Decorated style has been denominated "the perfect Gothick"; and with reason, if it be allowed to comprise the Edwardian period, when Architecture and the Fine Arts had doubtless attained their greatest excellence. In its mouldings and details, this style bears a closer affinity to the preceding, while its general contour is more like that of the subsequent period. It is generally rich in constructive decoration; but its chief beauties seem to lie in its windows, and in the abundance and repetition of canopy or crocketed work; and its principal parts are often of plainer character than in either the preceding or the subsequent style. *Pure* Decorated churches are of comparatively rare occurrence: perhaps the finest example in England is Heckington, Lincolnshire.

* It is very difficult to say when battlements were first introduced. They occur at the East end of Salisbury Cathedral; and are represented in illuminations and sculptures of the 13th century.

(10.) The beautiful and strictly English style which, about the year 1377, succeeded to the Decorated, is usually called the Perpendicular. As, however, this term includes all the modifications of Gothick architecture till the time of the Reformation, a period of nearly two centuries, it has been thought better to arrange it under two distinct heads, the *Early*, from 1377 to 1485, and the *Tudor*, or *Late*, from 1485 to the Reformation. There is a sufficient difference of style to warrant this new classification, though there is yet much room for research to determine all the precise variations in detail by which each may be distinguished *.

Of the transition from the Decorated to the Early Perpendicular, the Nave of Winchester, and the Choir of York Cathedrals, are the best examples.

The most striking and general feature of this style is the peculiar form of the window-tracery, which consists of vertical lines, continued parallel with the mullions through the heads of windows. Many doorways, (and sometimes, as at Haslingfield, Cambridgeshire, the windows) have a square hood-moulding above them, the spandrils of which are ornamented with feathered loops and circles, or other devices. Richly ornamented wooden roofs, generally distinguished by the trefoiled or cinquefoiled form of the trusses, and by the absence of tie-beams, now became general, though comparatively few examples remain. We usually find clerestories lighted by much larger and more closely set windows than in the preceding styles: and the roofs and gables are seldom of a high pitch. One very marked and almost universal feature of this style is a wide but shallow cavetto in jamb and architrave mouldings, which is often, in rich examples, filled with square pateræ, &c. placed at intervals, as in the entrance arches to the Lady Chapel, Peterborough. These ornaments, generally representing foliage, are almost peculiar to this style, and are often placed at regular intervals in cornices, across strings, or in bosses, being sometimes of considerable size. There is a peculiar sharpness and hardness of outline in all Perpendicular sculptures and mouldings, which is very different from the gracefully curved and rounded forms of Early English work.

The walls and buttresses are often very richly panelled; there is a general predominance of surface sculpture, and much repetition of decorative parts. The capitals and bases of piers have a peculiar character; the latter are frequently raised or stilted from the ground, as under the west tower of Ely Cathedral, and the piers themselves are arranged in a peculiar manner, their plan being generally a parallelogram, set north and south, with the angles cut away in a bold hollow, in continuation of the large architrave cavetto, and a half shaft attached to the east and west faces, and sometimes a vault-

---

* In the third edition the terms *Plantagenet* and *Tudor* were adopted for the two divisions of the Perpendicular style. On this nomenclature, see a valuable Letter in the *Ecclesiologist*, Vol. I. p. 193.

ing-shaft north and south. This may be seen at Great S. Mary's church. The windows in this style are usually of a great size, and divided into one or more parts by transoms, under which the heads of the lights are cinquefoiled. Transoms are very seldom found in Decorated windows. Shafts now become a much less prominent feature, and appear to be merely ornamental, without any constructive use: the capitals and bases are generally octagonal, and the former frequently embattled. Fan-tracery was now first introduced in vaulted roofs, as at the Lady Chapel of Peterborough Cathedral; though it was much more frequently used in the Tudor period. Battlements were often richly panelled, or pierced after the manner of the window tracery, as in the last-mentioned example. A beautiful parapet of the Tudor flower may be seen in the Porch of Yaxley, Suffolk. Below the battlements and at the basement of the walls, broad bands or borders of squares, circles, or lozenges, containing quatrefoils, &c. are very frequently found. The mouldings of doorways are either continuous, or intercepted by the capitals of engaged shafts: and very often a crocketed canopy, either with or without the square hood-moulding, is carried above the arch. After this period Gothick Architecture, though it had a short reign of extraordinary splendour, was rapidly on the decline.

(11.) The distinguishing feature of the Tudor style is the constant, though by no means invariable, use of the low four-centered arch. This is found (as in the Porch of Bainton church, Northamptonshire) even in Decorated work, and not unfrequently in the Early Perpendicular style. But its general use in the Tudor age, when it became extremely depressed, caused, by violating that great principle of Gothick Architecture, vertical ascendancy, the gradual decay of the art till it received its death-blow at the Reformation.

Of Tudor edifices, three magnificent examples exist; King's College Chapel, Cambridge, S. George's Chapel, Windsor, and that of Henry VII. at Westminster, besides many other very exquisite specimens on a smaller scale. A degree of richness which is so gorgeous as to confuse and bewilder rather than to please the eye, as will be felt on beholding the Chapels of Bishops West and Alcock in Ely Cathedral, characterised this period. There is such a predominance of surface sculpture, that in some cases no space of plain walling is anywhere left. The vaulting spaces are almost infinitely subdivided by ribs, and the interstices are filled with delicate tracery, or have rich pendents hanging from the centers. A good example of plainer Tudor groining is the entrance-gateway of Queens' College. Angels with spread wings are very often to be found; and a common distinguishing mark is the repetition of the rose and portcullis, and of the fleur de lys. Shields charged with heraldick devices also very often occur. We meet with piers in which the architrave mouldings are continued, without the interruption of capitals, to the bases; or they are discontinuous, that is, die into the pier where the arch springs, as at Croyland Abbey. The windows were made very broad and low; and the transoms were generally embattled. Hood mouldings or labels are frequently supported by slender shafts; or they are terminated by large and heavy square or diamond-shape returns. The peculiar ornamental cusping called *double feathering* frequently occurs, as in King's College Chapel, and the Sedilia at Chesterton* and Milton churches. The mouldings became shallower and plainer; or they are so very wide and deep as to weaken the jamb as in the west window of Grantchester church. The ornament called the Tudor flower is most frequently found at this period. There is sometimes a partial recurrence to Decorated tracery, as in the smaller side windows of King's College Chapel. Octagonal turrets were used as buttresses; and these and the pinnacles were sometimes terminated by a domical head, as in the corner turrets of the last-mentioned example. The pinnacles are usually panelled in the shaft.

Perpendicular edifices, especially of the later kind, are generally remarkable for external richness of sculpture; for flat terminations, as square towers without spires; low roofs hardly seen above the strongly marked lines of battlements; depressed vaultings; and horizontal lines contrasted with the vertical tracery and panellings. As some of the most costly works in existence were built in this style, its capabilities are more fully known than perhaps those of any other, and it is allowed by all to possess great grandeur, beauty, and solemnity of effect. It is characterised by splendour rather than grace, and by striking prominence of parts rather than blended and harmonious disposition. By carrying decoration to excess it became meretricious, and by attempting too much soon brought about its own ruin.

(12.) The Flamboyant style is very rare in England, but on the continent occupies the place of our early and late Perpendicular. It is distinguished by the wavy flame-like character of its window-tracery, and the extravagance of its ornament in vaulting, fan-tracery, and porches. In some instances niches actually hang out of the soffits of the doors. Large windows often without any tracery; broad and poor soffits; shallow crockets and finials on the exterior; piers out of which the arch springs suddenly, "as if plunged into it while soft;" the "interpenetration" of mouldings, that is, the appearance of one member running into and passing through another, (a feature exaggerated in the Flamboyant, but occurring occasionally in Perpendicular work, as in the basement moulding of the corner turrets of King's College Chapel): Grecianised pendents; tracery of heart-shaped trefoils confusedly heaped together; figures of excessive size in the soffits; mouldings, where the naked form, and not the light and shade, was the principal object of care; and the occasional imitation of earlier styles, especially Early English, form the general characteristicks of this species of after-Gothick. The west window of S. Michael's, Cambridge, has much of Flamboyant character: and there are two engraved in p. 99 of the Glossary of Architecture of about the same date, and with decidedly Flamboyant tracery. Churches of Flamboyant character, or which have received Flamboyant additions, are found in this country on the coast, particularly where communication with France was common; as at S. Mary's, Sandwich, and one of the churches at Bristol.

(13.) About the time of the Reformation, the partial recurrence to classical forms, induced by the vitiated and unhappy taste for Italian architecture, completely corrupted the pure Gothick style by giving birth to various anomalous compositions, generally termed Debased Perpendicular. It is unnecessary to particularize all the barbarisms which but too frequently occur in churches of the subsequent period: but Italian doors, windows, and porches; the substitution of balustres for battlements, vases for pinnacles, and round balls for finials; exceedingly depressed and flat-sided pointed arches; square windows without labels or featherings, arabesque sculpture, and similar violations of the principles of the true Christian Architecture, will readily enable the learner to distinguish edifices of this description. The tower of Great S. Mary's, Cambridge, is in a degree liable to the stigma of barbarism; and the Chapel of S. Peter's College affords a good example of the style. There are, however, a few churches even of the seventeenth century of correct composition, though the details are for the most part clumsily wrought. A good example is the Tower of Godmanchester church. The Tower of Probus church, Cornwall, built in the time of Elizabeth, is a remarkable specimen of fine detail and effect: and the Chapel of Burford Priory, Oxon, is well deserving of notice.

(14.) The distinctive features detailed above are equally applicable to all ecclesiastical buildings in Great Britain; for as the ancient body of Freemasons had the sole superintendence and direction of all edifices of this kind erected in the land, the plans and drawings of them all emanated from, or at least, we may suppose, were examined, altered, and approved by, one body. Hence we must explain that extraordinary uniformity in details, even to the minutest mouldings, throughout the kingdom. It is certain also, that all repairs, additions, and alterations of pre-existing buildings were executed in the style *prevalent at the time*, however dissimilar to the original edifice; and thus almost all Cathedrals, and many parish churches, individually exhibit specimens of various styles which require to be carefully discriminated from each other.

(15.) It is proper that the attention of visitors should be directed to the *local peculiarities* of style, material, or composition and design, for which various counties are individually remarkable. Thus, Sussex, and generally the south-eastern coast, is distinguished for Early English work; Lincolnshire, Hunts and Cambridgeshire for Decorated; Somersetshire for its beautiful Perpendicular towers, and florid and elaborate specimens of wood-work; Norfolk and Suffolk for their round towers, flint masonry, and magnificent open roofs, as well as for the frequent absence of any external distinction between Chancel and Nave. Again, Cornwall is noted for its granite churches, its singular fonts, and its cradle roofs; Cheshire for its red sandstone; Derbyshire, Cumberland, and Lancashire, for their very poor and late Perpendicular work: Devonshire for its splendid rood-screens, rood-lofts, and open seats; Gloucestershire and Northamptonshire for their Norman remains. In some districts almost every tower has a spire; in others this feature is comparatively rare. That the Cathedral church probably exercised some influence in determining the character of the parochial churches of the diocese, we have elsewhere observed.

(16.) The student must bear in mind that some of the marks laid down as peculiar to one style may occasionally be met with in another. Thus, the toothed ornament occurs first in late Norman, and extends to Decorated; the ball-flower is found in Early English; the banded or filleted shafts occur in Decorated, and even in Perpendicular work, as in Canterbury Cathedral; the double-ogee moulding in Decorated; the chevron in Early English. Above all, windows are so frequently inserted and altered, that they must seldom be considered alone as certain proofs of the date of the building to which they belong. Some knowledge of the various mouldings peculiar to the styles is also an indispensable acquirement; since these furnish certain, and sometimes almost the only, indications of the date to which churches belong.

It is almost impossible to give a correct idea of mouldings by description; but a few hints shall here be added, which, if attended to, will be found useful. Early English arch-mouldings may almost always be known by the depth of the hollows; the bases of *shafts* by their capability of holding water; of larger columns, by one or more plain and bold roll-mouldings; of clustered columns, by their circular arrangement, or by standing on a square or octagonal plinth; the capitals, by the peculiar foliage, the bell-shape, and by having a deep hollow immediately under the abacus. Decorated capitals have also the bell-shape, and differ from Early English chiefly in this, that the abacus, instead of being undercut, has generally the scroll-moulding. The bases are usually formed by two or more quarter-rounds, or at least contain these members and very often the scroll-moulding also. The arch-mouldings of this style are often extremely plain, and in smaller churches usually mere chamfered edges. In the Perpendicular a peculiar moulding consisting of a double ogee is extremely common, especially in the Tudor. The large and shallow cavetto, with which it is often combined, has been before mentioned. The capitals lose their bell-shape, and the upper member is usually a bold ogee, not unlike the letter S in its section. The bases spread with a peculiar slope, which is not easy to describe, but is readily learnt by observation. In small shafts however the bases are much more varied than in any other style. Generally, Perpendicular mouldings have less depth, more angular edges, and a comparatively meagre appearance when compared with the rich depth and bold projection of the earlier styles.

(16.) The following churches in the county of Cambridgeshire will be found excellent subjects for the study of Architecture:

Balsham.	Harlton.	Over.
Barrington.	Haslingfield.	Soham.
Bottisham.	Histon.	Sutton.
Bourn.	Isleham.	Swavesey.
Burwell.	Ickleton.	Thorney Abbey.
Cherry Hinton.	Little Abington.	Trumpington.
Foulmire.	Little Shelford.	Willingham.

In the town of Cambridge, S. Benet's, S. Sepulchre's, S. Michael's, Little S. Mary's, Great S. Mary's, Jesus College Chapel, and King's College Chapel, are deserving of particular attention.

(17.) The following works are also especially recommended:—

The publications of the Oxford Architectural Society; Bloxam's *Principles of Gothick Architecture,* and *Monumental Remains;* Rickman's *Architecture;* Pugin's *True Principles of Christian Architecture;* Carter's *Specimens of Ancient Architecture, Painting, and Sculpture ;* Winkles's *Cathedrals;* Britton's *Cathedrals* and *Architectural Antiquities,* especially Vol. V., which contains a series of beautiful plates illustrative of the history of Architecture in England from Saxon to late Perpendicular; Lysons' *Britannia;* Weever's *Sepulchral Monuments ;* Willis's *Architecture of the Middle Ages;* Whewell's *Architectural Notes; The Glossary of Architecture,* in 3 Vols.; Grose's *Ancient Armour;* The *Monumental Brasses* of the Cambridge Camden Society ; Clark's, Gwillim's, and Edmonson's *Heraldry ;* and the Article on that subject in the *Encyclopædia Metropolitana.*

(18.) The annexed Table presents at one view the dates of the commencement of the different styles, with the reigning sovereigns during the continuance of each, and local examples by way of illustration.

The dates have been assigned from a comparison of English churches, the age of whose erection is certainly known; those given by Mr Rickman appearing to be in some cases incorrect.

2

STYLE.	DATE.	REIGNING SOVEREIGN.	EXAMPLES IN OR NEAR CAMBRIDGE.
Saxon	600—1066		Tower of S. Benedict's, and perhaps Chancel Arch of S. Giles, Cambridge.
Norman	1066—1154	William I. .... 1066 William II. .... 1087 Henry I. .... 1100 Stephen......... 1135	Nave of S. Sepulchre's, Cambridge: Nave of Ickleton: Doors and Chancel-arches of Milton, Hauxton, and Duxford S. John's: Coton Font.
Transition or Semi-Norman	1154—1189	Henry II............ 1154	Jesus College Chapel: Soham: Bourn: West Tower of Ely Cathedral: Oakington Font.
Early English	1189—1272	Richard I............ 1189 John............ 1199 Henry III. 1216	Chancels of Cherry Hinton and Foxton: Barnwell S. Andrew's: Transepts of Histon: Witcham and Foxton Fonts.
Decorated	1272—1377	Edward I............ 1272 Edward II. .... 1307 Edward III. 1327	Chancel of Grantchester: The Chapter House, Ely: Little S. Mary's, Cambridge: Bottisham: Lady Chapel at Fordham: Carlton Font.
Early Perpendicular	1377—1485	Richard II. .... 1377 Henry IV............ 1399 Henry V............ 1412 Henry VI............ 1422 Edward IV. ....1460 Edward V. .... 1483 Richard III. 1483	Transepts of Trinity church, Cambridge: South Chapel, Little Shelford: Landwade: March: Font of S. Edward's, Cambridge.
Late Perpendicular	1485—1546	Henry VII............ 1485 Henry VIII............ 1509	King's College Chapel: Nave of Great S. Mary's: S. Neots: Trumpington Font.
Debased	1546—1640	Edward VI............ 1546 Mary............ 1553 Elizabeth .... 1558 James I............ 1602 Charles the Martyr 1625	All Saints: S. Clement's: S. Peter's College Chapel: S. John's College Library: the Law Schools: Font of Great S. Mary's.

Of Transition from Early English to Decorated, the Chancel of Trumpington church is an example: of that from Decorated to Early Perpendicular, Harlton, and the Chancel of Fen Ditton: and from Tudor to Debased, Trinity College Chapel.

(19.) If, in filling up the Church-schemes for the use of the Society, it should be found necessary to use abbreviations, it is indispensable that the following, for the sake of uniformity, should be adopted by all. To this point the Society have to request that particular attention be paid.

A. aisle, arch.

C. chancel.

Ch. chapel.

Cont. continuous.

D. Decorated.

G.D. geometrical Decorated.

Db. debased.

Discont. discontinuous.

Dr. dripstone.

E. east.

EE. Early English.

L. light.

M. moulding.

Mt. mutilated.

N. north, nave, Norman.

P. Perpendicular, pier.

PA. pier arch.

S. south.

Sg. stage.

Ss. spandril space.

Sup. supermullioned.

T. Transept: transition (*i.e.* from N. to EE.)

Td. Tudor.

T.D. transition from EE. to D.)

T.P. .... D. to P.)

W. west.

Wd. window.

3f. trefoil, trefoiled.

4f. quatrefoil, quatrefoiled, &c.

8 l. octagonal.

c.f.p. crocketed finialed and pinnacled.

The eight forms of arches may be thus described:

a, or ½ *cir.* semicircular.

b, or *seg.* segmental.

c, or *lan.* lancet.

d, drop.

e, or = *lat.* equilateral.

f, or *Tud.* fourcentered.

g, or *og.* ogee.

h, or *hors.* horseshoe.

(20.) The mouldings of piers, and the like, may be copied exactly by means of a leaden tape; and the rough sketch reduced to any

2—2

required size by the Pentegraph. Great nicety, however, is required in using the tape, and considerable practice is necessary before the sketches thus made can be depended upon. They should in every case be carefully tested and corrected by measurements. In describing a church the piers are to be numbered from E. to W., or from N. to S., as the case may be. A window is said to be *super-mullioned*, when from the heads of the principal lights smaller vertical mullions spring up, thus dividing the upper part of the window into panel-like compartments. By *disengaged* lights are meant lights which, being under one dripstone, have yet no tracery in common.

(21.) It is the Society's wish to procure a complete and accurate description in detail of as many churches as possible; but especially of such as either, from their antiquity or any other causes, may contain objects peculiarly worthy of record, or, from their remote situation, may have hitherto escaped the researches of Ecclesiologists. It is with this view that the church-schemes have been prepared; and as a specimen of the manner in which they should be filled up by visitors, the descriptions of Trumpington and Cherry-Hinton churches are given at the end.

It is feared that the abbreviations may at first occasion some little difficulty: but they have not been adopted hastily, nor till the description by them of many hundred churches has sufficiently proved their utility.

REMARKS ON THE CHURCH SCHEMES.

It is plain that the only safe way to arrive at any general principles of Ecclesiology, is to observe and describe the details and arrangements of unmutilated churches, or parts of churches; and from a large collection of such observations, if carefully recorded, much advantage may accrue to the science. But it is equally plain, that if all these are to be sketched, a visit to the poorest church would scarcely be comprised in the longest day; and a degree of trouble, attended with no results of proportionate value, would ensue. For this reason the Cambridge Camden Society, on its first formation, issued those Church Schemes which have now reached an eleventh edition, and the value of which has been amply proved by the experience of four years. They are by no means intended to supersede sketching, but simply to assist and corroborate it, and to supply its place in the less valuable details of the churches examined. The arrangement adopted has been founded on the principle of allowing the describer to remain in one spot till that is finished, and to spare him the trouble, as much as may be, of walking backwards and forwards while he proceeds with his work.

There are two impressions of the Church Schemes; the one on a long strip of folio paper, on which the visitor will take an account with his pencil in the church, and which, by being torn into several parts, will allow as many persons to take at once different portions of the same church; the other on a quarto sheet, into which the account will afterwards be transcribed before it is presented to the Society, or placed in a private collection. The quarto schemes may readily be bound in volumes or preserved in portfolios according to counties, styles, or any other convenient arrangement.

The visitor of a church will do well to provide himself, in addition to drawing apparatus, with heel-ball and paper (long pieces of thin glazed paper may be had for the purpose) for rubbing brasses; a measuring line of not less than twenty feet, a foot-rule, and a leaden tape for taking mouldings. A pocket telescope and a compass will also be very useful.

It has been thought proper to add the following remarks to explain the terms used in the Church Schemes, and to point out the reasons why certain particulars have been inserted therein.

I. *Ground Plan.* It is of course desirable that a plan with measurements should be drawn and sent in together with the scheme; but where, from want of time, this cannot be done, it will be sufficient to measure the length of the Chancel and Nave; a measurement which should never be omitted; and to mention the several parts of the church, beginning with the former. Care must be taken, when the church has quasi-Transepts, not to confound them with Aisles. In such cases, the Aisles run one arch to the east of the Nave or Chancel arch, and in the same line with this is an arch across each of the Aisles. This arrangement occurs chiefly in city churches, or where the builders were cramped for want of room, but may be found elsewhere, as at Ketton, Rutland, which would have been a cross church had the Transepts projected beyond the aisles.

I. 3. *Orientation.* It is important to notice the deviation of a church from due east, because it is supposed that the Chancel points to that part of the horizon where the sun rises on the Feast of the Patron Saint; and it would be interesting to ascertain the truth of this belief. It may here be observed, that some churches diverge northward at the Chancel arch from a true line drawn east and west. A very remarkable example is S. Michael's, Coventry; more frequently the direction is southward, as at Bosham, Sussex. The symbolical reason is, that the inclination of our Lord's head on the Cross is thus represented.

II. 1. *Apse.* A circular or polygonal east end. There are but few of these in England, though they are common on the continent; but the list given in the Glossary of Architecture does not contain a tenth part of the number. Co-existent with an Apse, we sometimes find a triple division of the church into Sanctum Sanctorum, Chancel, and Nave. (Kilpeck, Herefordshire; Bishopstone, Sussex; Compton, Surrey.)

II. 11. 3. *a. Altar Stone, fixed or removed.* Before the Reformation the Altar usually consisted of a large slab of granite, marked with a small cross at each corner and in the center, symbolical of the Five

Wounds, and raised about four feet from the ground, sometimes on a solid mass of masonry, sometimes on brackets, more rarely on legs. At the Reformation these were allowed to be removed; and those which then escaped were so effectually displaced in the Rebellion, that scarcely one High Altar is known to exist. A few Chantry Altars however remain. They are described in the Glossary of Architecture, p. 7; and we may add five more; one at the Abbat's house, Much Wenlock, one in Lidbury church, Salop, one in Compton, Surrey, one at Burton Dasset, Warwickshire, and one at Arundel, Sussex. But the altar-slab or stone was sometimes used as a flagstone, generally with the crossed face reversed. An altar-stone is to be found at

Cherry Hinton, Cambridgeshire.
All Hallows, Barking, London.
Irnham, Lincolnshire.
Streatham, near Ely.
Myton, Yorkshire.
S. Mary Magdalen Chapel, Ripon, (where it is still used.)
S. Nicholas', Yarmouth.
Little Welnetham,
Hayle,
Flixton,   } Suffolk.
Fressingfield,
Dunster, Somersetshire.
Hove, Sussex.
Several in Lincoln and in the triforia of Gloucester Cathedrals.
The Bede House, Stamford.
Cookham, Berks, (where the Crosses are inlaid with Brass.)
Burlington Abbey, Yorkshire.
S. Mary's, Barton-upon-Humber.
S. Martin-le-grand, York.
S. Alban's Abbey Church, (on the summit of a high tomb in the south aisle of the choir.)
Cottingham, Yorkshire;
Selmestone,
Coates,   } Sussex.
Boxgrove,

These altar-stones are very easily overlooked, and great care must therefore be taken in searching for them. They were for the most part purposely placed near a door, or in the centre of the Nave, as at Cherry Hinton, or in some position where they could most frequently be trodden upon. At Coates, the altar-stone is reverentially laid down under the Table. It is needless to add, that where they are known to occur, it is highly irreverent to subject them wilfully to further indignity. They should always be taken up, and carefully protected from profanation. In ancient Missals we sometimes find the central cross omitted, and in a few instances there is a small hollow instead. This was designed either to hold the Chalice or to contain the Alms offered. Examples of this occur in S. Robert's Cave, near Knaresborough, and the Holy Chapel, S. Madron, Cornwall.

II. II. 3. β. *Reredos*, or *dossel*, a screen of wood or stone behind the Altar. There are fine examples of the latter at Harlton, Cambridgeshire, and Geddington, Northamptonshire.

II. II. 3. γ. *Piscina, orifice*, and *shelf.* It might perhaps be more correct to term these *Fenestella, piscina*, and *shelf.* Piscinæ, or *water-drains*, as they are called by Rickman, were the necessary appendages of an Altar, for pouring away the water in which the chalice was rinsed, and that in which the priest washed his hands. They generally appear as small niches in the south wall near the High or Chantry Altars: more rarely they are inserted in the east wall. They are usually single; but sometimes double (Jesus College Chapel); very rarely triple (Rothwell, Northamptonshire). When they are double (*i. e.* of two compartments, divided by a central shaft, which is only the case in Early English examples), one orifice was probably used for the former of the above-named purposes, and the other for the latter. The orifices of Early English piscinæ are generally either shallow and circular, or deep and reversed pyramidal. They are, however, sometimes 8-foiled (Skelton, Yorkshire) or 10-foiled (Histon). Sometimes two orifices are differently foliated, as at Cherry Hinton and Histon. In Decorated, they are 4-foiled, 5-foiled, &c. up to 17-foiled; which last is very unusual, but occurs in Ardingley church, Sussex. A Chantry piscina in Over church, Cambridgeshire, has a 12-foiled orifice. Other forms are square, segmental, three-quarter circular, lozenge, semicircular, or 8-foiled within a raised rim, covered with a pierced flower, or with a dog or lion keeping guard over the orifice. Norman piscinæ are very uncommon, and, where they do occur, of the rudest form. Sometimes piscinæ are found in the north wall, as at Ditchelling, Sussex, which is of Early English date, and appears to have been found inconvenient, as a Perpendicular one is inserted in the usual position. At Castor church, Northamptonshire, there is an Early English piscina both in the north and south walls of the Chancel. A shelf of wood or stone, or a small bracket, as at Stoughton, Sussex, frequently occurs across the middle of piscinæ: the use of this is not certainly known. Some think that it formed the Table of Prothesis (see below, II. II. 3. μ.); but this, from the small space commonly afforded, seems impossible. Others suppose that it held the soap; but it was more probably the receptacle of the cruets for the holy oil. A recess sometimes runs inwards, on either or both sides, from the piscina: this should be observed: its use is unknown.

Some piscinæ have no recess or fenestella, but project after the manner of brackets: some are supported on a small shaft, and some, as in Christ-Church, Hants, have a niche in the interior of the fenestella. In some Constitutions of the thirteenth century, it is ordained that where there is no piscina, a hole in the floor, to the south of the

Altar, should serve the purpose. None such have as yet been described; but it will be well to look for this arrangement.

Some few churches (Castor, Northamptonshire, Thurlby, Lincolnshire,) have a small square recess near the ground to the east of the piscina. This should be noticed, though its use is unknown, and it seems hitherto to have escaped observation.

II. II. 3. δ. *Sedilia.* Seats for the priest, deacon, and sub-deacon, at the administration of the Holy Eucharist. They vary in number from one to five: but the usual number is three. They almost always occur on the south side of the Chancel, though sometimes on the north: at Helpstone, Northamptonshire, there are three of Early English date on both north and south sides. At Hauxton, Cambridgeshire, they are at the east end of the north aisle, there having been a Chantry Altar there. Sometimes they are of equal height; sometimes the eastern seat is higher than the two others, and sometimes (chiefly in early examples) they descend in regular gradation towards the west. Examples, Teversham, Cherry-Hinton, S. Michael's, Cambridge. They often occur in the sill of the south-east chancel-window, and are then easily overlooked. Sometimes the sill is graduated, as at Goldington, Beds, and Little Wilbraham. Sometimes, as at Fulbourn, there is no division of seats, but one canopy covers space sufficient for three. Norman sedilia are very uncommon: a fine specimen has been uncovered at S. Mary's, Leicester. The piscina is almost always to the east of the sedilia: very rarely to the west, as in a south chantry in S. Mark's Chapel, Bristol. We often find adjacent to the sedilia on the western side, a larger recess, as at Great Hasely, Oxon, and Meysey Hampton, Gloucestershire*; which may be called the *magnum sedile.* Its use is unknown; but it may have been an Easter Sepulchre. It is certainly incorrect to regard it as a common sepulchral recess. There is a fine one of Norman date in Thurlby church, Lincolnshire.

II. II. 3. ε. *Aumbrye,* or locker. A plain recess, for the safe preservation of the sacred vessels, and the like. They are exceedingly common in all parts of the church, especially on the north side of an Altar. A perfect example, with the original door and shelves, remains in the south aisle of Barrington church, Cambridgeshire. Traces of hinges should be looked for; as other recesses, probably for different uses, may often be met with.

II. II. 3. η. *Brackets.* The hole for the serges, or wax-tapers, is sometimes to be found in these: they must not, in that case, be mistaken for piscinæ.

II. II. 3. θ. *Easter* or *Holy Sepulchre.* A recess for the reception of the Elements consecrated on the Cœna Domini, or Maunday Thursday, till High Mass on Easter-day. They are generally shallow, under an obtuse or broad ogee arch, rising about three feet from the ground. They usually occur on the north side of the Chancel, but

---

* Engraved in Part IV. of the *Illustrations of Monumental Brasses*, Plate 4.

often in Kent, Sussex, and Hampshire, on the south; and may be found of all degrees of magnificence, from the plain oblong recesses in the Weald of Sussex, to the gorgeous sculpture representing the Resurrection, in Heckington, Lincolnshire. They are almost invariably of Decorated date. Cambridgeshire does not furnish many examples; but there is one in Grantchester church. Sometimes a high tomb on the north of the Altar, especially in the Tudor age, served as an Easter Sepulchre. A beautiful instance occurs at Exton, Rutland. At East Wittering, Sussex, is a curious example: here the monument consists of two parts, one in the north wall, the other jutting out at right angles to it, at a distance of about three feet from the eastern wall. In ancient wills we sometimes find requests that tombs might be built so as to serve for the holy sepulchre. This may possibly be connected with the early practice of using the martyrs' tombs for Altars. (See Rev. vi. 9). Fosbroke (Antiq. II. 703.) quotes the following from a will of 1479: " I will that there be made a playne tombe of marble of a competent height, to the intent that yt may ber the blessed body of our Lord, and the sepultur, at the time of Estre, to stand upon the same, with myne arms, and a convenient scriptur to be sett about the same tombe." The sepulchre itself was usually a moveable wooden structure: it appears also to have been called the *Paschal.* At Fulbourn, a curious wooden frame over a recumbent effigy near the altar seems to have been thus used. The ceremony of the Passion and the Resurrection performed at the sepulchre on Good Friday and Easter-day, is accurately described in the Antiquities of Durham Abbey.

II. II. 3. κ. λ. *Altar-rails* and *Table.* These, when of the date of King James I. or King Charles the Martyr, deserve especial notice. They were not in use before the Reformation: a long linen cloth held up before the communicants (as is still the case abroad) served the purpose: and in some churches, as at Holy Rood, Southampton, a linen cloth is, at the Communion, put over the rails.

II. II. 3. λ. *Steps.* Three, or some multiple of three, is the most usual number: but four and seven also occur. On the fronts are sometimes engraven the founder's name, and the date of the church, as at Geddington, Northamptonshire. See below, II. II. 12.

II. II. 3. μ. *Table of Prothesis,* or *Credence.* The place whereon the Elements were deposited previously to their oblation. It sometimes appears as a plain square recess, or a low large bracket, on the north of the Altar. In the former case it may easily be mistaken for an aumbrye. Credences of the 17th century are occasionally found; but they are of rare occurrence under any circumstances, and perhaps the only perfect specimens of note are those at S. Cross' Hospital near Winchester, and Compton, Surrey.

II. II. 6. *Window-arch.* In deeply recessed windows the internal arch generally differs in shape from the external, and in Early English and Decorated frequently has jamb-shafts and a hood-moulding above.

II. II. 10. *Misereres.* The elbowed stalls, so frequently occurring in Cathedrals, where the seat lifts up, and folding back, forms a higher and smaller seat. The carving on the under part is often very curious. Those in the choir of Ely Cathedral are perhaps the finest examples extant. There are very beautiful specimens at Nantwich, Cheshire.

II. II. 11. *Chancel-seats.* Low stone seats continued, as at Trumpington, along one or both walls of the Chancel, and even, as at Little Bytham, Lincolnshire, along the east end also. They are sometimes furnished with raised ends carved in stone after the manner of poppy-heads. These seats are sometimes to be found in the Nave also. See *History of Pews,* p. 12. They are still used at Waterbeach, Cambridgeshire.

II. II. 12. *Elevation of Chancel.* In Standon church, Herts, Walpole S. Andrews', Norfolk, S. Stephen's, Bristol, S. Mary's, Guildford, and a few others, the Chancel is raised on a flight of six, ten, or twelve steps. This arrangement is now very rare, the Puritans having been (as the journal of Will Dowsing attests) most zealous for the levelling of the Chancel with the rest of the church. Yet where this has been done, its former height may be often judged of from the elevation of the piscina from the ground. It is remarkable that ancient writers sometimes speak of the Chancel as *lower* than the Nave. Original examples of this would seem still to occur, as in S. Giles' church, Cambridge.

II. II. 9. *Chancel-arch.* This is sometimes triple, as at Capel le Ferne, and Barfreston, Kent, and Branford, Suffolk.

II. VIII. 2. *Panelling above Nave-arch.* That this is not an unnecessary enquiry is evident from Burwell, Great S. Mary's, and Saffron Walden churches.

II. VIII. 3. *Rood-screen.* The screen which separates the Chancel from the Nave; in Latin *cancelli,* whence the former name. Here, before the Reformation, a Rood, or Crucifix, and the images of the Blessed Virgin and S. John, were placed. The doors represent death, as the entrance from the Nave, the Church Militant, to the Chancel, the Church Triumphant; and the sculpture with which they are adorned will usually be found to bear some reference to this. For example, in Guilden Morden church, Cambridgeshire, the following legend is painted round the screen:

> Ad mortem duram Jhesu de me cape curam
> Vitam venturam post mortem redde securam
> Fac me confessum rogo te Deus ante secessum
> Et post decessum cœlo michi dirige gressum.

It is perhaps in accordance with this idea that the doors always open inwards and never outwards. The Rood-screen was generally richly decorated with painting and gilding: the gilding still remains at Eye, Suffolk. The original doors however very seldom remain, as they do at Martham, Norfolk. The lower part of the screen is not pierced:

it is often painted with figures of Apostles and Saints, as at Therfield, Herts, Yaxley and Eye, Suffolk, where eighteen figures remain. Magnificent examples exist at Walpole S. Andrew's, Ranworth, and Worstead, Norfolk. The paintings of this kind are of a peculiar school, and well deserving of more examination than they have yet met with. Several have recently been brought to light in consequence of our calling attention to the fact, that the lower panels were seldom removed, but merely hidden by pews: as at Blyth, Yorkshire. This will afford encouragement for further investigations. Examples of Rood-screens in wood, are Bourn, Lolworth, Foulmire, Balsham, Barton, and Quy: in stone, Harlton and Bottisham, Cambridgeshire, Great Bardfield, Essex.

II. VIII. 4. *Rood-staircase.* The staircase by which the Priest ascended to the Rood-loft. It is sometimes concealed in a pier, and sometimes, when the tower is central, forms part of the staircase to the belfry. More rarely it winds round a pier externally (Fairford, Gloucestershire.) Generally it has a Rood-turret for its reception (IV. 20.), as at Great S. Mary's, Great Shelford, and Harlton. Many Norfolk churches have two such turrets with doorways opening on to the roofs of the Aisle, Chancel, and Nave. When there are two staircases, it has been suggested that they were intended for the Gospeller and Epistler to ascend different ways. At Bainton, Northamptonshire, the Rood-turret rises above the gable of the Nave, and perhaps contained the Sancte Bell (IV. 17).

II. VIII. 5. *Rood-doors.* By these are meant, not the door in the Rood-screen to the Chancel, but the door to the Rood-staircase, whether below or aloft. Concerning these it is to be observed on which side of the Chancel-arch they occur, and whether there be two or four. The Rood-door is sometimes found in the wall of the aisle, and a wooden passage was thrown across it to the Chancel-arch; an arrangement frequent in Somersetshire.

II. VIII. 6. *Rood-loft.* In addition to what has been said above, we may further remark that these were so effectually destroyed at the Reformation that very few now remain. Guilden Morden church has its Rood-loft still in existence; and considerable portions remain at Balsham; and there is a very fine one, though much altered and mutilated, in S. John's College Chapel. The magnificent one at Llanegryn, Merionethshire, was for the first time described by the Cambridge Camden Society in the summer of 1840. There are perfect Rood-lofts at Sleaford, Lincolnshire, Bettws Newydd, Monmouthshire, Flamborough, Yorkshire, Norton-Fitzwarren, and S. Aldred's, Somerset; and large portions remain at Gaddesby and Buckminster, Leicester, and Ashelworth, near Tewkesbury. The Roods were taken down by order of government in 1548, when the Royal Arms, that unfortunate disfigurement of our ancient churches, were often, though apparently without sufficient authority, substituted in their places, and hence their common position over the chancel-arch.

II. VIII. 7. The half-piers at the east or west of the Nave are called "responds:" where there are two arches there are therefore one pier and two responds, and so on. Sometimes, but rarely, these responds resemble brackets, the upper half, bevilled to a point, being alone used to support the arch. There are examples, beautifully floriated, at Teversham.

II. VIII. 9. *Triforia,*

> " The cloister-galleries small,
> That at mid-height thread the chancel wall,"

were passages giving access to different parts of the fabrick, and were sometimes used for letting down tapestry on high feasts: they principally occur in Conventual or Collegiate churches, and are often elaborately beautiful. An ancient name was " Blindstory."

II. VIII. 10. *Clerestory.* The old way of spelling clear story: that part of a church which rises above the aisles, and which in late Perpendicular sometimes presents almost a continuous window, so closely is it pierced for lights, as at Great S. Mary's church. Sometimes, especially in Staffordshire, there is a clerestory to the aisles. The earlier clerestories in parish churches are lighted by foliated circles, as at Trumpington and Bourn. But clerestories were not generally used, except in very great churches, till the fifteenth century.

II. VIII. 15. *Poppy-heads,* or *poppies* (perhaps *pupa-heads,* i. e. little wooden images) the terminations of the ends of open seats, often exquisitely carved in heads, animals, foliage, &c. Drawings and measurements of these are of great value to the Society.

II. VIII. 17. *Parvise turret.* The little tower enclosing a stair-case to the parvise. See below IV. 5.

II. VIII. 18. *Roof and groining.* Particular attention should be paid by visitors to the ancient examples of wooden roofs, as few now remain unmutilated. The earliest kinds have tie beams; the *foliated* roofs are extremely beautiful, but do not appear to occur of earlier date than the fifteenth century. The points which should be especially noticed in ancient roofs are (1.) the pitch; (2.) the general construction; (3.) the particular arrangement of collars, braces, king-posts, &c., and the number and position of the trusses. Tudor-roofs are almost flat, as in the chapels of Trinity and S. John's Colleges, and S. Sepulchre's church. A very rich and magnificent one of this date remains at S. Neot's. Anciently many roofs had a ridge-moulding externally, which is a kind of serrated tile-work projecting upwards, and shewn in relief against the sky. It is now very rarely found; but vestiges of it occur in the Chancel at Impington, and Compton, Surrey. *Pack-saddle* or gable-roofs to towers are uncommon in England, though frequent on the continent. Examples, Tinwell, Rutlandshire, Colne S. Aldwin, Gloucestershire, Carhampton, Somersetshire.

II. VIII. 19. *The Pulpit* ought properly to stand at the north side of the Chancel-arch; facing the north-west. If it stands anywhere else, it has assuredly been removed: and enquiry may be made when and whence. The reason of this position is, that the Priest may have his face to the people without turning his back to the Altar; the people of course facing the east. Stone pulpits are not common: but their stem or base occasionally remains, surmounted by a modern wooden erection: and sometimes, as in the fine pulpit of S. Mary's, Bridgewater, the stem being stone, the upper part was originally carved wood. A good many stone pulpits remain in Somersetshire, as at Wrington, Nailsea, Kew-Stoke. Sometimes they have a stair-case externally, as at S. Peter's, Oxford. Ancient wooden pulpits are also to be found, as at Thurning, Suffolk, Castle Acre, Hun-stanton, Snettisham, Burnham-Norton, in Norfolk. The last is a magnificent example, hexagonal, richly painted with the four Doctors of the Church, the builder, John Goldale, and Katharine his wife. The fine stone pulpit at Cheddar, Somersets, has one side of oak, forming the door of entrance, and carved similarly to the stone part.

II. VIII. 20. *Hour-Glass Stand.* A relick of Puritanick times. They are not very uncommon; they generally stand on the left hand of the preacher, close to the pulpit, and are made of iron. Examples, Coton, Shepreth, Impington (in the Font). A curious revolving one occurs at Stoke D'Abernon, Surrey, and in S. John Baptist, Bristol, where the hour-glass itself remains, as it does at Brooke, near Nor-wich, and S. Alban's, Wood-street, London. Though a Puritanick innovation it long kept its place: for Gay in his Pastorals writes,

> " He said that Heaven would take her soul no doubt,
> And spoke the *hour-glass* in her praise quite out:"

and it is depicted by the side of a pulpit in one of Hogarth's paintings.

II. VIII. 22. 23. *Pews* or *Pues;* and *Galleries.* This article is inserted, not as expressing any approval of these abominations, but rather from the desire of showing how late is their introduction. The earliest yet described bears date 1601. The date of these, as well as of the Reading pew and pulpit and gallery, should be care-fully noticed. See the Society's *History of Pews.*

II. IX. 2. X. 2. *Chantry Altar.* The same things are here to be noticed as in the High Altar, though, for the sake of brevity, they have not all been specified. Chantry sedilia are not common, and occur chiefly in large churches.

II. XI. 1. *Parclose.* The screens which separate chapels, more especially at the East end of the Aisles, from the body of the church. They are sometimes of stone, more frequently of wood; and in all re-spects resemble Rood-screens. There are good examples at Bottisham.

II. XI. 8. *Benatura,* or Holy-water stoup, placed at the entrance of churches, generally on the right hand of the outer or inner-porch door, or both. A very good example occurs at Horseheath: they are almost invariably much mutilated. Examples, Barrington, and Harlton. Sometimes there is a shelf over them.

II. xi. 9. *Corbels* often represent persons living at the time of the erection of the church, and who were connected with it as founders, benefactors, or otherwise. Hence, especially in female heads, by attention to the costume, much light may be thrown on the date of the church. The principal head-dresses are, the Wimple, used from the time of King John to about Edward II. It concealed the throat and chin, like a kerchief tied high over the face. During the 14th century, the Coif or Mantilla, a kind of veil flowing from the back of the head, was generally used; and the Reticulated (a net confining the hair on each side of the forehead) was prevalent in the reign of Edward III. In this century, however, the varieties of female head-dress were very numerous. At the commencement of the 15th century, the Lunar was in fashion, resembling a crescent with the points upward. Afterwards, till about 1460, succeeded the *Horned*, which is not unlike the upper part of a heart. The Wired, or Butterfly, is often found during the age of Richard III., in Brasses; as in the Peyton Brass, at Isleham, Cambridgeshire. It is a preposterously large structure of wire and gauze projecting from the back of the head. The Kennel is common in the Tudor period. It is an angular peak projecting above the forehead, and continued down both sides of the face. A dripstone is often terminated by the head of a king on one side, and of a prelate on the other; the reigning monarch and the bishop of the diocese.

II. xiii. *Font.* If this be not at or near the west end, and by a door, we must enquire when and by whom it was moved; and a few words on the impropriety of the alteration may not be out of place. See below, VI. 15.

III. 12. *Bells.* The inscription on these may be taken, where it is too dark to do more than to feel it, with the black lead and rubber. *Alphabet bells,* those in which the letters of the alphabet supply any other legend, are very scarce, and should be noticed. The oldest bells have wooden crowns.

III. 12. ζ. *Saint's Bell.* Called in Puritanick times *sermon bell,* and forbidden by the orthodox prelates to be rung, as it now is at Godalming, Surrey, when a sermon is preached. It is a small bell generally on the outside of a church: its present employment is commonly to "ring in" the minister. It was formerly rung to give notice that the *Sanctus, sanctus, sanctus, Dominus Deus Sabaoth,* in the celebration of the Mass, had commenced, and to warn the people of the approaching elevation of the Host. The custom of ringing a bell on the commencement of the Eucharist is still retained at S. John's College. A Saint's bell, long disused, still hangs in the tower of Great S. Mary's, Cambridge. In the parish accounts of Steeple Ashton, Wilts, occurs: "1609. Item. In yᵉ Tower five greater Bells and a little sance Bel,' which is curious as shewing the pronunciation.

III. 13. *Beacon or Belfry-turret* *. The turret at the angle of a Tower, sometimes in border counties, as in Westmoreland, Cumberland, Northumberland, and Herefordshire, used to contain the apparatus for kindling, at the shortest possible notice, the *need-fire*. In some, the caldron which held the fire is still said to remain, as it does in the Church of Fontaine, near Havre de Grace, in Normandy. And at Oystermonde, near Caen, it is surmounted by a small piece of ordnance, of the time of Francis I. The *licentia crenellandi*, or permission to make defensive arrangements, was frequently given about the time of Stephen: though by Church Canons the use of the church as a fortress was strictly forbidden. In the border counties, however, such may be found, as at Burgh on the Sands, and Newton Arlock, Cumberland. There is a Beacon-turret at Paul (S. Paulinus), Cornwall.

III. 14. γ. *Spiral bead.* This serves sometimes as a bannister in stone staircases, as at Kingstone-by-sea, Sussex.

III. 17. *General character of Tower.* It is interesting to determine why churches so completely run in lines as to the character of their towers or spires. The example of the Cathedral is usually assigned as the reason, and probably is so, if only we bear in mind that the spires of many Cathedrals have been destroyed: so that the example might be taken from what they were, rather than from what they are.

IV. 4. *Porch.* Porches of Norman date are extremely rare. A fine one occurs at Malmsbury. A few instances of Transition date may ccasionally be found. In Early English Porches the outer arch is often pointed while the inner one is semicircular, as at Barnack, where there is a very magnificent example. Some Porches are of wood, as at Impington; and these are usually of very beautiful and varied design, though sometimes, as at Great Eversden, quite plain.

IV. 5. *Parvise.* The small room frequently, as at Girton, occurring over the porch. It was generally the abode of a Chantry-priest. Probably the largest in England is that at Cirencester.

IV. 14. *Gurgoyles.* Images of men, monsters, beasts, or demons, on the exterior of the church, and more especially at the angles of the tower, serving as water-spouts.

IV. 17. *Sancte-bell cot.* A small but frequently elegant erection at the east end of the nave, for the reception of the Sance bell. Sometimes, but rarely, the bell itself remains, as at Over, Cambridgeshire. At Baston, Lincolnshire, the cot is placed over the west end of the south aisle, of which there is perhaps no other instance. The word *sancte* should be pronounced as one syllable, being only the Anglicised form of a Latin termination.

IV. 18. *Lych-gate*, or corpse-gate, from the Anglo-Saxon "*leich,*" a dead body, (whence Lichfield, Lich Street, in Worcester, and the like)

---

* The notice in the second edition on this subject has been misunderstood, as if it intended to assert that *all* angular turrets served the purpose of beacon-turrets, which is, of course, by no means the case.

a gate at the entrance of the church-yard, where the coffin was for a
few minutes set down before burial, to await the arrival of the minister. They are generally of wood, and thatched; but they are
of uncommon occurrence in England, though extremely frequent in
Wales. Examples, Fen Ditton, Horningsea. This gate was also
called "lich-stile," or "churchstile," corrupted into *churstele,* (Parish
Registers of Warrington, 1658.) A Lich-gate, when perfect, com-
prises a lich-path, lich-seats, a lich-cross, and a lich-stone on which
to rest the coffin. The three last occur at S. Levan, Cornwall, and
lich-stones are common through that county.

IV. 19. *Coped coffins.* These are of sufficiently common occur-
rence, and usually have a floriated cross sculptured upon the lid.
The date is very difficult to determine in the present state of ecclesi-
ology, but the smaller, plainer, and flatter examples, seem the earliest.
There are several good ones in the south aisle of Trumpington church.
Those of unquestionably Norman date are excessively rare. A most
beautiful one, covered all over with intricate sculpture, exists in
Hickling church, Notts.

IV. 21. *Masonry.* This article is inserted with a view principally
to the discovery of Saxon work. A church bearing any traces of
"long and short" work should be carefully examined in the belfry-
arch, the chancel-arch, the interior angles of the tower, and in the
belfry windows. Herringbone masonry is also deserving of attention.

VI. 3. *Hagioscope.* By this term are meant those singular and
not uncommon apertures which were made through different parts of
the interior walls of a church, generally on one or both sides of the
chancel-arch, as at S. Sepulchre's, in order that the worshippers in the
Aisles might be able to see the elevation of the Host. The technical
term in use is "Squint;" that used by some Ecclesiologists, "Lori-
cula." The former is every way objectionable, the latter unmeaning,
since *lorica* signifies, not the hole pierced through a breast-wall, but
the breast-wall itself. *Elevation aperture* was sometimes substituted
for this: a term, to say the least, very awkward. It is hoped that
the new term, formed as it is according to analogy, and expressive,
may be thought useful*. These apertures are usually oblong slits
in the chancel-wall, opening obliquely, generally into a chantry.
At Tillbrook, Beds, is an example of a chantry piscina serving also
for a Hagioscope, as there likewise is at Castle Rising, Norfolk: and
at S. Mary's, Guildford, a benatura was thus used. In early Norman churches, their place is sometimes supplied by a smaller, on
each side of the great, chancel-arch. Rodmell church, Sussex, has
a very curious Hagioscope, supported by a spirally-fluted Transition
shaft; and S. Giles', Cambridge, has a good one of Perpendicular
date. Sometimes these apertures appear to have been glazed, as in
the Mayor's Chapel, Bristol. Hagioscopes vary much in size, and

---

* This hope, expressed in the second edition, has been fully verified, and the word seems
to have become a recognized term in Ecclesiology.

are sometimes very large. There are two very remarkable ones in the north Chancel-wall of Wingfield, Suffolk.

VI. 11. *Church Chest.* These occur sometimes of Early English date, as in Clymping, Sussex; or Decorated as at Derby, S. Peter: but their date is seldom easy to determine. A very curious double one, of enormously massive oak, and with singular locks, is built into the wall and floor in the Chapel of South Lynn: the outer lid alone requires a strong man to lift it.

VI. 12. *Fald-stool.* More correctly, Litany desk. A beautiful kneeling desk is to be seen in the carved seats of S. Ives, Cornwall. For an explanation of the word see the Rubrick to the Coronation Service.

VI. 14. *Oratory.* A small chapel attached to the church for the purpose of private devotion. They are very seldom found; but a perfect one exists at Maxey church, Northamptonshire. It is a small room with a groined roof, entered by a double door from the Chancel, to which it forms a south Transept.

VI. 15. *Chrismatory.* A recess like a piscina, above or near the place where the Font originally stood, to contain the Chrism, or holy oil, with which infants were after Baptism anointed. Examples occur at S. Mildred's, Canterbury, and Thoyden Garney, Essex.

VI. 16. *Lychnoscope.* In the third edition the following account of this singular arrangement was given, though further investigations have induced us to think it untenable: "The small and low side window at the south-west or north-west of the Chancel, or the south-east or north-east of the Nave. This generally occurs in Early English churches; and the window is frequently transomed. The use of this arrangement has been much questioned. Some have thought it a confessional; some, for lepers to view the Elevation of the Host; but the position of the window often made it impossible that the Elevation of the Host should be seen through it. Others think that it served as an external Hagioscope from the Aisles, or to see when the priest advanced to commence the service at the Altar. The following hint is thrown out as to its real use. During the three last nights of Passion Week lights were kept burning in the Holy Sepulchre[*], and at all times in Chantries and upon High Altars. This window probably served for those whose business it was to keep them in, to satisfy themselves that all was right: the other windows being too high for the purpose. Hence they generally occur on the south side, because the Easter Sepulchre is generally found on the north. And they are less common in Perpendicular churches because the windows are usually so low as to render them unnecessary. In old parish registers we sometimes find the item "Paid for watching the Pasch-light." It has been observed that traces of shutters may sometimes be found inside; and it

[*] This was usually a temporary wooden erection: the existence therefore of this window where no sepulchre now remains, does not disprove what is here advanced.

3

is probable that this window was opened only on the above occasions, because it would materially interfere with the uniformity of the Chancel windows, and impede the prospect through the Hagioscope. It is rare to find Lychnoscopes on both north and south sides of the Chancel, as at Ufford, Northamptonshire. The above term has been introduced in conformity with this view of the use of such an arrangement, no received or satisfactory name having yet been assigned to it: though the subject is, of course, open to further investigation."

The opinion stated above appears to be untenable, both from the occurrence of lychnoscopes in positions, and under circumstances, which are irreconcileable with the theory, and from the consideration that, although the item "for watching the Paschlight" occurs perhaps not unfrequently, yet devotion was seldom at so low an ebb, particularly in the twelfth century, as to make such a provision in the fabrick of the building necessary. From investigations made since the publication of the third edition, it appears that in particular districts the features and position of the lychnoscope are varied in a more remarkable way even than might have been expected from the acknowledged prevalence of peculiar architectural forms and arrangements in different localities. Thus in some places the lychnoscope is always transomed, that is, forms part of an original window, being divided from the upper part by this unusual member in windows of this period: in others a somewhat later window has been added, perhaps clumsily, at the bottom of an original one: as may be seen at Addington in Surrey. In other churches it is found as an entirely distinct window from the ordinary Chancel windows, unlike them in character, and placed at a lower level in the wall. In some cases the lychnoscope has two lights divided by a mullion. The eastern part of the county of Kent presents some curious examples. In the fine Norman church of S. Margaret at Clyffe, there may be seen at the south-west of the Chancel the blocked remains of a very low broad window, with a segmental head. This is the earliest example we have heard of. At Ringswould a trefoliated Early English lychnoscope has been inserted at the north-west of a Norman Chancel. In Preston church there are *two :* one, an elegant trefoliated light at the south-west of the Chancel; the other, apparently of Early Decorated date, at the north-west of a north Chantry. Here it would seem an appendage of an Altar rather than of an Easter Sepulchre. Walmer has, in an Early English Chancel, a low square lychnoscope at the south-west; and, what is more remarkable, a second, of Early Perpendicular date, at the south-east of the Nave. These two lights must together have commanded the north pier of the Chancel Arch. Whether any remarkable arrangement exised here, cannot now be known, owing to the miserable mutilation of the church.

In Ewell church an Early English lychnoscope of very rude work occurs at the south-west of the Chancel. It is square, and divided by a rude mullion into two oblong lights. A Decorated example occurs at Elmstone, at the south-west of the Chancel. In three nearly contiguous churches of the same district, the lychnoscope occurs in the remarkable position of the north-east of the Nave, or North Aisle. At Lyddon it is a plain light in the back part of a sepulchral recess of rude character and workmanship. At Tilmanstone there is a low plain oblong aperture in a sort of sepulchral recess in the same position. In Eythorne it is a mere small oblong opening apparently without internal splay.

The most curious lychnoscope however that has yet been described occurs in Buckland church, in the same neighbourhood. At the north-west of the Chancel is a tall niche, splayed very slightly in its eastern jamb, but very much in its western, so as to allow a person from without to see the western face of the south pier of the Chancel Arch. In the upper part of the niche is a trefoiled light, apparently divided by a transom from a lower light, now blocked. In the inside, on the western jamb, remains the hinge of a wooden shutter. In this church the Chancel is much narrower than the Nave, but the north walls of both are in a line: so that south of the Chancel Arch there remains an eastern wall to the Nave. Here there might have stood an Altar, commanded by this lychnoscope, except that there seem to be traces of a smaller arch of communication here into a south Chancel Aisle, which exists, but in a mutilated state.

The form of these windows is extremely varied, but they almost invariably have transoms. At Littlebury, Essex, a transomed lancet occurs; at Comberton, a Decorated window of two lights, with the western only transomed. At Essendine is a quatrefoiled circle.

The lychnoscope must not be confounded with a little window sometimes, as at Bishop's Bourne, Kent, found in the same position but high up in the wall. This was to throw light into the Roodloft. Sometimes also, as at Preston, Sussex, the Chancel windows are all on a different level, descending from the east. In such cases the interior of the Chancel was formerly on an ascent of steps.

The attention of church visitors is particularly invited to this subject, and any information will be gladly received by the Society. The points to which the attention of Ecclesiologists is more particularly directed are the following:

The position of the lychnoscope considered with reference to the ground-plan of the church.

Their adaptation to an external or internal point of sight.

The direction of their internal splay; it being ascertained, if possible, what parts of the church are commanded by them from without.

Whether they have any external splay; which might have been expected if they were to be used from without.

Whether they were ever glazed, and if so, whether with coloured glass.

3—2

Whether they were transomed; whether furnished with internal shutters; if so, the arrangement of the hinges.

Their height, outside and inside, from the basement moulding or line of floor.

VI. 18. *Paintings on Wall or Roof.* Anciently, besides the windows being filled with gorgeous stained glass, the interior walls of churches were covered with fresco paintings, and the roofs adorned with beautiful heraldic devices or mosaic patterns, or made to represent the blue sky with gilt stars and constellations, as at Empingham, Rutland. The frescoes on the walls were at first flowers or patterns, as at S. Sepulchre's; afterwards legends of Saints, or historical events, as the Martyrdom of S. Thomas of Canterbury at Preston, Sussex. They gave special offence to the Puritans, who effaced them wherever they could. Many considerable portions however have recently been brought to light, concealed by coatings of whitewash, though in most instances they have unfortunately been effaced or destroyed. Wherever any trace is discovered, careful search should be made for more in every direction; but great pains must be taken in removing the paint or wash from them, since much mischief may be done by injudicious haste and impatience. It is probable that in many instances fine paintings were purposely concealed from the Puritans by covering them with coarse whitewash, and that many invaluable examples to this day exist in a perfect state. One of the commonest representations is of S. Christopher, who, being a saint *boni ominis,* is often found opposite the chief entrance. Upon the discovery of any considerable portions of fresco painting, intimation should be sent to the Society at Cambridge, who will give directions for its restoration. The groining and canopies of niches, and the capitals and shafts of columns were often adorned with red, blue, and gilt decorations, traces of which may generally be found by carefully removing the outer coatings with a knife. At Coton the capitals of the nave piers were painted vermilion, and much of the original colouring remains.

VI. 24. *Ancient Armour.* A very brief summary is here inserted to guide the visitor in determining dates. From about 1150 to 1310, a *complete* dress of mail (the hauberk) was used, made of small steel rings. Effigies of this kind are almost always of Knights Templars. During the 12th century the head was covered with a hood of mail (coif de mailles), and the crown was protected by a flat or trencher-shaped steel plate worn underneath. In the time of Richard I. a cylindrical or spherical helm (chapel de fer), horizontally pierced in front, was much worn. Over the hauberk was a loose surcoat. The arms were, a long kite-shaped shield, a mace, or pole axe, (martel de fer), and a long sword, usually with the hand on the hilt. The feet were cased in mail, and armed with a pryck spur.

Effigies scarcely occur before about 1250, though a few Knights Templars of earlier date remain. In the time of Henry III. plates of steel began to be added to the elbows and knees. The shields were worn shorter; on the head was a simple hood of mail; and a quilted shirt (gambeson) was worn under the hauberk. A little before 1300, *ailettes* (or small shields charged with arms over each shoulder) were introduced. Steel plates on the arms and legs (in front only) succeeded, and the surcoat was charged with the armorial bearings. Horses were *barded*, or enveloped in drapery bearing the rider's arms. The conical helm (bascinet) seems to have come in use about 1320. Circular plates at the joints, as shoulders and elbows, were often bosses with lions' heads, &c. Pointed shoes (sollerets) were now first used. The loose surcoat still worn over the mail. Brasses and effigies of this age are extremely rare.

From 1340 to 1390, the bascinet, camail, or mail tippet, jupon, or jerkin, fitting tight over the body, and escalloped at bottom, below which the mail shirt (haubergeon) appears, were in fashion. A long sword, and *anelace*, or dagger, are the offensive arms. The legs and arms are cased in steel. Sollerets and rowel-spurs on the feet. The arms were sometimes blazoned on the jupon. Sometimes the SS collar occurs: a vizor to the bascinet; and a chaplet or wreath round the helm. Effigies and Brasses of the date of Edward III. are very common.

About 1400, the camail gave way to a gorget of plate. Below the waist hung *taces* of steel laminæ. The head often rests on a tilting helm, with crest above it. On the elbows are fan-like pieces of steel: on the arm-pits *pallettes*. The toes of sollerets are now blunt. In the time of Richard III. armour attained its greatest perfection. Still later (Henry VII. and VIII.) we find pendent *tassets* or *tuilles* below the waist: broad-toed shoes (*poullains*), and frequently fluted armour. The mail appears below the tassets, which hang like a flap over each hip. The elbow plates are sometimes preposterously large.

VI. 26. *Images of Saints.* The images of patron saints often occur in niches on the exterior, particularly the Tower: as at Yaxley, Suffolk, Bourne-Bridge, Kent: S. Loup near Bayeux. Some statues remain in the east wall of S. Mary le Crypt, Gloucester. The following account of the symbols of the most commonly occurring Saints, will be found useful in examining stained glass, ancient paintings, &c.

The Holy Apostles:

S. Peter. With a key; or two keys with different wards. Usually represented with S. Paul: in which case S. Peter has an open book, S. Paul a closed one.

S. Andrew. Leaning on the Cross called from him.

S. John Evangelist. With a Chalice, in which is a winged serpent. (In this case the eagle is rarely represented.)

S. Bartholomew. With a flaying-knife.

S. James the Less. With a fuller's staff, bearing a small square banner.

S. *James the Greater.* With a pilgrim's hat, staff, scrip, and escallop shell.

S. *Thomas.* With an arrow; or with a long staff.

S. *Simon.* With a long saw.

S. *Jude.* With a club.

S. *Matthias.* With a hatchet.

S. *Philip.* Leaning on a spear; or with a long Cross in the shape of a *T.*

S. *Matthew.* With a knife or dagger.

S. *Paul.* With elevated sword.

S. *John Baptist.* With an Agnus Dei, generally on a book.

S. *Stephen.* With stones in his lap.

[Some of the above are doubtful.]

S. *Agatha.* V. M. Her breast torn by pincers.

S. *Agnes.* V. M. With a lamb at her feet.

S. *Aidan.* B. C. A stag crouching at his feet.

S. *Alphege.* Abp. M. His chasuble full of stones.

S. *Anagradesma.* V. C. Covered with the leprosy.

S. *Anne.* Teaching the Blessed Virgin to read: her finger usually pointing to the words *Radix Jesse floruit.*

S. *Antony the Eremite.* The Devil appearing to him like a goat.

S. *Antony of Padua.* C. With a pig, a T Cross, and a Rosary.

S. *Apollonia.* V. M. With a tooth and pincers.

S. *Augustine the Doctor.* B. D. By the sea-side.

S. *Barbara.* V. M. With a tower in her hands.

S. *Blaise.* B. M. With a wool-comb.

S. *Boniface.* B. M. Hewing down an oak.

S. *Bridget.* V. Holding a Crucifix.

S. *Britius.* B. C. With a child in his arms.

S. *Canute.* K. M. Lying at the foot of an Altar.

S. *Catharine.* V. M. With a wheel and sword.

S. *Cecilia.* V. M. With an organ.

S. *Christopher.* M. A giant, carrying the infant Saviour on his shoulder across a stream: a monk or female figure with a lantern on the further side.

S. *Clement.* B. M. With an anchor.

S. *David.* Abp. C. Preaching on a hill?

S. *Denys.* B. M. With his head in his hands.

S. *Dorothy.* V. M. A nosegay in one hand, a sword in the other.

S. *Dunstan.* Abp. C. With a harp.

S. *Edith.* V. C. Abbess. Washing a beggar's feet?

S. *Edmund.* K. M. Crowned, fastened to a tree, and pierced with arrows.

S. *Edward.* K. C. With the Gospel of S. John in his hand.

S. *Enurchus.* B. C. A Dove lighting on his head.

S. Etheldreda. Q. V. Abbess. Asleep: a young tree blossoming over her head.

S. Eustachius, or *S. Hubert.* M. A stag appearing to him with a cross between its horns.

S. Fabian. B. M. Kneeling at the block, with the triple crown at his side ?

S. Faith. V. M. With a bundle of rods.

S. George. M. With the dragon.

S. Gertrude. V. Abbess ? With a loaf?

S. Giles. Abbat C. A hind with an arrow piercing her neck standing on her hind legs, and resting her feet in his lap.

S. Gudula. V. M. With a lantern.

S. Guthlac. C. With a whip.

S. Helena. Q. Holding the true Cross.

S. Hilary. B. C. D. With three books.

S. Hippolytus. B. M. Torn by wild horses.

S. Januarius. M. Lighting a fire.

S. Joachim. With a staff and two doves in a basket.

S. Laurence. Deacon. M. With a gridiron and a book, and in Deacon's Vestments.

S. Leonard. C. With two long fetters.

S. Longinus. A Soldier, with a long spear.

S. Magnus. M. Restoring sight to a blind man ?

S. Margaret. V. M. Trampling on a dragon : a crozier in her hands.

S. Mary Magdalen. With dishevelled hair and box of ointment.

S. Martin. B. C. Giving half his cloak to a beggar.

S. Michael. As an Archangel ; often with scales.

S. Nicholas. B. C. With three naked children in a tub, in the end of which rests his pastoral staff.

S. Odilo. Abbat. With two goblets.

S. Pancras. M. Trampling on a Saracen : a palm-branch in his right hand.

S. Raymond. In a boat with a sail up.

S. Richard. B. A chalice at his feet.

S. Roche. With wallet, dog, and loaf of bread.

S. Rosaly. V. With a rock in her arms ?

S. Sebastian. M. as S. Edmund, but without a crown, and naked.

S. Ursula. V. M. Surrounded with virgins much less in size than herself.

S. Vincent. D. M. On the rack ?

S. Walburga. V. Oil distilling from her hand ?

S. Waltheof. M. Kneeling at the block : the sun rising.

S. Winifrid. V. Abbess. With her head in her arms.

S. Wulfstan. B. C. Striking his Pastoral Staff on a tomb.

The Blessed Virgin is principally represented :

1. At the Annunciation : the almond-tree flourishing in the flower-pot.

2. At her Purification : with a pair of turtle-doves.

3. In her agony: a sword piercing her heart.

4. In her "repose": *i.e.* death.

5. In her Assumption.

6. With the Blessed Saviour in her lap.

7. In her ecstacy: kneeling at a prayer-desk, which faces the Temple : the Holy Dove descending on her.

Martyrs hold palms: Virgins, lamps; or, if also Martyrs, lilies and roses: Confessors, lilies : Patriarchs, wheels.

The glory round the head is circular, except where living Prelates, eminent for holiness, are represented, when it is square.

VI. 27. *Stone Sculptures.* Though these are intended to include all kinds of carved work in stone, attention should especially be directed to *stone effigies*, since this part of ancient Christian art, has, in our blind admiration for pagan statuary, received much less notice than its extraordinary merit deserves. Nothing is more affectingly beautiful than the recumbent figure of a Bishop or Abbat; nothing more truthful and striking than that of the knightly founder of a church, a holy nun, or a venerable priest. The exquisite beauty of the drapery, the peaceful countenance, and the clasped hands, are all worthy of careful study, as they are oftentimes among the most interesting relics of antiquity. The statues in niches (as on the west fronts of Wells Cathedral and Croyland Abbey) are equally fine, though of much less common occurrence. The date of all such effigies may readily be known by the style of the dresses, mitres, crowns, armour, or other ornaments. The statuary in the Chapter-house of Ely, though much mutilated, is of the most exquisite design and execution.

VI. 28. *Merchants' Marks.* A device, generally inclosed in a shield, on monuments, fonts, stained glass, brasses, or corbels, taken up by merchants for the sake of distinction, they being then prohibited by the heralds from bearing arms. See *"Illustrations of Monumental Brasses,"* Part 2, for an account and some specimens of them.

VI. 30. *Well, connected with church.* Examples of this occur in S. Lo, Notre Dame, and Coutances Cathedral, Normandy.

VI. 32. *Brasses.* A volume might be written on the subject: for the present the briefest sketch must here be given, and the student referred for general information to the Society's larger work, the *" Illustrations,"* &c. just named.

1. As to the method of copying them.

There are two methods: the first by employing a soft leathern rubber, a mixture of black-lead and oil, and tissue paper; the second with the heel-ball and paper of a somewhat thicker kind. The former has the advantage of being more accurate, less laborious, and requiring less practice: but it is a dirty and disagreeable process, and the impression is found to fade by time, besides that tissue paper is unsuited for large collections. The latter is more spirited, requires no apparatus, and is less liable to rub or to tear.

2. As to the brasses themselves:

Brasses are not found before 1300: nor (to any extent) after the Restoration. They may be divided into three classes: ecclesiastical, military, civil.

Ecclesiastical brasses fall under seven heads:

I. Priests in Eucharistical vestments:—

    α. The *alb* (alba): to the lower part is appended the *orfray*, or *orphrey* (aurifrisium), anciently ornamented with stripes of purple. It signified innocency and purity of soul.

    β. The *zone*, or *girdle* (zona), emblematick of chastity: used to confine the *alb*.

    γ. The *girdle* (cingulum), typifying freedom from the world, concealed by *ε*.

    δ. The *stole* (stola or orarium), typifying the yoke of the Gospel. This was a long narrow strip, fringed at the ends, thrown over the neck and crossed on Priests, but worn by Deacons over the left shoulder.

    ε. The *chasuble* (casula), a circular vest without sleeves: having an aperture in the middle, for the head to pass through. The peaks before and behind, in which it fell down when the hands were raised, designated love to GOD, and to our neighbour.

    ζ. The *maniple* (manipulum), hanging from the left arm: it typified the troubles of the present world. It was a strip of fine linen, similar to the stole, but shorter, and originally used to wipe the fingers.

Priests in Eucharistical vestments occur,

    (1). Without the chalice, (Saffron Walden: Fulbourn):

    (2). (Which is much more rare) with it, (Littlebury): in which case it is sometimes placed below the hands (North Mimms, Hertfordshire).

II. Priests in Processional Vestments:—

    1. The *alb*, as before.

    2. The *amice* (humerale, amictus), a square piece of linen thrown over the shoulders, formerly worn on the head like a hood, and typifying the helmet of salvation. The long ends were kept down by pieces of lead.

    3. The *cope* (pluviale or cappa): this was originally used in processions, to keep off the rain, whence its first name: the derivation of the latter is uncertain.

These were in general elaborately ornamented: one at Ely was so rich as to be called "The Glory of the World." At Durham*, "The Prior had an exceedingly rich one of cloth of gold, which was

---

* *Antiquities of Durham Abbey.*

so massy that he could not go upright with it, unless his gentlemen, who at other times bore up his train, supported it on every side whenever he had it on." The *fibula*, or *morse* (i. e. clasp), is often sculptured with the Saviour's head. The border is sometimes adorned with flower-work (Girton); sometimes cancellated (Queens' College Chapel); sometimes enriched with figures of Saints (Dr John Sleford, Dr John Blodwell, Balsham; Dr Walter Hewke, Trinity Hall); sometimes with the initials of the Priest (Fulbourn, Great Shelford, Wilburton); sometimes with an inscription, as "Credo quod Redemptor meus vivit;" sometimes with a rebus of the name, as in the brass of Dr Mapleton, Broadwater, Sussex, where is an M alternately with a Maple-leaf. A Cope is preserved in Ely Cathedral. The Cope is very seldom seen in stone effigies. An example before the Reformation occurs in S. Nicholas, Guildford; which also retains the original colours; after the Reformation, in Bishop Heton's Monument, Ely Cathedral.

The use of the Cope and of the *Vestment*, or Chasuble, is still ordered by the Anglican Church.

III. Priests in Academical Dress.

Examples: in hood and gown, Dr Richard Billingford, S. Benedict's: Provost Hacomblayne, King's College Chapel: in cap, hood and gown, Dr Walter Toune, in the same Chapel.

IV. Canons, or Deans.

These wear a white woollen hood, with bell-shaped pendents, (Luton, Beds: Byfleet, Surrey: Great Hasely, Oxfordshire.)

V. Monks.

The *principal* divisions of these are: Benedictines, Cistercians, Cluniacs, Carthusians, Austin and Præmonstratensian Canons. To particularize the difference in the robes of each, would lead us too far from our subject: and they are fully explained and illustrated in Churton's Early English Church. A Benedictine Monk occurs in Sawston church.

VI. Bishops.

The full vestments were Alb, Zone, Tunic, Dalmatic, Stole, Chasuble, Maniple, Sandals, Gloves, Mitre, Pastoral Staff with Vexillum, Ring. Bishop Goodrich, Ely, is a good example. The hands are sometimes joined in prayer: oftener the left grasps the Pastoral Staff, the right is extended in the attitude of benediction.

An Archbishop has the Pall, (which may be seen in the arms of Canterbury and Armagh) in addition: he has, or ought to have, a ducal coronet round the Mitre, and he holds a Crozier instead of a Pastoral Staff.

Mitred Abbats have exactly the same appearance, except that generally they hold the Pastoral Staff in the right hand, and give the benediction with the left. If they hold it in the left, the crook is turned *inwards:* Bishops hold it outwards. A list of Mitred

Abbeys, as likely to prove useful and not easily procurable, is here given:

St. Alban's, the first in dignity.

Abingdon.	Malmesbury.
Bardney.	Peterborough.
Battle.	Ramsey.
Bury S. Edmunds.	Reading.
Canterbury S. Austin's.	Selby.
Cirencester.	Shrewsbury,
Crowland.	Tavistock (doubtful.)
Colchester S. John's.	Tewkesbury.
Evesham.	Thorney.
Glastonbury.	Waltham.
Hide.	Westminster.
Hulme, (of which the Bishop of Norwich is to this day titular Lord Abbat.)	Winchelcombe.
	York S. Mary.

The Priors of Coventry and S. John of Jerusalem.

VII. Priests after the Reformation. These are not common. Example: Wimpole.

Military Brasses, as coming less within the province of an Ecclesiological Society, may be dismissed with a few examples from this county.

1289	Sir Roger de Trumpington	Trumpington.
1330	Sir John de Creke	Westley Waterless.
1360	Sir Henry Englysh	Wood Ditton.
1382	Sir John de Argentein	Horseheath.
1401	Sir Thomas Braunstone	Wisbeach.
1416	Sir William Skelton	Hinxton.
1420 (circ)	Sir —— Parys	Linton.
1425	Sir Baldwin St George	Hatley S. George.
1450 (circ)	Sir —— ——	Sawston.
1484	Sir Thomas Peyton	Isleham.
1500	Sir John Burgoyne	Impington.

Civilians are not common in Cambridgeshire. Fulbourn and Milton will afford examples.

Of female head-dresses we have already spoken.

The symbols usually found with Brasses are:

A Heart pierced with the Five Wounds.

The Holy Trinity: either under the form of the Father seated in His Glory, embracing the Crucifix, the Holy Dove hovering over it: or in the monogram,

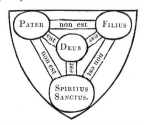

A Rose with Glory, which must not be confounded with the Tudor "Rose en soleil."

The Evangelistick symbols: S. Matthew's Angel: S. Mark's Winged Lion: S. Luke's Ox: S. John's Eagle.

The four Doctors of the Western Church are sometimes also thus represented: S. Augustine by the first: S. Ambrose by the second: S. Jerome by the third: S. Gregory by the fourth.

A Lily terminating in a Crucifix.

The Instruments of Crucifixion.

Rebuses, such as the following:

An arrow in a cask	Bolt-tun	Bolton.
A lamb and dove	Lamb-bird	Lambert.
A hatchet and cask	War-bill-ton	Warbleton.
TON	Long-ton	Langton.
A dog in a barrel	Cur-tun	Kirton.
An ash tree in a barrel	Ash-tun	Ashton.
A man falling	I-slip	Islip.
Three pieces of gold	Gold-stones.	Goldstone.
A skein of silk and a horse	Silk-steed	Silkstede.

and such like.

These Rebuses should be carefully looked for, as they may often determine the date of a building, font, &c., where they were frequently added where the modesty of the donor or founder would not allow his name.

The arms of the person represented: of his company, guild, diocese, or hospital.

 Merchant's marks.

 Implements of trade, as gloves for a glover.

As a general rule, the narrower the rim of the legend the older the Brass.

Legends from the mouth are of the following kind:

Sancta Trinitas, unus Deus, miserere nobis.

or, as it would be written, Sc̄a Trinitas, un' de', misere nobis.

Mcy, īhu, and gramcy. (Mercy, Jesu, and gramercy!)

īhu, mey. ladye, helpe.

īhu yat us made—and with thy blood us bought—forgive us our trespasses.

Mater sc̄a ihu, me serva mort' ab esu.

Sit sc̄i Thomæ suscepta precacio pro me.

Chor' Apostolic' sit nobis semper amic'.

Sanguis Xpi, salva me. Passio Xpi, conforta me.

īhu fili Dei, miserere mei.

Nos jungat thronis vere thronus Salomonis.

Virgo coronata duc nos ad regna beata.

Nos cum prole pia benedicat Virgo Maria.

Credo q̄d̄ Redemptor me' vivit, et in die novissima stabit sup'
terram : et rurs' sup' inducar pelle meâ, et in carne mea
videbo dēu : reposita hæc spes est in sinu meo.

Ordo prophetar' minuat penas animar'.

Laus Deo.

Magnificat anima mea Dn̄um.

Martir scē Dei, duc ad loca me requiei.

Legends at the feet, or round the circumference, resemble the
following :

Ralph de Cobham de Kent Esquier,

Qe morust le vingtieme jour de janvier

L'an de grace MCCCC. gist ici :

Priet a du par charite pur lui.

Orate p̄ aīa dn̄i Willi' Bisshop, Clcī q' obiit v° die Maii a° do'
MCCCCCXII, cui' aīe ppiciet ds.

Orate pro anima domini Wilhelmi Bisshop, Clerici, qui obiit
quinto die Maii, anno Domini 1512. cujus animæ propicietur Deus.

Pray ffor the sowlys of Willi' Kemp and M'get his wyf. ye wʰ
Willi' dep'ted in the yere of our Lord 1539.

Of yoʳ charite py ffor yᵉ soulis of Willm̄ Byrd and Margaret his
wife which decessid ye xv day of Apl. yᵉ yerᵉ of oʳ lord M.CCCC.XVI.
on whos soulis ihū have mcy.

Heere lyeth Maistre Peter Andreye, gen. whoos sowle god p'don.

In gracia et misericordia īhu hic requiescit Dnus Johēs Taylor,
q̄dam huj' ecclīe rector : cuj' aie ppiciet altissimus. Amen.

Orate p' ana Johīs Bancroft, et Alicie ux'is ej, qui q̄dem Johēs
obiit vi° die mens' Junii, a° dn̄i MDXXI : et predicta Alicia obiit—die
mens'   a° dn̄i   , quorum aīabs et omnium fidelium
defunctorum ppiciet' ds. Amen. The omission of the date for the
wife or husband (the survivor) is very common.

Of your charite pray for the sowlys of John Peyton, and Katerine
his wif. on whoos sowles and all Crysten sowles īhu have mcy.

Of a later style the following is a specimen :

In memoriam Ricardi White, infantuli beatissimi

	in			
Qui	a	peccato	re	natus
	sine		de	

a lavacro simul et vitâ decessit, in vitam auspicato albatus eternam.

One of the commonest epitaphs is the following :

Es test' Xpe, q̄d non jacet hic lap' iste

Corp' ut ornet' s' spirit' ut memoret'.

Hem tu q' trans' magn' medi' puer' an sis

Pro me funde prec', quia sic mihi sit venie spes.

The last two lines often run thus :

Quisq' er' qui transier' sta perlege plora

S' qd er', fueramque qd es, pro me precor ora.

Rare brasses are:

> Priests with a chalice containing the host: particularly when the latter has the letters Ihc.
>
> A chalice by itself, exceedingly rare.
>
> Knights or squires with tabards or surcoats.
>
> Figures of the 17th century, with hats; in some counties.
>
> Painted brasses.
>
> Three-quarter priests.
>
> Hearts with legends issuing from them.
>
> Children in grave-clothes.
>
> Emaciated figures, or skeletons with shrouds, (Fulbourn,) or without (Hildersham, Sawston). An absurd legend, that the person represented died of hunger, or of love, is usually related of these.
>
> Figures with churches in their hands. These represent the founder or re-founder of the church.

VI. 8. *Chest for Alms.* These but rarely occur and generally are of late date. They are varied in form and design. In Branford, Suffolk, is one of 1591, with the following inscription:

> Remember ye pore; the Scripture doth recorde
> What to them is given is lent unto the Lorde. 1591.

VI. 33. *Monuments.* The fuller the account of all, late or early, in the church, of course the better: but all previously to the Rebellion should be carefully described.

The Founder's tomb generally occurs at the north-west of the altar, generally in a mural recess; and is usually an essential part of the original church, not an after addition. There is one in the south wall of the Chancel (seen externally) at Trumpington.

VI. 34. *Lombardicks.* These generally are of granite or alabaster, having a coffin shape: there is a slightly raised cross in the center, and the legend runs round it. By the side of the cross are sometimes represented a chalice, a hand with a ring, a sword, a distaff, and many other devices. Probably, as the science of Ecclesiology advances, we shall find that the various forms of the cross refer to the different situations in life of the parties whom it commemorates: all sketches of these are very valuable. The legends are often very difficult to read: they may be copied with the rubber and black lead: and are more easily to be decyphered on the paper than in the stone. There are fine examples in Jesus College chapel, and in S. Clement's church, Cambridge. The inscription on the latter, and on a very well preserved one in Little Shelford, are here given:

+ Ici: gist: youn: de: helysingham: clerk: jadis: mayr: de: caynbrigge: par: charite: priet: pur: lui: qe: lalme: en: pais: endormie: qi: pur: lui: priera: qarante: jours: de: pardon: avera: qi: morust: la: qarte: jour: de: julli: le: an: de: grace: de: nostre: seysnour: mile: tres: cent: vint nevime.

+ Ici . gist . sire . johan . de . friu
ile . qi . fust . seigniour . de . ces
te . vile . vous . qe . par . ici . passe
t . par . charite . pur . lalme . priet.

The latter, though not metrically arranged, is in verse, and would, in modern French, read thus:

Ici git sire Jean de Freville,
Qui fut seigneur de cette ville:
Vous qui par ici passez,
Par charité pour l'âme priez.

There is a fine specimen of a Lombardick Cross at Rampton, and several at Lolworth, Cambridgeshire.

Sometimes a brass figure is surrounded by a Lombardick inscription in stone, as at Bottisham church.

Lombardicks must not be confounded with the sculptured alabaster slabs (Lolworth, Tadlow,) which are of much later date. They are called 'alabaster,' as being indeed so in the best specimens: in the poorer they are of plain stone, and sometimes even of chalk. Lombardick letters are of early English date. Black letter inscriptions (as they are commonly called) were introduced early in the fourteenth century. The forms of letters in ancient legends should be very carefully studied, as the date of inscriptions may hence be determined with considerable accuracy.

VI. 36. *Stained Glass.* It is needless to say anything on this subject, (beyond a request to our members to be most particular in their accounts of the glass,) in consequence of the excellent article furnished by Mr Williment to the Glossary of Architecture. As this however is one of the most beautiful as well as interesting objects of Ecclesiological research, a few additional remarks may not be out of place.

The earliest glass consists almost entirely of three colours, gold, blue, and red; but these, and especially the two last, are of greater purity, depth, and richness, than that of later ages, owing partly to the greater thickness of the material. The early devices are for the most part mosaic patterns with broad and rich borders, but very little glass remains of a date earlier than the fourteenth century. That in the Chancel of Trumpington is Early Decorated, and very fine. Almost every village church in England was anciently adorned with stained glass; and most of the churches near Cambridge still contain fragments. In some cases, as at Landbeach and Eaton Socon, considerable portions exist in tolerable preservation.

The glass of the fourteenth century usually exhibits single figures of Saints or Bishops in their vestments, under canopies, the ground being often diapered. Some portions of this date may be seen in the Chapter House, Ely. In the fifteenth century the grouping of figures was introduced, and they are often in a kneeling posture, with scrolls proceeding from their mouths, held in their hands, or thrown across the body, bearing scriptures in the black-letter character. In the earlier examples the letters are of Lombardick or Early English character, and placed only at the feet of effigies. A very elegant and simple device was to glaze windows in diamond panes of a thick and dull glass, containing in the middle an elegant flower, leaf, initial letters, or a badge. Specimens remain in the side Chapels of King's College Chapel, and at Waterbeach and Harlton; and in the north Chantry at Hacconby, Lincolnshire. Coats of arms often occur. Architecture when represented, which it commonly is in the later examples, is usually of singularly incorrect design and perspective, and appears quite debased even though the work of pure ages. The same may be remarked of ancient Illuminations and Brasses. The best test of the age of stained glass is the costume represented, especially the armour, since even a fragment, as a helmet, arm, leg, or foot, will be sufficient to determine its age with considerable accuracy. The arrangement of the lead-work, often very beautiful, may also be noticed. This in the earlier specimens is *cast*, not *milled*.

Much stained glass may often be found in blocked windows, or by turning up the soil near the church-walls.

We trust, that in pursuing these researches, our members will always be on the alert to use every opportunity of speaking a word in due season, for restoration, and against destruction; and that in the case of the contemplation of any extraordinary barbarism, such as the decapitation of a Chancel-Arch as useless, or the removal of a Rood-Screen, as being in the way, they will lose no time in transmitting the information to head-quarters.

Before we conclude, a few words may be allowed on that part of our study which, as it is the most interesting, so must it be kept constantly before our eyes, if we would enter into the feelings of the great church-builders of other days, now with GOD.

We enter the Church Militant by Holy Baptism; therefore the Font is placed by the entrance at the west end: a Church built upon the foundation of the Apostles and Prophets, as the earthly building rests on the Piers of the Nave, often twelve in number: we pass along this, keeping our eyes fixed on the Passion of CHRIST, depicted in the great eastern window, and trusting to the merits of His One Sacrifice, as represented by the one Altar, till we arrive at the close of our life, imaged by the Chancel-Arch. This we pass through Faith, some symbolism of which often occurs; as the Blessed Saints and Martyrs have gone before us, whose figures are depicted on the Rood-Screen: and thus enter the Church Triumphant, represented by the Chancel.

We conclude by a passage from one of the Canons of our Church, too little observed in the present day.

"Whereas the church is the House of GOD, dedicated to His holy worship, and therefore ought to remind us both of the greatness and goodness of His divine majesty; certain it is that the acknowledgement thereof not only inwardly with our hearts, but also outwardly with our bodies, must needs be pious in itself, profitable unto us, and edifying to others. We therefore think it very meet and behoveful, and heartily commend it to all good and well-affected people, that they be ready to tender unto the LORD the said acknowledgement by doing reverence and obeysance both at their coming in and going out of the said churches, Chapels, or Chancels, according to the most ancient custom of the primitive Church in the purest times, and of this Church also for many years of the reign of Queen Elizabeth."

Cambridge Camden Society.

The Society trusts that its Members, while pursuing their Antiquarian researches, will never forget the respect due to the sacred character of the Edifices which they visit.

Date. *Name of Visitor.*

Dedication,	Parish,	County,
S. Mary and S. Michael.	Trumpington.	Cambridgeshire.

I. **Ground Plan.** *C. N.* 2 *A.* 2 *Ch. Tower at West end.*

1. Length } of Chancel {39 ft.} Nave {57 ft.} Aisles {57 ft.} Porches { }
2. Breadth } {16 ft.} {20 ft.} {9 ft.}

Transepts { } Tower { } Chapels {37 ft.} {13 ft.}

  3. Orientation.

II. **Interior.**

  I. Apse.

   1. Plan.
   2. Windows.
   3. Apse-Arch.
   4. Groining.

  II. Chancel.

   1. East Window. *5 l. 3 f. Geomet. tracery of 4 fs. 3 fs. and 5 fted triangles. Ext. dr. horizontally returned. A 4 fted circle in gable.*
   2. Window Arch. *d. with label and internal jamb-shafts.*
   3. Altar.
     α. Altar Stone, fixed or removed.
     β. Reredos.
     γ. Piscina. *Large double EE. 3 f. a. 3 f. in head, the whole under a d. label continued down the sides.*
       (1) Orifice. *deep 4 f. in each.*
       (2) Shelf. *Narrow chamfered stone ledge across spring of arch.*

4

δ. **Sedilia.** *Wd. cill used as such.*

ε. **Aumbrye.**

ζ. **Niches.**

η. **Brackets.**

θ. **Easter Sepulchre.**

ι. **Altar Candlesticks.**

κ. **Steps—number and arrangement.** 2 *modern brick, by rails.*

 λ. **Altar Rails.** *Well carved, but of late arabesque character.*

 μ. **Table.** *Good plain oak.*

4. **Clerestory, N.**
  S.

5. **Windows, N.** 2 *elegant early D. lancets, of 2 l. 3 fted with large 3f. in head. Ext. and int. labels with notch-head terminations.*
  S. i. 3 *plain intersecting ls. D.* ii. iii. *as on N. side, but* ii. *partly blocked.*

6. **Window Arches, N.** ⎱ *as ext. Arch.*
     S. ⎰

7. **Piers, N.**
  S.

8. **Pier Arches, N.**
   S.

9. **Chancel Arch.** *Dies into wall at impost, without piers.* **Plain** *d. with chamfered edges. A small label on west side.*

10. **Stalls and Misereres.**

11. **Chancel Seats, exterior or interior.**

12. **Elevation of Chancel.** *Level with Nave.*

13. **Corbels.** *Five modern heads in each int. cornice string.*

14. **Roof and Groining.** *Semi-decagon cieled vault, with wooden ribs and bosses, modern.*

III. North Chancel Aisle.

 1. **Windows, E.**
   N.
   W.

 2. **Roof and Groining.**

IV. South Chancel Aisle.

 1. **Windows, E.**
   S.
   W.

 2. **Roof and Groining.**

V. North Transept.

 1. **Windows, E.**
   N.
   W.

 2. **Transept Arch.**

 3. **Roof and Groining.**

VI. *South Transept.*

    1. Windows, E.
                  S.
                  W.

    2. Transept Arch.

    3. Roof and Groining.

VII. *Lantern.*

    1. Windows.

    2. Groining.

VIII. *Nave.*

    1. Nave Arch.

    2. Panelling above Nave Arch.

    3. Rood Screen.   *Lower panels remain, but concealed by pues.*

    4. Rood Staircase.

    5. Rood Door.

    6. Rood Loft.

    7. Piers, N. ⎱ *Six fine lofty D.* i.—v. *4-clustered, each cluster of*
                ⎰ *3 semi-circ. beaded shafts, finely moulded bell-caps and*
            S. ⎱ *bases.* vi. *respond,* ½ *a 4-clustered pier. Base to* vi. **S.**
              ⎰ *of very wide spread, and EE. character, on sq. plinth.*

    8. Pier Arches, N. ⎱ *Slightly d. of* 2 *richly moulded orders. labels*
                 S. ⎰ *terminated by heads not reaching to caps.*

    9. Triforia, N. 1st tier.
                  2nd tier.
             S. 1st tier.
                  2nd tier.

   10. Clerestory, N.   *Four circ.* 4 *fted lights, with bold deep int. and ext. M s.*

                 S.   *Four single* 3 *fted lancets, without int. splay. d. labels ext. and int.*

   11. Windows, N.
                 S.

   12. Window Arches, N.
                   S.

   13. Belfry Arch.   *Lofty D. d. with fine cont. M s. and label horizontally returned, bases stilted, blocked with boards.*

   14. Parvise Turret.

   15. Roof and Groining.   *Low pitched mod. king-post.*

   16. Eagle Desk.

   17. Lettern.

   18. Poppy-heads.

   19. Pulpit, (*position and description*).   *On north side of P.* ii. **S.** *good modern.*

   20. Hour-Glass Stand.

   21. Reading Pew.   *As Pulpit.*

   22. Pews.   *All mod. but* 2 *in N. with arabesque Jacobean panels. At west end, mod. open seats.*

   23. Galleries.   *One mod. at west end.*

IX. North Aisle.

    1. Windows, E.   1 *D*. 3 *disengaged ls.* 5 *f. jamb-shafts, and int. label only.*

                N.   2 *D*. 3 *l*. 3 *f*. i. 4 *fted net-tracery.* ii. *intersecting* 3 *fted.*

                W.

    2. Chantry Altar.

                α Piscina.

                β Aumbrye.

                γ Niches.

                δ Bracket.

    3. Roof and Groining.   *Mod. sloped open timber.*

X. South Aisle.

    1 Windows, E.   *Same as in N.*

                S.   *As in N.*

                W.

    2. Chantry Altar. α Piscina. (*in S. Ch.*) *Small* 5 *f. g. stone shelf.* 6 *f. orifice. bold d. label.*

                β Sedilia.

                γ Aumbrye.

                δ Niches.

                ε Bracket.

    3. Roof and Groining.   *As in N.*

XI. " Ornaments."

    1. Parclose.   *Pier* i. *of S. Ch. mt. as if by insertion under A.* i.

    2. Shrine, fixed or moveable.

    3. Niches.

    4. Brackets.

    5. Mouldings.   *A triply moulded string round the int. under wds. of A s. and Ch s. and a plain square edged one ext.*

    6. Arcades.

    7. Sepulchral Recesses.

    8. Benatura.

    9. Corbels (*date of head-dress, &c.*) *4 heads built in S. wall of S. Ch. to support a Db. Monument* (1681.)

    10. Arches of Construction.

    11. Interior Surface of Arch toward Aisles.

    12. Spandril Spaces.

    13. Vaulting Shafts.

    14. Woodwork.

    15. Pavement.   *Modern brick.*

XII. Belfry, E.

          N.

          W.

          S.

XIII. Font.

    1. Position.   *West end of Nave, close to Belfry Arch.*

2. **Description.** *Good P. 8 l. Each side panelled with 4 f. circles, charged with roses and blank shields alternately. At lower corners of bason, male and female heads alt. on a receding M. Stem 8 l. panelled in manner of 2 l. wds. 5 fted and 5 fted under embatt. transoms. At each angle a circ. bead. Base of 2 plain slopes, i. with heads and flowers, ii. with alt. square and circ. sockets.*

3. **Cover.** *Modern.*

4. **Kneeling-stone.**

5. **Measurements.**

III. **Tower.** *Fine early D.*

1. **Form.** *Square.*

2. **Stages.** *3.*

3. **Spire Lights.**

4. **Lantern.**

5. **Parapet.** *Embatt. of 4.*

6. **Pinnacles.**

7. **String-Course.** *Below parapet, with lion-head gurgoyle in middle of each.*

8. **Belfry Windows.** *Plain d. of 2 l. without cusps.*

9. **Windows of Tower, S.** *A single 3 f. lancet light, with a similar one, but 5 f., below.*

   W.

   N. *As S.*

   E. *B. wd. without mullion. A very high-pitched weather-moulding reaches up to it.*

10. **Buttresses.** *4 sgs. at W. end, 2 at rt. angles at each corner, at E. one do.*

11. **Construction and age of Woodwork and Floors of the Tower and Spire.** *3 floors of massive old oak.*

12. **Bells.** α **Number.** *Five.*

    β **Tone.**

    γ **Inscription and Legendal History.** *i. in old black letter without date: "Qui regnat et unus Deus det munus." ii. "Cano busta mori cum pulpeta vivere desi. Omnia fiant ad gloriam Dei. T. Eayre, 1749. John Hailes, Thomas Spencer, Churchwardens." iii. 1723. iv. "John Darbell made me 1677. Thomas Allen gave me a treabell for to be." v. MC.*

    δ **Chime.**

    ε **Remarkable Peals rung.**

    ζ **Saint's Bell.**

    η **Arrangement, &c. of Frames.**

13. **Beacon or Belfry Turret.**

    α **Situation.**

    β **Form.**

γ State of Defence.

δ Line of Beacons.

14. Staircase. α Construction. *Spiral newel at S. W. angle, of little ext. projection.*

    β Doorways. *Flat 3 f. headed, with old oak door.*

    γ Spiral Bead.

15. Defensive arrangements of Tower.

16. Thickness of walls.

17. General Character of Tower as peculiar to the district, or adapted to scenery and situation.

IV. Exterior.

1. West Window. *Fine D. 3 l. 5 f. (lately restored, and side lights transomed.) a 3 f. above middle l. label returned horizont. to buttresses.*

2. Window Arch. *Equilat.*

3. West Door. *Fine deep cont. roll mouldings; bold label with heads. Inside: jamb-shafts supporting depressed flat-sided A. with deep Ms. and label.*

4: Porch, N.

 α Inner Doorway. *D. d. of 4. cont. uniform og. members.*

 β Benatura.

 γ Windows, $\left\{\begin{array}{l} \text{E.} \\ \text{W.} \end{array}\right.$ *A door into N. Ch. d. internally flat-sided, deep Ms. with string carried over it.*

 δ Groining.

 ε Outer Doorway. *d. cont. Ms. label falling into ext. string.*

Porch, S.

 α Inner Doorway. *As N. but much mt.*

 β Benatura.

 γ Windows, $\left\{\begin{array}{l} \text{E.} \\ \text{W.} \end{array}\right.$

 δ Groining.

 ε Outer Doorway. *Modern.*

5. Parvise.

 Windows, E.

    N. or S.

    W.

6. Doors in α Chancel or Chancel Aisles, N. *One blocked, formerly opening into a Sacristy, d. A. with bold int. label.*

       S. *Priest's door near west end. Small pointed of 2 plain cont. orders. Label with mt. notch-heads.*

  β Nave or Aisles, N.

      S.

  γ Transepts, &c.

7. Niches.

8. Buttresses. *Plain and bold D. of 2 sgs.*

9. Pinnacles.

10. Arcades.
11. Parapet. *Plain.*
12. Mouldings.
13. Pinnacle Crosses. *Mt. stem. over E. Wd.*
14. Gurgoyles.
15. Eave Troughs, and general arrangement of Drains.
16. Crosses in Village or Church-yard. *1 mt. on N. W. 8 l. stem bevilled from a square, on square bevilled base.*
17. Yew in Church-yard.
18. Sancte Bell Cot.
19. Lych-Gate.
20. Coped Coffins. *3 in pavement of S. Aisle, with crosses pattée and floriated stems.*
21. Rood Turret.
22. Masonry. *Of Tower, internally squared and fine-jointed clunch. Most of the ext. covered with plaister.*
23. Nature of Stone. *Clunch and Barnack or Ketton.*
24. Composition and age of Mortar.
25. Joints in Arches.
26. Door and Stanchions.
27. Roof. α Present pitch. *Of C. original height: of N. low.*
       β Original pitch. *Of Nave, equilat. (See III. 9 E.)*
      γ Nature.

V. Crypt.

1. Form.
2. Arrangement.
3. Vaulting.
4. Piers.
5. Dimensions.
6. Windows.
7. Door.
8. Stairs.
9. Altar Appurtenances.
10. Lavatory.

VI.

1. Evangelistic Symbols.
2. Confessional. *A recess in north wall of tower commonly supposed to be so : seems to have been used for ringing the sance bell in the tower.*
3. Hagioscope.
4. Lychnoscope. *A low square recess (not visible ext.) at S.W. corner of Chancel.*
5. Painted Tiles.
6. Texts, (Canon 82.)
7. Church Terriers, (Canon 87.)
8. Homilies, &c. (Canon 80.)
9. Chest for Alms, (Canon 84.)
10. Commandments, (Canon 82.)

11. Church Plate.
12. Church Chest. *Old, in S. Ch. iron clamps, 2 padlocks and lock.*
13. Fald Stool.
14. Reliquary.
15. Oratory.
16. Chrismatory.
17. Sun Dials.
18. Royal Arms—Date and Position.
19. Paintings on Wall or Roof.
20. Tradition of Founder.
21. Connexion of Church with Manor.
22. Time of Wake or Feast. *S. Peter's Day.*
23. Conventual Remains.
    (α) Situation of Church with respect to other buildings.
    (β) Situation and Description of Cloisters.
    (γ) Situation and Description of Chapter-House.
    (δ) Abbat's or Prior's Lodgings.
    (ε) Gate-House.
    (ζ) Other Buildings.
24. Antiquity of Registers.
25. Funeral Atchievements, viz. Banners, Bannerets, Pennons, Tabard, Helm, Crest, Sword, Gauntlets, Spurs, Targe.
26. Embroidered work.
27. Images of Saints.
28. Stone Sculptures.
29. Merchants' Marks.
30. Library attached to Church.
31. Well connected with Church.
32. Heraldry. *A Hatchment in N. Ch. (See 35 and 38.)*
33. Form of Churchyard, and situation of Church in it.
34. Brasses. *On high tomb in N. Ch. (See 35.) a Brass of a Knight with hauberk, surcoat, ailettes, shield, sword, prick spur, head on helm. Effigy, size of life, Sir Roger de Trumpington, (died 1289.) Legend lost. Arms, 2 trumpets pile-ways between 8 cross crosslets, 3, 3, and 2.*
35. Monuments. *A. i. of N. A. filled with perpeyn wall, embatt. at top, in which a high tomb under og. D. arch, 5 f. double feathered, sides of cusps flowered. An int. and ext. label with heads, jambs of engaged shafts. On N. side of tomb a series of 11 canopied panels, 5 f. with blank shields in spandrils. On the tomb in a slab of Purbeck marble, a Brass (see 34).—On north of the above a low oblong stone with Brass, George Pitchard, 1650. 2 shields : i. a fesse between 3 escallops. ii. 3 Scotch spurs empaling a fesse between 3 cross crosslets fitchée.*
36. Epitaphs.
37. Lombardics.
38. Stained Glass. *The original of early D. date in wd. ii. on S. of C. and fragments in middle light of E. wd. (engraved in Lysons'*

Cambridgeshire.) *Some fragments, of mod. date, in* wd. iii. *of* **N. A.** *A shield azure 2 trumpets pile-ways between eight cross crosslets or.* (*Trumpington.*)

39. **Chapel, N.** *N. of C. Formerly a Ch. or Sacristy. On outside remain corbels wh. supported roof. N. of Aisle, opens into it by* **2 D.** *equilat. As. Ps.* 4 *clust^d. each shaft having vert. bead, and richly moulded cap. Lighted by* **3** *wds. as in* **N. A.** *on west end a door with flat-sided* **A.** (*See* **IV. 4.** γ.)

    α Dedication.

    β Sides, N.

          E.

          W.

          S.

    γ Roof and Groining.

40. **Chapel, S.**   α Dedication.

        β Sides, N.   *Ps. and As: as in* **N. Ch.**

              E.   *wd. mod. round A.*

              W.   1 *wd.* **D.** 2 *l.* 5 *f. and* 4 *f. in head. mt. by insertion of door.*

              S.   2 *wds.* **D.** *same as in Aisles.*

        γ Roof and Groining.

GENERAL REMARKS.

General state of repair.

Late alterations—when—by whom—and in what taste.

Notice to be taken of any recess **E.** or **W.** of the Sedilia: of the capping of Norman and Early-English Towers; of niches in the West soffit of the S.E. Nave Window; and of *gabled* Towers.

S. ANDREW, CHERRY HINTON, CAMBRIDGESHIRE.

[*N.B. Those particulars which do not apply to the present instance have not been repeated in the Scheme.*]

I. **Ground Plan.** *Chancel, Nave, 2 Aisles, Tower at west end.*

  1. Length   ⎰of Chancel ⎰ 44 *ft.* ⎱ Nave ⎰ 68 *ft.* ⎱ Aisles ⎰ 68 *ft.* ⎱
  2. Breadth ⎱   ⎱ 21 *ft.* ⎰   ⎱ 24 *ft.* ⎰   ⎱ 10 *f t.* ⎰

         Transepts ⎰   ⎱Tower ⎰   ⎱ Chapels ⎰   ⎱

  3. Orientation.

II. **Interior.**

  II. Chancel. Character. *Fine EE.*

    1. East Window. 5 *l. disengaged,* 5 *f. late Tud. insertion, flat* 4 *cent. A.*

  5

α Altar Stone, fixed or removed. *Laid down in centre of Nave, with 5 plain crosses nearly effaced.*

β Reredos. *Ugly modern panels in Italian style, painted.*

γ Piscina. *Beautiful EE. double, triple detached shafts, labels fall into vert. bead, which forms with string under windows a square compartment, dog-tooth in Arch M.*

(1) Orifice. *Of Eastern, 8f. the other 6f.*

δ Sedilia. *3 graduated fine large EE. on single shafts. d. As. deeply moulded, with labels as Piscina.*

κ Altar-Rails. *Modern.*

λ Table. *Plain and mean wooden.*

μ Steps—number and arrangement. *2 by Altar-rails, of stone; modern.*

5. Windows, N. *All blocked, but originally as S.*

   S. *Fine lofty EE. arcade of 13, 5f. deeply moulded and labelled heads and banded shafts, pierced with lancets in couplets, with blank arch between each couplet, behind wh. a buttress. A cornice string above, and one below windows both ext. and int. The couplet above Priest's door shorter than the rest.*

9. Chancel Arch. *Fine lofty EE. d. of 3 channelled or fluted orders; piers complex, a front shaft with 2 receding on each side, and a bead between each. A modern square wd. above it, mutilating the Ms. at the crown.*

10. Stalls and Misereres. *A plain Stall with small poppy head on each side against screen.*

12. Elevation of Chancel. *Level.*

14. Roof and Groining. *Flat modern, painted, and cieled between timbers.*

VIII. Nave.

3. Rood Screen. *P. of 2 compartments on each side of door, each comp. of 2 l. flat 3f. above which sup. Door d. A. 5f. double feathered, 4f. circles and loops in spandrils. Below lights, a string of 3f. circles on east side: below this plain panels.*

7. Piers, N. *EE. clustered of 4, set diamondwise, with bead between each. Bases on square plinth.*

   S. *Ditto.*

8. Pier Arches, N. *5 very fine EE. d. Ms. of two orders, each triply M'd. all with labels.*

   S. *Ditto.*

15. Poppy heads. *5 in N. A. curiously but rather rudely worked in flowers and leaves: one with mt. inscription.*

16. Western Arch. *T. Norman. Heavy wall-piers, with shallow underchannelled abacus at impost: on east sides an edge-shaft. Arch 4 cent. late Tud.*

18. Roof and Groining. *Flat modern tie-beam: pseudo-queen post.*

19. Pulpit, (*position and description*). *By N. pier of C. A. Late arabesque.*

21. Reading Pew. *Modern.*
22. Pews. *A few shabby deal towards east end, but mostly open seats in mod. deal.*

IX. *North Aisle.*

1. Windows, E. 1 *P. of* 3 *l. d. Arch. lights* 5 *f. g. sup. middle l. with secondary transom: flat* 4 *f. in head, and* 4 *fs. above side-lights.*

    N. 4 *as* E. } *Below windows an* EE. *string, carried*
    W. 1 *as* E. }   *round* N. *door.*

3. Roof and Groining. *Sloping Tud. tolerably good.*

X. *South Aisle.*

1. Windows, E. 1 *P.* 3 *l.* 5 *f. sup. flat* 4 *cent. A. large* 4 *f. in head.*

    S. 4 *do.* } *String as in* N. *A.*
    W. 1 *do.* }

3. Roof and Groining. *As* N. *A.*

XI. *" Ornaments."*

9. Corbels (*date of head-dress, &c.*) *In* N. *A. embattled, supporting roof, winged angels underneath, bearing charged shields on breasts.*

11. Interior Surface of Arch toward Aisles. *As Nave side.*

15. Pavement. *Modern brick.*

XIII. *Font.*

1. Position. *On west side of* 5*th nave pier, near entrance.*

2. Description. *Plain circ. T. N. bason, large leaded orifice, on mod. round stem.*

3. Cover. *A board, mod.*

4. Kneeling-stone. *Low square mt. mass of masonry.* 2 *steps towards S.W.*

III. 𝕿𝖔𝖜𝖊𝖗. *Very late Tudor.*

1. Form. *Square, low, and very plain.*

2. Stages. 3, *as divided by strings.*

5. Parapet. *Embattled.*

7. String-Course. *All plain.*

8. Belfry Windows. *Small plain* 2 *l. square-headed.*

9. Windows of Tower, S. 1 *small square, very plain, in* 2*nd. sg.*

10. Buttresses. *Diagonal, at western corners.*

IV. 𝕰𝖝𝖙𝖊𝖗𝖎𝖔𝖗.

1. West Window. *Tud.* 4 *cent.* 3 *l.* 5 *f. set northward with respect to B. A., a staircase turret being at the S.W. corner, not seen ext.*

2. Window Arch.

4. Porch, S. *Late Tud. faced with brick.*

    α Outer Doorway. *A. of clunch, much mt.*

    β Inner Doorway. *Fine EE. with deep Ms. and label: jamb-shafts gone, but caps remaining.*

    γ Windows, { E. } *Plain ones blocked.*
                 { W. }

δ Benatura. *Perhaps remains in square plinth of stone by inner door on E. side.*

6. Doors in α Chancel or Chancel Aisles, N.

> S. *A beautiful EE. priest's door, d. A. with deep and rich Ms. much mt. single jamb-shafts, internally with deep cont. Ms.*

> β Nave or Aisles, N. *One in N. A. EE. string round it int. and arch chamfered as far as the spring. Outside, fine bold cont. Ms.*

> S. *Int. same as N.*

8. Buttresses. *Of Chancel, bold but plain EE. with weathered heads and a set-off midway. Of Nave, P. of considerable projection, but very plain.*

11. Parapet. *Plain.*

14. Gurgoyles. *2 lions' heads in parapet of N. and S. Aisles.*

16. Crosses in Village or Church-yard. *Fragment in latter. square chamfered to 8 l. on 8 l. plinth.*

19. Coped Coffins. *A plain early stone one, flat, near Sacristy door in Chancel.*

22. Nature of Stone. *Clunch internally; externally Barnack or Ketton ashlar.*

25. Door and Stanchions. *That in S. Porch good ancient oak.*

26. Roof α Present pitch. *Of Chancel, flat. Nave of good pitch, but mod. as Clerestory existed 50 years ago.*

32. Brasses. *One EE. taken up, a floriated cross with marginal Lombardic letters traceable at E. end of Nave, placed N. and S. One magnificent floriated cross in Chancel, also taken up, slab 9ft. long, by 3ft. 10in. wide, flowers on stem, and resting on a Holy Lamb. Marginal legend in brass also removed.*

33. Monuments. *Some costly but tasteless modern marble in Chancel.*

37. Chapel, N. α Dedication. *A Sacristy on N. of Chancel, by east end, opens from Chancel by a Tudor doorway, 4 cent. with meagre discont. mouldings. On west side an ugly brick chimney.*

A Few Words to Church Builders, first edition, 1841

The motive claimed for the production of this pamphlet was that of filling an identified gap in the available literature: 'while so many have written [on the subject of the design of churches] as architects, so few ... have treated it as Churchmen' (p. 3). Although the opening sentence suggests that the publication should be seen 'in some measure as a preface to the *Designs for Churches* about to be published' (p. 3) this, it seems, never appeared. Thus *A Few Words to Church Builders* may be taken to represent the closest the Society came to producing a formal set of ideals to be incorporated in the design and arrangement of churches. The stated aim of treating the design of churches from the perspective of the layman underpins the whole of the work; while the title suggests a practical manual, the content is clearly

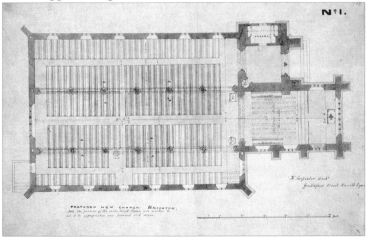

28. St Paul's, Brighton, R.C. Carpenter, 1848. The long chancel, the replacement of box pews by uniform, east-facing benches and the steps leading to the altar are all typical of the changes in church planning which the Camdenians initiated. Only the placing of the tower in the north-east corner – dictated by the cramped site – was unusual. This plan should be compared with the following illustrations for St Stephen, Kirkstall, Leeds and Hunslet Chapel in Leeds.

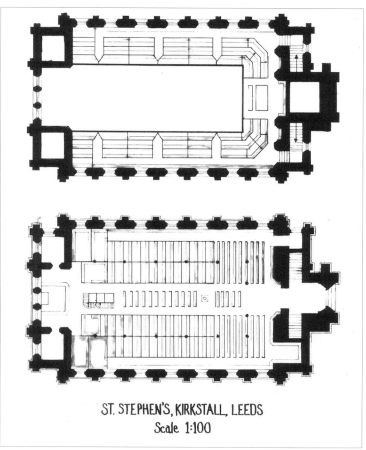

ST. STEPHEN'S, KIRKSTALL, LEEDS
Scale 1:100

29. St Stephen's, Kirkstall, Leeds, R.D. Chantrell, 1827-9, plan drawn by
Christopher Webster. Arrangements such as this and the one illustrated in the
Hunslet Chapel represent the two most widely used types in the early-nineteenth century. The free benches are in the rear part of the nave and in the central aisle, and the three-decker pulpit is in front of the altar.

addressed elsewhere. It is 'to church-building committees …
[that the words are written] rather than architects, who generally know what is right if they be only allowed to practise
it' (p. 4). Perhaps predictably, it argues that 'the whole superintendence [of the building project] should be vested in the
Clergyman of the parish, the only man who, in most country villages, understands anything about the matter' (p. 4)
,although the generous opinion of the knowledge of the

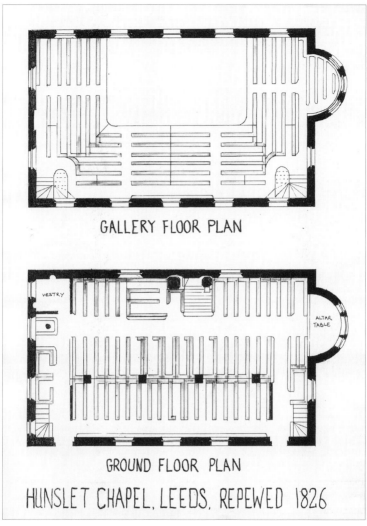

GALLERY FLOOR PLAN

GROUND FLOOR PLAN

HUNSLET CHAPEL, LEEDS, REPEWED 1826

30. Hunslet Chapel, Leeds, early-nineteenth century repewing. Plan drawn by Christopher Webster. Placing the pulpit on the long north or south wall, and orientating the seats towards it, was a popular arrangement.

architectural profession is in marked contrast with the Society's later views of it. But since Neale recognises the proliferation of committees in the process of appointing architects, in accepting or rejecting their designs and perhaps in suggesting modifications, he is keen to educate them in Camdenian principles. Thus they are told of the importance of having a deep chancel, separate from the nave; of placing the font in the correct place; of having the altar raised on steps; of including a sedilia and aumbry etc. And while acknowledging that it is unlikely that all the 'suggestions' could be followed, 'to describe a church such as it ought to be' will also show 'how very far below this model are most of the buildings to which we now by courtesy give that name.' (p. 4). A further example of Neale's pragmatisim is to be found at the end of the document when he states: 'If every thing else is forgotten, and two points only remembered, THE ABSOLUTE NECESSITY OF A DISTINCT AND SPACIOUS CHANCEL, and THE ABSOLUTE INADMISSIBILITY OF PUES AND GALLERIES in any shape whatever, I shall be more than rewarded.' (p. 30). Although intended for mid-nineteenth century consumption, it is equally helpful to twenty-first century scholars, eager to distil the essence of Camdenian thinking.

Many of the prescriptions set out in the pamphlet were highly contentious: the prominence given to the chancel; the introduction of a reredos or rood-screen; the use of candlesticks on the altar, for instance. The pamphlet deals with the controversies that are likely to ensue with commendable rationality. For some issues there is a specific section to ward off critics, for instance, 'Objections [to roodscreens] answered' (p. 19). Elsewhere, Camdenian 'innovations' are justified by reference to a range of criteria, for instance to the symbolism used by 'ancient architects', or by reference to Durandus[1] 'the great authority on such points' (p. 7). Other items are justified by reference to English pre-Reformation examples. However, mindful of the need to avoid appearing to be leading the Church of England in an unacceptably 'Roman' direction, Neale more frequently quotes precedents from the post-Reformation period –

'the Reformed Anglican Church in its best times' (p. 5) to support his views, for instance, the building and decoration of churches under Archbishop Laud, or by referring to sixteenth and seventeenth century Visitation Articles (pp. 10 and 15), or by reference to the *Book of Common Prayer* rubrics. Despite 'so many controversial points … If anything contained in [this pamphlet] can be shewn to be contrary to the Rubrick or the Canons of the Holy Anglican Church, the writer will be thankful to be told of it and the first to expunge it.' (p. 30). Despite the best efforts of critics to prove otherwise, it seems clear that the Society had positioned itself firmly on the Anglican side of the religious divide.

A Few Words to Church Builders was written by J. M. Neale and was first published in 1841. It was available in two versions; one containing the four plates reproduced here, priced at 6d., and one priced at one shilling without the plates but with four appendices A, B, C and D, the first three of which are reproduced here. A second edition appeared in 1842 and an 'entirely rewritten' and greatly expanded third edition was published in 1844. In the second and third editions, the number of appendices is reduced to three.

Notes

[1] William Durandus (*c.* 1230-96) was Bishop of Mende and author of the *Rationale Divinorum Officiorum,* a compendium of liturgical knowledge with mystical interpretation. This work was translated by Neale and Webb, and published in 1843, together with a lengthy introduction by them. The publishers were Rivingtons in London, Stevenson in Cambridge and T. W. Green in Leeds.

A FEW WORDS

TO

CHURCH BUILDERS

𝔓𝔲𝔟𝔩𝔦𝔰𝔥𝔢𝔡 𝔟𝔶 𝔱𝔥𝔢 ℭ𝔞𝔪𝔟𝔯𝔦𝔡𝔤𝔢 ℭ𝔞𝔪𝔡𝔢𝔫 𝔖𝔬𝔠𝔦𝔢𝔱𝔶

"EXCEPT THE LORD BUILD THE HOUSE: THEIR LABOUR IS BUT LOST
THAT BUILD IT"

CAMBRIDGE

AT THE UNIVERSITY PRESS

STEVENSON CAMBRIDGE PARKER OXFORD
RIVINGTONS LONDON

M DCCC XLI

Price Sixpence

CAMBRIDGE CAMDEN SOCIETY.

Instituted May, 1839.

PATRONS.

His Grace the LORD ARCHBISHOP of CANTERBURY.
His Grace the DUKE of NORTHUMBERLAND, Chancellor of the
University of CAMBRIDGE.

The Right Honourable the LORD HIGH CHANCELLOR OF ENGLAND,
High Steward of the University of Cambridge.
His Grace the LORD ARCHBISHOP of ARMAGH.
The Right Hon. and Right Rev. the LORD BISHOP of LONDON.
The Right Rev. the LORD BISHOP of WINCHESTER.
The Right Rev. the LORD BISHOP of BATH and WELLS.
The Right Rev. the LORD BISHOP of LINCOLN.
The Right Rev. the LORD BISHOP of GLOUCESTER and BRISTOL.
The Right Rev. the LORD BISHOP of CHESTER.
The Right Rev. the LORD BISHOP of ELY.
The Right Rev. the LORD BISHOP of HEREFORD.
The Right Rev. the LORD BISHOP of WORCESTER.
The Right Rev. the LORD BISHOP of NOVA SCOTIA.
The Right Rev. the LORD BISHOP of NEW ZEALAND.
The Right Rev. the BISHOP of Ross and ARGYLL.
The Right Rev. the BISHOP of EDINBURGH.
The Right Rev. the LORD BISHOP of NEW JERSEY, U. S.
The Hon. and Rev. the MASTER of MAGDALENE COLLEGE.
The Rev. the MASTER of CLARE HALL.
The Rev. the PROVOST of KING'S COLLEGE.
The Rev. the MASTER of DOWNING COLLEGE.
The Very Rev. the DEAN of PETERBOROUGH, Regius Professor of
Divinity.

PRESIDENT.

The Venerable THOMAS THORP, Archdeacon of Bristol,
Tutor of Trinity College.

OFFICERS.

CHAIRMAN OF COMMITTEES.
The Rev. JOHN MASON NEALE, Downing College.

TREASURER.
ARTHUR SHELLY EDDIS, Esq., Trinity College.

HONORARY SECRETARIES.
BENJAMIN WEBB, Esq., Trinity College.
James Gavin Young, Esq., Trinity College.
FREDERICK APTHORP PALEY, Esq., St John's College.

A FEW WORDS TO CHURCH BUILDERS.

Introduction. 1. THE following pages are intended in some measure as a preface to the DESIGNS FOR CHURCHES about to be published by the CAMBRIDGE CAMDEN SOCIETY: but as it is hoped that they may by themselves be not altogether useless to the practical enquirer, it has been thought well to print them separately, and in a more portable form. They are intended for the use of those to whom GOD has given, not only the means, but the will, to undertake a work, the noblest perhaps in which man can engage, the building a House in some degree worthy of HIS majesty: and who feel at the same time their want of the knowledge which is necessary to the correct and successful accomplishment of so great a design. It is needless to say that the writer is not an architect; it is rather his intention to dwell on the Catholick, than on the architectural, principles which ought to influence the building of a church; and he wishes to bring forward from the stores of a Society a larger number of examples for the illustration of his remarks, than would be easily procured by an individual.

What books useful. 2. IT is somewhat strange that, while so many have written on this subject as architects, so few should have treated it as Churchmen, though every one will allow that Ecclesiastical Architecture is a thing in which the Church mainly is, or ought to be, interested. Yet though no systematic treatise has appeared, setting forth how churches may best be built in accordance with Catholicity and antiquity and the voice of the Anglican Church, there are several works from which much information may be gained on this point. Among these we may especially notice—Mr Bloxam's Catechism of Gothick Architecture; the Rev. F. E. Paget's S. Antholin's; the Rev. G. A. Poole's Lectures on Churches and Church Ornaments; Mr Pugin's True Principles of Pointed or Christian Architecture; and the articles on the subject which appeared in the 55th and 58th numbers of the British Critic. I may also refer to the first part (Ninth Edition) of The Few Words to Churchwardens by the Cambridge Camden Society; and to the second part (Second Edition) of the same Tract which has just been published.

Design of this Tract. 3. IT is not supposed that all the decorations recommended in this tract can be adopted in every church, especially where the building is carried on

1—2

under the controul of a committee. But to describe a church such as it ought to be may perhaps have the advantage of shewing how very far below this model are most of the buildings to which we now by courtesy give that name. And here we may address ourselves to church-building committees, for whom, rather than for architects, who generally know what is right if they be only allowed to practise it, these words are written. The smaller these committees are, the better ; and the whole superintendence should be vested in the Clergyman of the parish, the only man who, in most country villages, understands anything about the matter ; and whose tastes, and feelings, and views are far more likely to be correct than those of any other person. Above all, if the Incorporated Society for building and enlarging Churches and Chapels be consulted, care must be taken that the beauty of the building be not sacrificed to the accommodation of worshippers, a fault into which that great Society is—I say it with grief—too apt to fall.

4. THE style in which a church ought to be built must depend on several considerations. It will, generally speaking, be better to adopt that (if any) which prevails in the district in which the church is to be built. The number of worshippers will much affect the style.. Nothing for example can be better suited to a small chapel than Early English; for a larger building either of the two later styles may be employed with more effect. It is cheapness alone which has induced modern architects to build churches of every shape and size exclusively in the Early English style, without any regard to the many circumstances which may render it less applicable in particular districts. But yet it is ill-suited to a large "cheap church," because Early English buildings are remarkable, when large, for the elaborateness and expensiveness of their decorations, as the Minster churches of Southwell and Beverley may shew.

Style depends on locality,

and size.

5. IN a cold and faithless age like this, to attach any importance to the selection of a Patron Saint will probably provoke a smile in some, and in others may cause a more serious feeling of displeasure at the superstition of those who do it. We are well content, if it be so, to lie under the same charge, and for the same cause, as Andrewes, Hooker, and Whitgift. Let us give an example or two of the motives which lead to the choice of a Patron Saint now. In a large town in the south of England a meeting-house was built by a dissenter, who called it, out of compliment to his wife, Margaret chapel. This, being afterwards bought for a church, is now named *Saint* Margaret's. In the same town is another chapel called All Souls, "because all souls may there hear the word of GOD." Other dedications are now given, which were

Patron Saint.

rarely, if ever, in use among our ancestors. Such are—S. Paul, instead of SS. Peter and Paul; Christ church, and S. Saviour's, for a small building; Emmanuel church, and the like. But who would found a church in England—once the " England of Saints"—without some attention to the local memory of those holy men whose names still live in the appellations of many of our towns? Who, in the Diocese of Lichfield, would forget S. Chad? in that of Durham, S. Cuthbert? in those of Canterbury and Ely, S. Alphege, and S. Etheldreda? Surely, near S. Edmund's Bury, a church-founder would naturally think of S. Edmund, or in the west of Wales, of S. David! Still it may be as well to confine ourselves to the holy men commemorated in our own Calendar; not as undervaluing others, the Blessed Saints and Martyrs of the Most High, but in order that we may not give occasion to be accused of Romanism.

6. THERE ARE TWO PARTS, AND ONLY TWO PARTS, *Ground Plan.* WHICH ARE ABSOLUTELY ESSENTIAL TO A CHURCH— CHANCEL AND NAVE. If it have not the latter, it is at best only a chapel; if it have not the former, it is little better than a meeting-house. The twelve thousand ancient churches in this *Chancel abso-* land, in whatever else they may differ, agree in this, that *lutely essen-* *tial: and why.* every one has or had a well-defined Chancel. On the least symbolical grounds, it has always been felt right to separate off from the rest of the church a portion which should be expressly appropriated to the more solemn rites of our religion; and this portion is the Chancel. In this division our ancient architects recognised an emblem of the Holy Catholick Church; as this consists of two parts, the Church Militant and the Church Triumphant, so does the earthly structure also consist of two parts, the Chancel and Nave; the Church Militant being typified by the latter, and the Church Triumphant by the former. But in nine-tenths of " new churches," we shall find no attempt whatever at having a distinct Chancel, or it is at best confined to a small apsidal projection for the Altar. And this, one of the most glaring faults of modern buildings, has not met with the reprobation which it so well deserves; nay, has even been connived at by those who knew better. To illustrate the respective sizes of ancient and modern Chancels, I subjoin [Plate 2] two ground plans, one of a church built about 1250, the other of one within a mile of it erected in 1835. And surely, if we had no other reason for the prominence we attach to a Chancel than that, without one exception, our ancestors attached such prominence to it, it ought to be enough for us who profess to admire their wisdom, and as far as we may, to tread in their steps. And this was the practice of the Reformed Anglican Church in its best times, as may be seen in the churches of S. Catherine Cree, and Hammersmith, consecrated by Bishop Laud;

Leighton Bromswould, built by George Herbert; Little Gidding, erected by Nicholas Ferrar; and above all in the church of S. Charles the Martyr, at Plymouth.

7. THIS division, essential in the interior, is not always to be traced in the exterior. It is far better indeed, generally speaking, that it should be marked in both; and to this end the breadth of the Chancel should be a little less than that of the Nave; a difference of four or five feet will be quite sufficient. The height of the Chancel is usually less, in the same proportion. Sometimes this latter is the only mark of division, as in the churches of Chailey and Southease, Sussex. In a cross church, it will be sufficiently marked by the Transepts. The only kind of church in which it cannot be externally shewn, is where there are Chancel and Nave, with two Aisles to both; but this is rarely the case, except in city churches, or where the builders were cramped for room. Where there is no exterior division, as in Wymington, Bedfordshire, there is only the more reason to make that in the interior more distinctly marked.

Division not necessary in the exterior:

yet desirable.

8. THE comparative size of Chancel and Nave is a point which, within certain limitations, must be left to taste. Yet, as a general rule, the Chancel should not be less than the third, or more than the half, of the whole length of the church. The larger, within the prescribed bounds, it is made, the more magnificent will be the appearance of the building.

Comparative size of Chancel and Nave.

9. A CROSS is of course the most beautiful form in which a church can be built. Yet those persons who think it necessary to a perfect building are in great error; not one tenth of the churches in this country having been erected in that shape. From this mistaken idea Transepts have been attempted with funds hardly sufficient for Chancel and Nave, often to the destruction of the fair proportion of the Chancel. The symbol conveyed by the Cross is certainly better adapted than any other for a Christian place of worship; yet that of a ship, which the other form sets forth, is by no means unsuitable, and was a very favourite one with the early Church, as S. Chrysostom and S. Hilary (writing concerning the SAVIOUR's walking on the sea) testify. A very general fault of modern cross churches is the excessive breadth of each of the four arms; whence the arches to the lantern, or central part of the cross, are made obtuse to an almost absurd degree; and sometimes are omitted altogether, as unneces-

The Cross a beautiful form:

yet not at all necessary:

and why.

sary. But if they are unnecessary to the safety of a church, they suggest (according to the great authority on such points, Durandus) an important symbolical meaning; namely, that by the writings of the four Evangelists the doctrine of the Cross has been preached through the whole world. And this is the reason that we so often find the Evangelistic Symbols on, or over, them.

10. IF however the funds should be more than adequate for the erection of Chancel and Nave,—and these ought to be built first,—the Aisles to the latter are of the next importance. For we thus gain another important symbolism for our ground plan, the doctrine of the MOST HOLY AND UNDIVIDED TRINITY, as set forth by the three parallel divisions which meet us as we enter the church at the west. There is no fixed rule as to the breadth of the Aisles ; about a third of that of the Nave seems a fair proportion to each. For instance, the plan, Plate I., has the Aisles too broad for beauty, though thereby it serves the better to illustrate the point for which it was given.

Aisles very desirable:

their breadth.

11. THERE is not the slightest objection, whatever the fastidious taste of modern times may think of it, against building at first one Aisle, if the funds are not sufficient for the erection of two. And it is far more in accordance with Catholick principles to build one Aisle as it ought to be, than to "run up" two cheaply; always supposing it in this, as in other cases of imperfect design, to be the intention of the builder, that the church shall, at some future time, though perhaps not by himself, be completed. And this leads to an important remark. It is not of consequence that the opposite sides of a church should correspond with each other. Churches with one Aisle, or one Transept, constantly occur. I will prove this by some examples, taken at random.

Churches with one Aisle.

Llanfwrog, Denbighshire, has	N. Aisle.
Tal-y-Llyn, Merion.	S. Transept.
Brandon, Suffolk,	S. Aisle.
Avening, Gloucestershire,	N. Aisle.
Rodborough, Gloucestershire,	N. Aisle to Chancel and Nave, and S. Transept.
Hunsdon, Herts.	S. Transept.
Stanford, Berks.	N. Aisle.
Erith, Kent,	S. Aisle to Chancel and Nave.

But now in most people's opinion, the great beauty of a church if it have two Aisles, consists, in having both sides the same in details, whereas nothing can be more opposite to the true principles of Ecclesiastical Architecture than this idea, so cramping to boldness of design and variety of ornament.

Position of Tower. 12. This remark applies particularly to the position of the Tower. Now-a-days it is almost universally placed at the west end of the church, that it may "stand in the middle;" whereas the following positions are equally good: the intersection of a cross church, or between the Chancel and Nave, where the church is not cross; these are very common. Other positions are

Middle of north Aisle, Vaucelles, near Caen.
Middle of Nave, Caen S. Sauveur.
North of Chancel, Berneval, Normandy.
South of Chancel, Standon, Hertfordshire.
North end of the north Transept, Montgomery.
South end of the south Transept, East Lavant, Sussex.
North side of the Nave, Goustranville, near Caen.
South side of the Nave, Midhurst, Sussex.
East end of the north Aisle, Patching, Sussex.
West end of the north Aisle, Clapham, Sussex.
East end of the south Aisle, West Grinstead, Sussex.
West end of the south Aisle, Amiens S. Loup. Holyrood, Southampton.
North-west angle of Nave, York S. Crux.
South-west angle of Nave, Sacombe, Herts.
Western part of the Chancel, Yainville, Normandy.

It shews the perverseness of modern times, that the only position in which a Tower never ought to be built, namely over the Altar, is almost the only one which in modern churches ever takes place of that at the west end; and it is adopted for the same reason, it is "just in the middle" too.

Tower not essential. 13. It must always be kept in mind, that the Tower, though a highly ornamental, is not an essential part of a church; and the really essential parts should never be sacrificed for it. A bell gable may be made a beautiful ornament, and is very well suited to a small church.

Building by parts. 14. Where the funds are small, or of uncertain amount, an excellent plan is to finish the Chancel and Nave first, leaving it to the piety of future years to raise Aisles. Of this a remarkable instance occurs in Ovingdean church, Sussex. It is a small Early English building, with Chancel and Nave; it was intended that a south Aisle should be subsequently built, and arches for it (like large arches of construction) appear in the south wall. That it never was built is evident from the Early English windows inserted in the flint work with which the arches are filled up. And such is the case in Irnham, Lincolnshire. Lamentable indeed it is when this intention of the pious founders is frustrated by modern "improvements". In a large and magnificent church in Derbyshire, where there was only a south Aisle, room was wanted on account of the increase of population. Instead of throwing out a north Aisle, the parish, at a greater expense, had a gallery built all round the church! Transepts and a Tower also may very easily be added. An instance of the intention to provide for future Transepts which has never been carried into execution, occurs in Iford, Sussex. Here the arches are Norman. Only where the church is cross, and the Tower is to be central, care must be taken to make the belfry arches strong enough for the future weight: the want of this precaution had nearly, as every one knows, caused the ruin of the Cathedral church of Peterborough. This way of building was often adopted by our ancestors, especially in the north of Devonshire, and with the happiest results; as it ought to be now in the Cathedral churches of Sydney, Montreal, and Calcutta.

15. The choice of the stone must of course depend in a great measure on the locality; for almost every county has its own kinds of stones. Brick ought on no account to be used: white certainly is worse than red, and red than black: but to settle the precedency in such miserable materials is worse than useless.

Stone.

Flint however may be used with good effect. Where the windows are faced with stone, the flints may be used either whole, as is generally the case in Norfolk and Suffolk, or cut and squared, as is usual in Kent and Sussex. The church of S. Michael and All Angels in Lewes (re-built in the middle of the 18th century) is a most beautiful model, so far as respects the materials. But if there be no local stone, and the situation be near the sea so as to admit of easy water-carriage, the best material would be Caen stone for the walls and windows, and Purbeck marble for the piers and shafts. Bath stone may be conveyed to almost any part of the country at a small cost: it is easily worked, and durable when properly selected. Caen stone was most deservedly a special favourite with our ancestors. When first taken from the quarries, it is so soft as to be carved easily: but it speedily hardens on exposure to the air, and never loses its colour. It can only be quarried in the spring and summer months, as when first taken out of the earth it is peculiarly liable to be spoilt by frost. It must, till used, be raised at least four inches from the ground,

Flint.

Caen stone.

and carefully covered over with straw in frosty weather. There has been very little demand in our own country of late years for this stone, inferior stones having taken its place: but with the reviving taste for church architecture an increasing demand for it has gone hand in hand. The stone is landed here in masses of about 70 cubic feet ; each foot weighs from 135 to 140 lbs.

Orientation. 16. THE Orientation, that is, the precise degree of inclination of the church towards the East, is the next point. It is well known that a direction to the *due* East was not thought necessary by our ancestors: they used to make the church point to that part of the horizon in which the sun rose on the day of the foundation of the church, the day also, it should be remembered of the Patron Saint. But many modern churches are built directly north and south, in total defiance of the universal custom of the Church in all ages: and some, as if out of pure perverseness, though they stand east and west, have the Altar at the west.

Chancel not to be entered by the laity on common occa-sions. 17. HAVING thus disposed of the ground-plan and the questions connected with it, we proceed to observe that the Chancel, except during the celebration of the Holy Eucharist, ought not to be used for the accommo-dation of worshippers. The reason is plain : this portion of the church ought to be set expressly and exclusively apart for our Holiest Mysteries. This is ordered by the Holy Ecumenical Council of Constantinople: and that it is the practice of the Anglican Church will be proved by the following extracts from Visitation Articles of the sixteenth and seventeenth centuries.

"Is your Chancel divided from the Nave or body of your church with a partition of stone, boards, wainscot, grates, or otherwise, wherein is there a decent strong door to open or shut, as occasion serveth, with lock and key, to keep out boys, girls, irreverent men and women?"—Bp. Montague, 1638. (Reprinted at Cambridge, 1841).

" Whether a partition be made and kept between the Chancel and the church, according to the advertisements?"—Abp. Parker, 1559.—Abp. Grindal (1571) directs that the Roodscreen be left to separate the Chancel from the Nave, and instead of the Roodloft, "some convenient crest put upon it."

" Whether is it [the Chancel] fenced in with rails or pales ?" Bp. Bridges, 1617.

This deplorable waste of "available space," to use the language of the cheap-church-builders of the present day; this due regard to the solemnity with which the worship of Almighty GOD ought to be performed, to speak as the great Prelates whom I have just quoted would have spoken; is doubtless the reason why Chancels have been so totally neglected in the ground plans of modern churches. They are pronounced, in short, an unnecessary expense.

Elevation of Chancel.
18. A VERY magnificent appearance may be given to the Chancel by raising it on a flight of nine or ten steps. I do not say that this is at all necessary; but where it can be done it has a fine effect, and renders the Chancel very dry. Every Chancel however should be raised at least two steps at the Chancel arch: a Chancel level with the Nave is all the more objectionable when (which however never ought to be) the Roodscreen is wanting.

Altar.
19. THERE is some difficulty in speaking on the subject of the Altar, on account of the vehement objections raised by many against the use of any thing beyond a Table, nay, to the very name ALTAR. For those however, who consider a stone Altar, though not necessary, desirable, the great difficulty is where to find a model since their almost universal destruction in the great rebellion. It seems that a solid mass of masonry about six feet by four in size, and about four feet in height, is the most suitable form. This also gives scope for panelling of any design and to any extent. In the Prior's house at Wenlock Abbey, Shropshire, is a fine specimen of a stone Altar quite perfect, and panelled in front. In the Altar we are left more to our own judgement than in any other part of the church; and having few actual models we must be especially careful not to admit anything at variance with the purity of the style in which we are working; for it must always be remembered that the Altar is something more than a piece of church furniture; that it is an actual and essential part of the church.

Reredos.
20. THE reredos, dossel, or Altarscreen, when wrought with all the richness of which it is capable, is one of the most beautiful ornaments of a church. We are unfortunately in possession of but few examples. The Cathedral churches of Gloucester, Bristol, Wells, Winchester, and Worcester, the Abbey churches of S. Alban's and Selby, and Christ Church Hampshire, the churches of S. Saviour's Southwark, Geddington Northamptonshire, Tideswell Derbyshire, and Harlton Cambridgeshire, all furnish examples which may at least be useful in affording the leading idea of a modern reredos.

Sedilia.
21. THE sedilia I would restore, if I could, because at least they are ornaments; but if their restoration would give offence I would not insist on them, because they are only ornaments. However great the offence may be which

the Catholick arrangement of a Chancel causes, we must bear it rather than give up an arrangement which is of the essence of a church; the case is not the same with sedilia. It may tend to remove objections to their use to observe that one of the alterations which Romanism has introduced into modern churches as seen on the continent is the disuse both of them and of the piscina: the latter being too often (like our Fonts) appropriated to the reception of lumber, and the place of the former supplied by chairs.

Table of Prothesis, or Credence.   22. MANY opinions have been entertained as to the situation in our ancient churches, of the Table of Prothesis; that is, the place whereon the Elements were placed previously to their Oblation. As this is a point on which we cannot speak positively, three ways remain in which we may supply the want. We may make a recess like a small Easter Sepulchre on the north side of the Altar, in which case we can easily find many excellent models, as Shottesbrook, Berkshire; or we may have an octagonal projection on the south, supported on an octagonal shaft, after the manner of some piscinæ; or, better still, a large low bracket, which, as in Barholme, Lincolnshire, and Hardham, Sussex, seems to have answered this purpose. At Southease, Sussex, is a plain oblong recess on the Gospel or north side with a slightly projecting base, which was doubtless a Table of Prothesis, and the slab in Compton, Surrey, was probably the same. The Credence table in the church of S. Cross, Hampshire, is on the south side of the Altar.

Aumbrye.   23. THE Holy Vessels were anciently kept in an aumbrye or locker, as they are to this day in Irnham church, Lincolnshire. They should always be kept in the church; and, of course, if an aumbrye be used, due attention must be paid to its security. The usual position of aumbryes was on the Gospel side of the Altar, though sometimes they are found in the east wall. They are seldom much ornamented, though the door, where it remains, is sometimes elaborately carved. A good model, from Chaddesden, Derbyshire, is figured in Bloxam's Catechism of Architecture.

Elevation of Altar.   24. THE Altar should be raised on one, two, or three flights of three steps each. "Are there ascents to the Altar?" asks Bp. Montague in his Visitation Articles. The sides of these steps may be panelled in a series of quatrefoiled circles, or in many other ways; sometimes, as in Geddington, Northamptonshire, and Wimborne Minster, Dorsetshire, the dedication and date of the church are or have been carved on them.

Chancel arch. 25. VERY much of the appearance of a church depends on its Chancel arch. A very excellent effect is given by throwing a highly ornamented "squinch" across each corner of the lantern: this gives the lantern of the Cathedral church of Coutances its great beauty.

It is the intention of the Cambridge Camden Society to publish shortly, as an appendix to this tract, a collection of lists of windows or other parts of a church, arranged in order of date.

Use of lists. 26. THE use of such lists is threefold. Firstly, it is possible that the enquirer may find among them some church in his own immediate neighbourhood. Or, secondly, he may be able to procure without difficulty working drawings from some church mentioned in them. Thirdly, they may at least be useful to those in whose churches they are found, by directing their attention to them, and tending to the preservation of the things themselves. And on all these accounts, a catalogue raisonnée of windows, and the like, now existing in England would be of inestimable value to the ecclesiologist.

Early English Windows. 27. WE now come to speak of windows, and first of Early English. In very small churches, especially in Wales, we find the east window consisting of a single lancet (Llanaber, Merionethshire), but the effect is poor, though it may do well enough for the west end. A great improvement upon this is to have two equal lancets (Patching, Sussex). These lancets are sometimes trefoiled (Up Waltham, Sussex), sometimes ogee and trefoiled (Chithurst, Sussex); in other cases at some height above them they have a plain circle (W. Hampnett, Sussex), a quatrefoil (Cherrington, Gloucestershire), a sexfoil (Portslade, Sussex), an eightfoil (Beddingham, Sussex), or a smaller lancet (All Saints, Hertford). Three lancets are the most usually adopted; these, it need not be said, symbolise the HOLY TRINITY. These are sometimes of equal height under one internal arch (Bosham, Sussex), or not (Foxton, Cambridgeshire); some have internal shafts (Clymping, Sussex). Oftener they are of unequal height, either under one interior arch (Onibury, Salop), or not; in which case they may be adjacent (Thakeham, Sussex), or not adjacent (Faringdon, Berkshire); and sometimes each lancet has internal shafts (Beaulieu, Hampshire). They sometimes nearly reach to the ground (Ringmer, Sussex). Again, the breadth as well as the height of the central light is sometimes greater than that of the others (The Temple). These lancets are sometimes trefoiled (Finden, Sussex), and the central light in this case is sometimes, though rarely, ogee (Jevington, Sussex). In other cases there are three plain circles in the head of the window (Ditchelling, Sussex), or near the apex of the roof is a circular window (Birdbrooke, Essex). We sometimes find two tiers; the lower of three equal, the upper of three unequal lights (Vanner Abbey, Merionethshire); and this arrangement has sometimes the circular window in the apex (New Shoreham, Sussex). Four equal lancets at the east end are unusual (Repton, Derbyshire); sometimes they are arranged two and two (Goustranville, Normandy). Five unequal lancets are exceedingly beautiful (Oundle, Northamptonshire). A still finer effect is produced by seven, as in Ockham, Surrey; an example almost unique. The chief thing which gives to modern Early English lights their wretched appearance is their double splay, as shewn in Plate III. This of course necessarily makes them larger, light pouring in and spreading through a single splay with so much more ease than it does through a dark one. Triple lancets are far too beautiful a feature to be used so cheaply as they frequently are now. The number of lights on each side of the Nave and Chancel is generally unequal. The Chancel of Cherryhinton, Cambridgeshire, of Jesus College Chapel, Cambridge, of Chailey, Sussex, of the church of S. Nicolas, near La Mailleraie, on the Seine, and the Chapel of the Seminary, Bayeux, are very fine specimens of this style; and the church of Clymping, Sussex, a plain but very good model of an unmutilated Early English building. Perhaps one of the most beautiful instances of an eastern triplet is at Castle Rising, Norfolk.

Decorated and perpendicular windows.   Of Decorated and Perpendicular Windows, as no description can convey an adequate idea, a large classified list will be given in the Appendix.

The deep symbolism however of many, perhaps all, of the former, is well worthy our attention. To take only one example. The east window of Dunchurch, Warwickshire, is figured in Bloxam's Catechism, p. 108. May we not see in it a most speaking type of the doctrine of the MOST HOLY and UNDIVIDED TRINITY? Its *three* *tre*-foiled lights, its tracery of *three* *tre*-foiled *triangles* round an *equilateral triangle*, and its *three* *tre*-foils interspersed between these; what else can they point to?

Font.   28. THE subject of Fonts is highly interesting; a list of models will be given in the Appendix. The reader cannot do better than consult Mr Poole's before-mentioned little work, where he will find much valuable information on the subject. To his remarks there we may add a few more.

The shape of the bason may be either square, circular, or octagonal; the greater number of examples in each style are octagonal; an octagon being a very ancient symbol of Regeneration. Where there is a central, and four corner shafts, the latter have capital and base, the former has neither. Hexagonal Fonts, though they do occur, are not to be imitated; yet they are not always late; that at Ramsey, which is Norman, is of this shape. A pentagonal Font, of which Mr Poole has not an example, occurs at Hollington, Sussex; a heptagonal one at Chaddesden, Derbyshire. I quite agree with Mr Poole, that coats of arms are to be avoided in ornamenting the instrument of our initiation into Him Who "was despised and rejected of men." Yet shields do occur in early Fonts: for example, at West Deeping, Lincolnshire, which is Early English. And shields with the Instruments of Crucifixion, and the like, would be no less beautiful than appropriate ornaments.

A kneeling stone at the west side appears desirable; it may be panelled to any degree of richness. It need hardly be observed that the cover should be richly carved in oak; there is a magnificent specimen in Castle Acre, Norfolk, about 16 feet in height. The pulley by which it is elevated is sometimes, as in Stamford S. George, curiously carved; the Fall of Man, the Baptism of our SAVIOUR, and His victory over the devil, are here frequently represented.

The position of the Font MUST BE IN THE NAVE, AND NEAR A DOOR; this cannot be too much insisted on: it thus typifies the admission of a child into the Church by Holy Baptism. The Canon orders that it shall stand in the ancient usual place; and I quote the following passages from the Visitation Articles of some of the Prelates before mentioned.

"Whether have you in your church or chapel a Font of stone, set up in the ancient usual place?" Abp. Bancroft, 1605.

"A handsome Baptistery, or Font, in the usual place." Bp. Bridges, 1636.

"Is there in your church a Font for the Sacrament of Baptism fixed unto the LORD's freehold? Of what materials is it made? Where is it placed? Whether near unto a church door, to signify our entrance into GOD's Church by Baptism?" Bp. Montague, 1638.

"A Font of stone, set up in the ancient usual place." Abp. Laud, 1636.

"A Font of stone, set in the ancient usual place." Bishop Wren; Hereford, 1635, and Norwich, 1636.

"A stone Font, towards the lower end of the church." Abp. Juxon, 1662.

29. WE now come to speak of the pavement. No
Pavement. doubt painted tiles* when they are really made well

---

* "Stones of course are best for the floor: then tiles, *as we make them now.*" A Few Words to Churchwardens (9th Edit.), part i. p. 14. "We do not think that stone is beyond doubt the best paving for a church. For our part, we like coloured tiles

are better than any other. This is the place for heraldic devices: we thus by treading them under foot symbolically express the worthlessness of all human dignity and rank in the sight of GOD. Excellent models both of devices and arrangements are to be found in the Cathedral church of Gloucester: in the Hospital church of S. Cross near Winchester; in the Chancels of Standon, Hertfordshire; of Poynings, Sussex; and Ludlow, Salop; and under a chantry in Christ Church, Hampshire. If stone be preferred, nothing can come up to white, and black Devonshire marble, chequerwise. Wood and brick are alike insufferable.

Doors. 30. IN the doors and porches of a church both the position and arrangement are matters of extreme importance. In a cross church we shall generally find five doors; three in the Nave, at the west, at the south-west, and at the northwest: one at the west of the north or south Transept, and one at the north or south side of the Chancel. This is called the Priest's door, and was always appropriated, as it ought to be now, to his entrance. Porches give great scope for beautiful groining; the devices here may be of a less chastened character than those in the church. Thus we meet with true-love knots, (because the earlier part of the service of Holy Matrimony was performed in this part), the zodiacal signs, and the like. In Early English, or early Decorated doors, a good effect will be given by terminating the drip-stone in those remarkable corbels called notch-heads, one of which is figured in the Glossary of Architecture, Vol. ii. pl. 39, fig. 3; and again in the corbel table, Vol. ii. pl. 28, fig. 4. Again, in the two later styles, why should we not adopt the beautiful custom which prevailed once, of terminating them in the heads of the reigning monarch and the Bishop of the Diocese? Neither are shields out of place here: when charged with armorial bearings, they are sometimes found in modern churches with the tinctures expressed; an architectural anachronism. There may be a stone seat on each side the porch, and a window of two lights on each side will add much to the richness of the whole.

Tower. 31. IN Mr Anderson's Ancient Models some excellent wood-cuts of spires are given, with a list of a few others. An additional list will be found in the Appendix.

Roof. 32. THE management of the interior of the roof, so as to look even decent, gives so much trouble to Churchbuilders, that they will perhaps be glad of some suggestions

tiles which are getting cheaper every day, just as well." British Critic, No. 59, p. 251. Both these sentences are equally true: if only sufficient emphasis be laid on the italicised part of the former.

on the subject, backed by sound reasons for adopting them. I am writing as a Churchman to Churchmen, and therefore must recommend that kind of roof which is most churchlike. As stone roofs are seldom thought of now-a-days, I shall confine myself to wooden ones. The common way of late is to have a tiebeam with king or queen posts: and no grant is given by the Incorporated Society for Churchbuilding except there be a tiebeam:—a rule which I earnestly hope will be dispensed with ere long. These unadorned beams and posts are either left bare, in which case (and it is the best) the church looks like a barn: or they are hidden by a flat cieling, which gives it the appearance of a drawingroom: or lastly, the cieling is coved, which is one degree less hideous than the last method. The remedy for all this is to do without the tiebeam. If the roof is a small one, over a Chancel for instance, it does not require a tiebeam, the rafters resting on the walls and being sufficiently tied by the collar: the interior may be boarded and panelled either as high as the collar or to the very ridges: this gives a handsome roof, and allows of abundant ornament in the shape of bosses, panelling, and the like. Or if there must be braces for strength, they may pass obliquely from the foot of the rafter on one side to the top of the corresponding rafter, as we find in some old roofs: either of these two kinds of open roof leaves an ample vaulted space internally, and on this account should be preferred, as more churchlike, to such as do not. But even these are less Ecclesiastical in their appearance, than could be wished: in the former the vault has a flatness and stiffness of outline; in the latter it is marred by the difference of shape in the rafters and braces: nor will either plan do for a large roof, as there will then be too much thrust on the walls. In all cases then, for a small church or a large, we heartily recommend the arched open roof, of all wooden roofs the most elegant and churchlike. In this the place of the tiebeams is supplied by arched braces pinned to the rafter and collars, and others again pinned under the hammerbeam. Of this kind of roof we have specimens both of the most elaborate and of the simplest kind: from the vast hall of Westminster down to the country church of ten yards by six. As all of these were erected in the 15th or early in the 16th century, they are so many standing refutations of the modern belief (acted on by the before mentioned Society,) that there is no safety without a tiebeam. There is an excellent article on this kind of roof in No. 58 of the British Critic, to which we refer for fuller details, and for engraved specimens from churches in Suffolk, a county famous for these roofs. We will only remark, that while they are the most churchlike as having the simplest and most uninterrupted vault consistent with safety, they are at the same time peculiarly beautiful. A small roof of two arches corresponds exactly with

2

a trefoiled light: a roof of three arches with a cinqfoiled light: the ornaments also generally found at the spring of the arches correspond to the richly feathered cusps of window heads, and in the spandrells of the arches, in the collars, cornices, purlins and the like, there is room for a variety of ornaments.

Ornaments.   33. OF these we may mention the following.

The monogram IHC, or IHS.

An Agnus Dei.

A pelican "in her piety."

A nest of young eaglets, the old one hovering over them: an allusion to Deut. xxxii. 11.

A boar rooting up a vine. Psalm lxxx. 11.

A salamander. When found on a Font, this animal symbolises the promise, "HE shall baptise you with the HOLY GHOST and with *fire;*" elsewhere it refers to Isaiah xliii. 2.

The Crown of Thorns.

The Instruments of Crucifixion.

All kinds of Crosses; especially a Cross botonnée, a Cross pattée, a Cross raguly, a Cross potence, a Cross moline.

The Crown of Thorns surrounding IHC.

A Chalice with Fruit.

A hart drinking. Psalm xlii. 1.

Two doves drinking out of one pitcher: an emblem of the peace and joy arising from the reception of the Holy Eucharist. A very ancient symbol.

The Tree of Life, with Adam and Eve, and the serpent.

On one boss, a barren tree; on the next, a tree in full bearing, swine generally revelling on the fallen fruit.

Our LORD in the ship (which was generally taken by the Fathers as a type of the Holy Church).

Bunches of grapes intermingled with wheat ears.

A Cross standing on a crescent.

A Rose and a Lily.

The Phœnix, which S. Clement adduces as a symbol of the Resurrection.

All these are strictly Catholick emblems, and might well be employed now. Sometimes, though less appropriately, the founder has alluded to circumstances connected with his own life; so the famous Norfolk legend of the pedlar who founded Brandon church, Norfolk, is worked in the open seats there.

Woodwork.   34. WE must now speak of the woodwork of a church. This includes the Roodscreen, Altar rails, doors, wood-seats, pulpit, faldstool, lettern, parish chest, alms box, and Font-cover.

Roodscreen. 35. WE have seen that the Chancel and Nave are to be kept entirely separate. This is done by the Rood-screen, that most beautiful and Catholick appendage to a church. We have also seen that the Prelates of the seventeenth century required it as a necessary ornament; and that they who were most inveterate against Roodlofts always held the Roodscreen sacred. Why is it that *not one* modern church has it? It constitutes one of the peculiar beauties of English buildings; for abroad it is very rare. There can be no objection to the erection of a Perpendicular screen in a church of earlier style; because such was the constant practice, and because that style is better adapted for wood work than any other. The whole may, and indeed ought to be, richly painted and gilded. The lower part, which is not pierced, may be painted with figures of Saints, as in Castle Acre, Norfolk; Therfield, Hertfordshire; Guilden Morden, Cambridgeshire: Bradninch, Devonshire; why S. Edmund the King so often occurs is not known. In the Appendix nothing will be given but what might well serve as a model, though some instances may be much mutilated.

Stone screens. Stone Roodscreens do not often occur. I may mention Ilkestone, Derbyshire; Harlton, Cambridgeshire; Great Bardfield, Essex; Merevale, Warwickshire; Christ Church, Hampshire, as examples; but the effect is not good in a small church.

Roodscreen retained by our Church. 36. Many Roodscreens were put up during the reigns of King James the First and King Charles the Martyr: there is a good instance in Geddington, Northamptonshire. It was erected by Maurice Tresham, Esquire, in 1618; probably as an expression (and a truly Catholick one) of thankfulness, as the words on the western side, "Quid retribuam DOMINO?" seem to imply. It is an arabesque imitation of the fine Decorated east window; and the effect is not bad. There are other instances in Stoke Castle, Salop, Isleham, Cambridgeshire, Middleton, Warwickshire, and Messing, Essex.

Objections answered. 37. Two objections have been made to the use of the Roodscreen now. The first is, that it is a Romish innovation, and is not to be met with before the 14th or 15th centuries. Now Early English screens, though not common, as might be expected from their material, do yet occur: as one at Old Shoreham, Sussex, the date of which is about 1250; and in Compton, Surrey, there is a Norman parclose, of the date of 1150. Add to which that modern Romanism, as we see it on the continent, has in almost every case removed the Roodscreen, and where the Roodloft is retained, it is mostly in the shape of an ugly twisted

2—2

beam thrown across the Chancel Arch. Secondly, it is said, that it prevents the worshippers from having a view of the Altar. But where this occurs, it is from the fault of the artist: for the "textilis aura" of such a Roodscreen as Llanegryn or Guilden Morden can prevent neither the Priest's being heard from, nor the people's looking to, the Altar.

Altar rails.   38. Since Altar rails were not known to our ancestors, any more than to the Romish Church at the present day, we must use our best diligence in adapting, where we cannot imitate. In modern churches, with hardly an exception, they are nothing better than eyesores. But, by exercising a little ingenuity, a model for them may be taken from the upper part of any perfect Roodscreen. But it may be questioned how far we are bound to retain Altar rails at all. At Orton, near Peterborough, they are not fixed, but only put up when the Holy Eucharist is administered: and many churches are without them altogether. The harm they have done to brasses and monuments is incalculable.

Door.   39. Our pious ancestors, who thought nothing in the service of God small or of no account, panelled their doors in the most elaborate manner possible ; the stanchions, locks, and handles were also very rich. Sometimes, as at Market Deeping, Lincolnshire, and Hickling, Nottinghamshire, the hinges ramify into tracery covering the whole surface of the door. Is it a proof of our modern wisdom that we now use deal doors grained in oak, or chesnut, as the case may be?

Seats.   40. We must now speak of the way in which the worshippers are to be accommodated. Those who have thought on the subject have long seen, and every day see more, the absolute necessity of getting rid, at any sacrifice, of those monstrous innovations, pews, or, to spell the word according to the most ancient spelling, pues. For remarks on the unmixed evil of which they have been the cause, I would refer the reader to Archdeacon Hare's first charge to the Archdeaconry of Lewes. The voice of the Anglican Church has been raised against the innovation long ago. For example: in the Visitation Articles of Bishop Bridges of Hereford, 1635, we find the following question [iii. 10]: "Whether doth any private man, or men, of his or their owne authority erect any pewes, or build any new seats in your church? and what pewes or seats have been so built? by whose procurement, and by whose authority? And are all the seats and pewes in the church so ordered that they which are in them may all conveniently kneel down in time of prayer, and have their faces towards the Holy Table?" And Bishop Montague, Bishop Wren, Archbishop Laud, and others, ask the question in nearly the same words. 'But people must sit somewhere, and they must be kept from the cold.' So they must. They will be sufficiently protected from the cold if the church be kept dry, and the doors during the time of worship shut close; above all, the daily service will do more towards making the church comfortable than anything else. And as to *sittings,*—our ancestors would have said *kneelings,*—they may easily be provided without pews. Two ways have been adopted for this purpose: the first, open wood seats; the second, chairs. The former was more prevalent in England, the latter on the continent.

41. I SHOULD not be disposed to adopt wholly either
Arrangement the one or the other: to use chairs alone would be to
of worshippers. deprive the church of some of its most beautiful ornaments; to use wood seats alone would be to leave hardly sufficient space unoccupied, and would occasion considerable difficulty in the arrangement of the Transepts. Plate 1 may make the arrangement which I would adopt more clear.

42. ON each side of the Chancel is to be a double,
Misereres. or, if needed, a triple row of misereres: these afford scope for an almost unlimited extent of carving. If the Chancel has Aisles, the misereres will not stand against the walls, but between and before the piers, and may have a canopy of tabernacle work thrown over them. Any Cathedral Church will afford excellent examples. Ripon, Winchester, and Dumblane have magnificent specimens. The row nearest the wall must, of course, have a slight advantage in point of elevation. It is needless to observe that this, and all the other wood-work in the church, must be of oak or chesnut. In smaller buildings we often find open wood seats, like those in the Nave, adopted instead of misereres.

43. WOOD SEATS are found of every degree of rich-
Chairs. ness. It is desirable that they should be somewhat inferior to those in the Chancel; and care must be taken that every one has ample room to kneel. The proper model for chairs, or prie-dieux (as they are called in France), may be seen by a reference to Plate 4. When used for sitting, the upper seat which moves on hinges, is shut down, and the back of the chair is towards the west; when wanted for kneeling, it is lifted up, the chair turned round, and the occupier kneels on the lower part.

44. WHERE shall the pulpit stand? is a question
Pulpit. which we continually hear asked. There are but two places where it ought to stand, namely, either on the north or south side of the Nave arch. It is better to have it of stone; in this case

it should be octagonal, richly panelled, projecting from the pier, and sloping off to a point, like that at Beaulieu, in Hampshire, figured in the Glossary of Architecture. The entrance is to be by a winding staircase in the pier itself. But the pulpit may also be of wood. It will then be octagonal, on an octagonal stem. And it may be sculptured, or painted, with the effigies of the eight doctors of the Church, or, which was more usual, with the four doctors of the Western Church, S. Ambrose, S. Augustine, S. Jerome, and S. Gregory the Great. Round the upper part may be carved, "Their sound is gone out into all lands: and their words unto the ends of the world." Excellent examples occur in Hatley Cockayne, Bedfordshire; Otterbourne, Hampshire; Castle Acre, Norfolk; and All Saints, Pavement, York.

But there are so many excellent pulpits of the time of King James the First, that I should have no objection to adopt this style. Some examples for the use of those who might wish to do so here follow:

1590. Ruthin, Denbighshire.	1632. Oxenhall, Gloucestershire.
1604. Sopley, Hants.	6633. Sep. 24. Clymping, Sussex.
1608. Kingstone next Lewes, Sussex.	1634. Ilkeston, Derby.
1616. Byfleet, Surrey.	1635. Barton, Camb.
1618. Geddington, Northampt.	1636. Sawley, Derby.
1624. Bristol Cathedral church.	1636. Pyecombe, Sussex.
1624. Rodborough, Gloucestershire.	1636. Wells—St Andrew.
1625. Breaston, Derby.	1636. York—St Cuthbert.
1625. Huish Episcopi, Somerset.	1637. Boston, Lincoln.
1627. Ashwell, Herts.	1638. Uppingham, Rutland.
1627. Keymer, Sussex.	1639. Iford, Sussex.
1630. Little Gidding, Hunts.	1640. Cerne Abbas, Dorsets.
1631. Steeple Morden, Camb.	1644. Whitchurch, Denbighshire.
1632. Bradford Abbas, Dorsets.	

45. ONE of the great abuses of modern times is the monstrous size and untoward position of the pulpit.

Position.

It, with the reading pue and clerk's desk, are in most modern churches placed immediately before the Holy Altar, for the purpose, it would seem, of hiding it as much as possible from the congregation. How symbolical is this of an age, which puts preaching in the place of praying! If prayer were the same as preaching, such a position would be more natural: but as the prayers are not offered to the people, but to GOD, our Church instructs us far otherwise. It is necessary to strike at the root of this evil, because some people seem still to fancy that the prayers ought to be preached; and what is called fine reading, in plain words, declamation, is preferred to the chant, or canto fermo, the primitive way of praying.

46. OTHER positions may be mentioned as occurring *Modern positions.* in modern times. In one of the most fashionable chapels in a fashionable watering place, the Altar stands in a low recess at the east end, and over it is a large room, with two openings in front, looking into the chapel; these serve respectively for reading-pue and pulpit. The church in a country town in Sussex has a large arch, thrown across the Chancel from pue to pue, *on* which is the pulpit, and *under* which is the reading desk, in the shape of a door, which shuts back or opens as occasion requires. This example has been followed in a village in Gloucestershire. In another village in Sussex, the clergyman mounts into a window seat, and there, without any desk or raised part before him, delivers his sermon from under a sounding board, erected above the window. Sometimes the pulpit is at the west end (alas! that it should be so in an University church!); and of course the worshippers, or rather the auditors, sit with their backs to the Altar. There are also parabolic sounding-boards, and semi-parabolic sounding-boards, and parabolic sounding-boards with a slice cut out to admit the light. Who can think, with common patience, on such enormities?

47. IT is, I hope, hardly necessary to caution you *Galleries.* against any approximation to a gallery. Bishop Montague (Articles of Inquiry, Cambridge, 1841) says of these (I. 10), " Is your church scaffolded" (*i. e. galleried*) " every where, or in part? do these scaffolds so made annoy any man's seat, or hinder the lights of any windows in your church?" Again Bishop Wren (III. 13), "What galleries have you in your church? How are they placed, or in what part of the church? When were they built, and by what authority? Is not the church large enough without them to receive all your own parishioners? Is any part of the church hidden or darkened thereby, or any of the parish annoyed or offended?" Still, if there be an organ, there must be a gallery for it; but it should be a shallow stone projection at the west end, such as we constantly meet with on the continent.

48. THE reading-pue is nothing but a modern *Reading-pue.* innovation, very ugly, very inconvenient, and totally repugnant to all Catholick principles of devotion. Who first sanctioned this mischievous and unhappy practice it is impossible now to determine: it certainly was not generally introduced before the 17th century. In its stead we ought to substitute two things, the faldstool, and eagle desk or lettern.

The faldstool, whence the Litany and other prayers *Faldstool.* are to be read, is a small desk at which to kneel; it is to be turned to the East, and may have rails on each side, as is the case in many of our Cathedral churches. The front admits of the most elaborate panelling. The proper place of this faldstool in a parish church is the entrance to the Chancel, on the east side of the Roodscreen. Its use is sanctioned, as indirectly by all parts of our Rubrick, so directly by the coronation service.

Lettern. The lettern is usually made of wood, though sometimes of brass. It may be described as a revolving desk, on the top of a stand about five feet in height. From it the lessons are to be read. Examples may be seen in the Glossary of Architecture. Brazen eagles are however the most usual, as well as the most beautiful ornaments: they are sometimes represented as trampling on a serpent. There are instances in many of our Cathedral, and in some of our parish churches, as Campden, Gloucestershire; Holy Rood, and S. Michael's, Southampton; Isleham, Cambridgeshire; S. Stephen, S. Alban's; Christ's and King's College chapels, Cambridge; S. Nicholas' and S. Margaret's, Lynn; Magdalen and Merton College chapels, Oxford; Croydon, Surrey; Salisbury S. Martin; Eton Chapel; and Wiggenhall S. Mary, Norfolk.

Parish Chest. 49. The Parish Chest, in better ages, often received a considerable degree of embellishment. In Clymping, Sussex, is one of good Early English character: Bignor, in the same county, and Luton, Bedfordshire, have good Perpendicular chests. This is not to be confused with the alms box: about the latter some curious particulars may be found in Bloxam's Catechism, with some specimens. In Castle Acre church, Norfolk, is a beautiful alms-box, said to have come from the priory. I would also recommend the adoption of another box, for the repairs of the church, which is always in use abroad.

Vestry. 50. A point of some difficulty is the position of the vestry. It is equally a disfigurement, whether it appears in the shape of a brick projection outside, or of a wooden one inside. Yet its erection has not done half the mischief in England that it has done in France, where, from the constant practice of throwing out a Sacristy behind the Altar, many a fine east window has been spoilt. The only way in which a vestry can be managed (unless the parvise, or room over the porch, be used for this purpose, which is in practice highly inconvenient) seems to be the following. A small chapel may be thrown out, as was often done, on the north or south side of the Chancel; and a parclose or screen being erected across its entrance, it will serve the purpose of a vestry very well. But the sanctity of God's House must not be profaned by parish meetings, or religious association anniversaries, which are too often held within its walls. An original Sacristy exists at Salisbury, S. Thomas; Stone, Kent; E. Bourne, Sussex.

Texts. 51. THE texts, which the 82nd canon commands to be written up in various parts of a church, were often during the earlier part of the -17th century admirably selected, generally from the Psalms. The references are all to the Prayer-Book version. A few are here given:

North and south of Chancel. Psalm xlii. 4, 5 ; l. 2 ; lxviii. 35 ; cxvi. 12.

West of the Chancel arch ; on which, it must be remembered, the eyes of the congregation would, when kneeling, be fixed: Psalm xviii. 5, 6 ; xx. 1, 2 ; xxxvii. 4 ; l. 15 ; cxxii. 6 ; cxxxii. 8, 9 ; cxxxiv. 1, 3.

North and south of Nave. Psalm vii. 7 ; ix. 14 ; xxii. 25 ; xxvii. 4 ; xlvii. 4 ; lxxxiv. 1 ; lxxxvii. 1 ; cxxii. 4.

Opposite the principal entrance : Psalm v. 7 ; xv. 1, 2 ; xxvi. 8 ; lxvi. 12 ; c. 3 ; cxviii. 19 ; cxxii. 1.

Opposite the pulpit. Psalm cxix. 43.

A chronogram was also sometimes employed. Thus in Mallwydd church, Merionethshire, we read: " A° ViVus et effICax." Heb. iv. 12.

That the commandments, if they must be put up, were not intended to assume the elaborate ugliness in which they now appear, is evident from the enquiries of Archbishop Grindal, and Bishop Cox, whether " they are written on fair sheets of paper, and pinned up against the hangings in the east end."

Needlework and embroidery. 52. NEEDLEWORK and embroidery are needed for the Altar-cloth, Corporas or napkin to be laid over the Elements, Altar carpet, the antependium of the faldstool, and pulpit cushion.

We may be allowed to ask, would not the time and ingenuity spent on worsted work, satin stitch, bead work, and the like frivolities, be better employed if it were occupied in preparing an offering to GOD for the adornment of His Holy dwelling places ? Hour after hour is cheerfully sacrificed in the preparation of useless trifles for those charity bazaars which would fain teach us that we *can* serve GOD and mammon: no time is then thought too much, no labour spared. But when an Altar cloth or carpet is to be provided, then the commonest materials and commonest work are thought good enough. Better examples were set in former times: as here and there a tattered piece of church embroidery still remains to tell us.

That such ornaments are employed by our Church, is proved by the following questions:

" A comely and decent Communion Table with a fair covering of some carpet, silk, or linen cloth to lay upon it." Archbishop Parker, 1559.

"A Table for the Holy Communion with a fair linen cloth to lay upon the same, and some covering of silk, buckram, or such like." Archbishop Grindal, 1573.

"A convenient Communion Table with a carpet of silk, or some other decent stuff, and a fair linen cloth." Archbishop Bancroft, 1605.

"A convenient pulpit with a decent cloth and cushion; a Communion Table with a handsome carpet or covering of silk stuff, or such like." Bishop Bridges, 1634.

"A Communion Table with a carpet of silk or some other decent stuff, continually laid upon it at the time of divine service." Archbishop Laud, 1636, and Bishop Wren, 1635.

"Have you a carpet of silk, satin, damask, or some more than ordinary stuff to cover the Table with at all times?" Bishop Montague, 1639.

There are very few specimens of Altar cloths now remaining, and those which do remain are so much mutilated that we are thrown almost entirely on our own resources in providing a pattern for them. Our forefathers provided more than one Altar cloth, according to the different Feasts on which they might be used. Thus, that employed on an ordinary Sunday was green: that on the great feasts, as Easter and Pentecost, purple and gold, the symbol of triumph; that on the Festival of any Martyr, scarlet, in reference to his resisting unto blood; that used on the Purification and Annunciation, white, the colour of purity. During Lent, a black Altar cloth was employed, excepting only on Easter Eve, when the Altar was entirely stripped. Any of the symbols mentioned in Section 33 might here be worked with gold thread on the velvet. The Altar cloth should not hang over the edge of the Altar more than six inches (otherwise the panelling would be concealed), and should be furnished with a thick gold fringe.

More than one desirable.

53. THE precious metals are now only needed for two things, the Altar candlesticks and the Holy Vessels.

Altar candlesticks.

Two Altar candlesticks are commanded by the first rubric in the Prayer book. The *thing* signifies "that CHRIST is the very true Light of the world:" the *number*, His Divine and Human Natures. They are to stand on the Altar, and not on the Altar rails.

The universal shape of the Chalice was, as it generally is, and always ought to be, an octagonal base and circular bason. In most of the Visitation Articles particular enquiry is made as to the silver cover of the Chalice.

54. STAINED glass is of much importance in giving a chastened and solemn effect to a church. Those who travel on the continent might find many opportunities of procuring, from desecrated churches, at a very trifling expense, many

Stained Glass.

fragments, which would be superior to any we can now make. But if it be modern, let us at least imitate the designs, if we cannot attain to the richness of hues, which were our ancestors'. In a window lately stained by Evans of Shrewsbury, for the church of the Holy Cross in that town, no one would at first believe that the four elegant figures which occupy a conspicuous place are the four Evangelists. And in the new window at Ely, by the same artist, the case is not much better, except that here the Evangelistick symbols are to be seen on close inspection, though in the wrong place and form. I will here give the usual symbolism used to represent those Saints who are recorded in our calendar:

The Holy Apostles:

S. Peter. With a key; or two keys with different wards.
S. Andrew. Leaning on the Cross called from him.
S. John Evangelist. With a Chalice, in which is a winged serpent. (In this case the eagle is never represented.)
S. Bartholomew. With a flaying knife.
S. James the Less. With a fuller's staff, bearing a small square banner.
S. James the Greater. With pilgrim's hat, staff, and cockle shell.
S. Thomas. With an arrow; or with a long staff.
S. Simon. With a long saw.
S. Jude. With a club.
S. Mathias. With a hatchet.
S. Philip. Leaning on a spear; or with a long Cross in the shape of a T.
S. Matthew. With a knife or dagger.
S. Paul. With elevated sword.

S. John Baptist. With an Agnus Dei.
S. Stephen. With stones in his lap.

We will proceed to other Saints in our calendar whose symbols are distinctly known:

S. Hilary. A Bishop, with three books.
S. Fabian. Kneeling at the block, the triple crown by his side.
S. Agnes. With a lamb at her feet.
S. Blaise. Holding a woolcomb; or with a woman at his feet, offering a pig.
S. Agatha. Her breast torn by pincers.
S. David. With Pall and Crosier, preaching on a hill.
S. Perpetua. With a child at her breast, surrounded by flames.
S. Gregory. A book in one hand, the triple Crosier in the other, and a triple crown.

S. Richard. A Chalice at his feet.

S. Alphege. An Archbishop, with a heap of stones in his chesible.

S. Dunstan. An Archbishop, with a harp in his hand.

S. Boniface. A Bishop, laying an axe to the root of an oak.

S. Margaret. With a crozier in her hand, and trampling on a dragon.

S. Mary Magdalene. With the alabaster box, and with loose long hair.

S. Anne. Teaching the Blessed Virgin Mary to read: her finger generally points to the words, " Radix Jesse floruit.'

S. Laurence. With a gridiron.

S. Giles. A hind, with an arrow piercing her neck, standing on her hind feet, and resting her fore feet on the lap of the Saint.

S. Edmund. Fastened to a tree, and pierced with arrows ; the royal crown on his head.

S. Enurchus. A dove lighting on his head.

S. Martin. Giving half of his cloak to a beggar.

S. Britius. With a young child in his arms.

S. Cecilia. With her organ.

S. Catherine. With her wheel, and a sword.

S. Clement. With an anchor.

S. Nicolas. With three naked children in a tub, in which rests the end of his pastoral staff.

S. Faith. With a bundle of rods.

It is to be observed generally that Virgins, not Martyrs, hold lamps ; if Martyrs, roses and lilies: that Martyrs have palm branches; that Confessors have lilies: Prophets, wheels: and when the four Evangelists occur together, the two first have closed, the two last, open, books.

Bells.   55. IT may not be out of place to say a few words on the subject of bells. You surely would not wish that instruments, consecrated like these to the praise of GOD, should be profaned by the foolish, profane, or self-laudatory inscriptions so often found on them. They, as all other parts of church furniture, are holy. The following are examples of ancient inscriptions on bells :

Defunctos ploro, vivos voco, fulgura frango.
Nos jungat thronis vere thronus Salomonis.
AGNUS Sancte DEI, duc ad loca me requiei.
Nomen Sancte JESU, me serva mortis ab esu.
Sanguis Xpi, salva me! Passio Xpi, conforta me!

Te laudamus, et rogamus	First bell,
Nomen JESU CHRISTI	Second bell,
Ut attendas et defendas	Third bell,
Nos a morte tristi.	Fourth bell.

Monuments. 56. BEFORE concluding, a word or two on monuments, as eventually exercising great influence, for good or for ill, on the beauty of a church. To learn what harm they may produce, we need only refer to Westminster or Bath Abbey churches, or the Ladye Chapel at Ely.

But let us imagine a church, like that we have been endeavouring to describe, filled with monuments befitting a Christian temple; what appearance would it in the course of years present? Between each of the piers in the Nave, but of course not touching them, would be seen a low altar tomb, the sides gorgeously panelled, the edges of the upper part indented with the brass legend, commemorating not the virtues or alliances or genealogy of the deceased except in the mute language of heraldry, but his name and his humble prayer for mercy; and on the top his effigy might be wrought in brass, or carved on stone. And why do we not, in the position of the figure, return to the constant practice of our ancestors? Why are the warrior and the orator to be represented as still occupied with the cares and excitement of their earthly professions, instead of resting, with clasped hands, in the holy repose of our earlier effigies? Till the great rebellion, the majority of figures, whether recumbent or not, were in the attitude of prayer, even when those whom they represent lived and died puritans. But to proceed: on the north side of the Chancel would probably be placed one or two canopied altar tombs, of still richer design than the last; these would commemorate the benefactors to, or joint-founders of, the church. And the poorer portion of the flock would be kept in remembrance by the simple brass legend, or sculptured Cross, scattered here and there on the church pavement. Some visible reference to the Death and Passion of our REDEEMER were surely not amiss, and what supplies it so beautifully as these Crosses? Where the church abounds with them, we could not enter it without thinking "These all died in faith."

The church-yard. 57. AGAIN, every effort should be made to prevent the intrusion of "headstones," "footstones," "breaststones," "tablet-boards," and the like, into the churchyard. These came in with the revolution, and were not common till many years later. And no small service would be rendered to our churches if an order could be taken to prevent the adoption of any more; and those at present existing, with their hour-glasses, weeping willows, death's heads, cherubims, scythes, and inscriptions of "afflictions sore," would quietly, and from their perishable nature, soon moulder away. A stone with a Lombardick Cross, or dosd'âne, is the fittest monument for those who can afford it; they who cannot might content themselves with a cross formed by sowing box in that shape. A yew should be planted south of the church, that at Easter, Whitsuntide, and Christmas, its boughs may be used to ornament the interior. Before the rebellion there was always a Cross of stone, either in the village or churchyard. Would there now be any impiety or superstition or profaneness in erecting such " A deare remembrance of our dying Lord?"

58. Thus then imperfectly, but not I hope
Conclusion.
quite uselessly, have we completed our survey of a church and its ornaments. If every thing else is forgotten, and two points only remembered, The absolute necessity of a distinct and spacious Chancel, and The absolute inadmissibility of pues and galleries in any shape whatever, I shall be more than rewarded. I have been writing in the name of a society, physically it may be weak in numbers and pecuniary resources, but morally strong in the zeal of its members and the goodness of its cause. It may indeed be years before the great truth is learnt, which that Society hopes to be one of the instruments of teaching—the intrinsic holiness of a church, and the duty of building temples to God in some sort worthy of His presence. But learnt sooner or later it will be; and to be allowed in any way to help forward so good a work, is a high privilege. This the society has already done by the little Tract to Churchwardens, the success of which has gone beyond its warmest hopes. There is scarcely a diocese from which accounts of its usefulness have not been received; and it has been distributed by more than one Archdeacon to the Churchwardens at his visitation.

In the present tract, touching as it does on so many controverted points, it can hardly be hoped that no mistake has been made, and no offence given. If anything contained in it can be shewn to be contrary to the Rubrick or the Canons of the Holy Anglican Church, the writer will be thankful to be told of it and the first to expunge it. These are matters "wherein" (to quote Hooker) "he may haply err, as others have done before him, but an heretick by the grace of Almighty God he will never be."

The above scheme of Churchbuilding may, and probably will, be called visionary: and some parts of it, not involving essential principles, may and probably do admit of difference of opinion, even among those under whose name and sanction it comes forth.—Page on page might be devoted to prove that as a whole the scheme is practicable, and ought to be adopted: and the reader, however his reason might be convinced, might yet scarcely be a convert to the principles here advocated.

Another method of proof is in contemplation by the CAMBRIDGE CAMDEN SOCIETY. Further notices and more detailed accounts will be issued in due course of time: at present we may state that it is intended, in a church to be dedicated in honour of S. ALBAN THE PROTOMARTYR OF ENGLAND, to exhibit, in the Decorated as the most beautiful style, a perfect model of a Christian temple.

PUBLICATIONS OF THE CAMBRIDGE CAMDEN SOCIETY.

The Report for 1841, *with the President's Anniversary Addresses, Lists of Laws, Members, &c.* 1s. 6d.

Hints on the Practical Study of Ecclesiastical Antiquities, 2nd Edit. 1s. 6d.

Church Schemes, Ninth Edition, 4to. 2s. 6d. per score.

Illustrations of Monumental Brasses. Parts I. and II. 5s., Part III. 8s.

Transactions of the Cambridge Camden Society. Imperial 4to. Part I. 5s. 6d.

An Argument for the Greek origin of the Monogram IHS. 1s. 6d.

A Few Words to Churchwardens on Churches and Church Ornaments. Part I. *Suited to Country Parishes.* Ninth Edition.

A Few Words to Churchwardens on Churches and Church Ornaments. Part II. *Suited to Town and Manufacturing Parishes.* Second Edition. Price of each Part, 3d; or 25 copies for 5s; 50 for 8s; 100 for 10s.

Nearly Ready,

AN ACCOUNT OF STOW CHURCH, LINCOLNSHIRE.

In the Press,

ILLUSTRATIONS OF MONUMENTAL BRASSES. Imperial 4to. Part IV.

Dr Haufurd, *from Christ's College Chapel, Cambridge.*

John Tame, Esq. *Fairford, Gloucestershire.*

Prior Nelond, *Cowfold, Sussex.*

Sir Andrew Luttrell, *Irnham, Lincolnshire.*

PLATE I. is intended to illustrate the Catholick arrangement of a church. The ground plan is that of a village church in Sussex; the arrangement, however, adopted in the original is sadly at variance with the principles inculcated in this Tract

> *S.* The Chancel.
> *T T.* The Transepts.
> *N.* The Nave.
> *O O.* The Aisles.
> *P.* The Porch.
> *A.* The stone Altar.
> *a.* The sedilia.
> *B.* The three flights of three steps.
> *C C.* Misereres. A double row on each side.
> *D.* Roodscreen.
> *Z.* Priest's door. [This might equally well have been on the other side.]
> *T.* The founder's tomb.
> *E.* The steps to the Chancel. Two are perhaps better than three.
> *ffff.* Lantern piers. These support a light Decorated spire.
> *F.* Font.
> *K K.* Piers.
> *H.* Pulpit.
> *I.* Eagle desk. Facing west.
> *G.* Faldstool. Facing east. A better position—at least on Litany days—would be on the east side of the Roodscreen.
> *W.* Transept door.
> *K.* S. western door.
> *V V.* Wooden seats.

The whole of *O O. T T.* are, if necessary, to be filled with chairs.

PLATE II. Fig. B. The modern chapel has four doors on the "ground floor"—one at each corner; and four in the gallery, in the same position. And the Tower stands over the Chancel, which otherwise would probably have been smaller.

PLATE III. Two Early English splays:

> Fig. 1. From Chailey, Sussex. The entire breadth is 4ft. 2 in.
> Fig. 2. From a modern Early English church in Sussex.

Plate I.

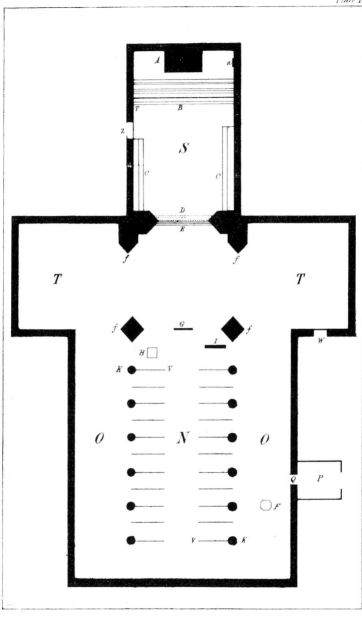

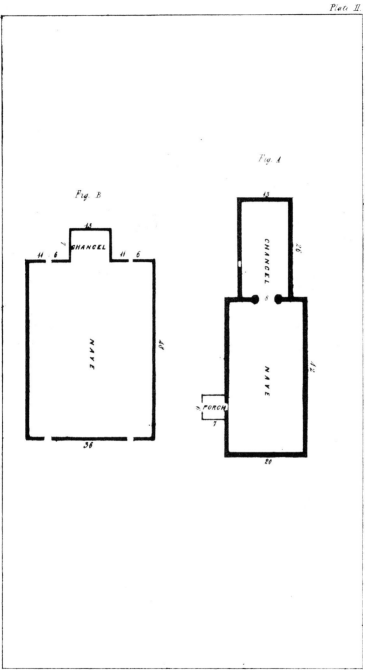

Fig. A

Fig. B

Plate II.

Plate III.

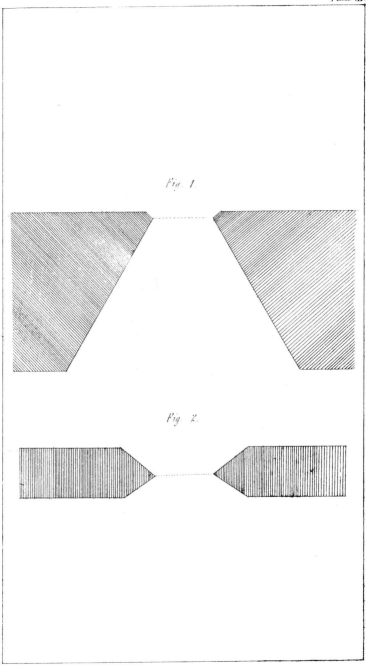

Fig. 1

Fig. 2

Plate 11.

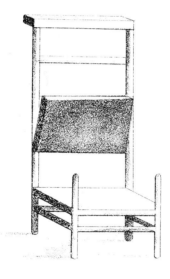

APPENDIX

TO

𝕬 𝕱𝖊𝖜 𝖂𝖔𝖗𝖉𝖘 𝖙𝖔 𝕮𝖍𝖚𝖗𝖈𝖍𝖇𝖚𝖎𝖑𝖉𝖊𝖗𝖘

CONTAINING LISTS OF

𝕱𝖔𝖓𝖙𝖘 𝖂𝖎𝖓𝖉𝖔𝖜𝖘 𝖆𝖓𝖉 𝕽𝖔𝖔𝖉𝖘𝖈𝖗𝖊𝖊𝖓𝖘

INTENDED TO SERVE AS MODELS

PUBLISHED BY THE CAMBRIDGE CAMDEN SOCIETY

𝔈𝔫𝔰𝔭𝔦𝔠𝔢 𝔢𝔱 𝔣𝔞𝔠 𝔰𝔢𝔠𝔲𝔫𝔡𝔲𝔪 𝔢𝔵𝔢𝔪𝔭𝔩𝔞𝔯 𝔮𝔲𝔬𝔡 𝔱𝔦𝔟𝔦 𝔪𝔬𝔫𝔰𝔱𝔯𝔞𝔱𝔲𝔪 𝔢𝔰𝔱
𝔈𝔵𝔬𝔡 𝔵𝔵𝔟 40

CAMBRIDGE
AT THE UNIVERSITY PRESS
STEVENSON CAMBRIDGE PARKER OXFORD
RIVINGTONS LONDON

M DCCC XLI

Price Sixpence.

APPENDIX A.

N.B. In the following list, the windows are reckoned from the East; so that "2 N. of N. Aisle" means the second window on the North side of the North Aisle, reckoning from the East.

LIST OF WINDOWS.

DECORATED:

Of two lights:

Bedfordshire—Melchbourne,	W.
Tillbrook,	1 and 2 S. of Chancel.
Wymington,	N. S. Aisles.
Essex—Colchester, S. Nicholas,	N. Aisle.
Holy Trinity,	1 N. of Chancel.
Heydon,	2 and 3 N. of N. Aisle.
Little Maplestead,	N. S. of Chancel.
Weathersfield,	N. S. of Chancel.
Huntingdonshire—Elton,	S. of Chancel.
Steeple Gidding,	N. of Chancel.
Hamerton,	N. S. of Chancel.
Northamptonshire—Abington,	W.
Barnack,	N. S. of Chancel.
Cottesbrooke,	N. of Chancel. S. Transept.
Helpstone,	E. S. Aisle.
Maxey,	S. of Chancel.
Wittering,	E.
Rutland—Caldecot,	W.
Egleton,	W.
Oakham,	W.
Staffordshire—Tamworth,	N. of Chancel.
Suffolk—Barham,	Clerestory.
Baylham,	1 S. of Chancel. S. of Nave.
Coddenham,	1 and 2 S. of S. Aisle.
Copdock,	N. of Nave.

Suffolk—Gosbeck,	1 S. of Chancel.
Hemingstone,	N. of Chancel.
Sproughton,	N. of N. Aisle.
Stowmarket,	N. of Chancel.
Washbrook,	1 and 2 N. of Chancel
Woolpit,	S. of Nave.
Surrey—Shiere,	Chancel.
Sussex—Ditchelling,	1 and 2 S. of S. Aisle.
Eastergate,	S. Aisle.
W. Ferring,	2 S. of Chancel.
W. Hoathly,	S. of S. Aisle.
Lindfield,	E. W. of N. Transept.

Of three lights:

Berkshire—Stanford,	3 N. of Chancel.
Shellingford,	E.
Caernarvonshire—Bangor Cathedral,	S. of S. Aisle.
Cambridgeshire—Arrington,	E.
Burrough Green,	E.
Fulbourne,	W.
Grantchester,	N. of Chancel.
Horningsea,	E. of S. Aisle.
L. Wilbraham,	E.
Newton,	W.
Essex—L. Chesterford,	E.
Colchester Holy Trinity,	E. of N. Aisle.
Weathersfield,	E.
Gloucestershire—Minchin Hampton,	N. of N. Transept.
Hatherop,	E.
Hertfordshire—Baldock,	W.
Huntingdonshire—Caldecot,	S. of Chancel.
Steeple Gidding,	N. of N. Aisle.
Kent—Erith,	E. of S. Aisle to Chancel.
Northamptonshire—Castor,	E. of S. Aisle.
Corby,	S. of S. Aisle.
Northampton S. Giles,	S. of S. Transept.
Northborough,	S. Chapel.
Scaldwell,	E. of S. Aisle.
Stanion,	E. of S. Aisle.
Ufford,	E. of S. Aisle.
Rutland—Stoke Dry,	E.
Staffordshire—Tamworth,	Clerestory.
Suffolk—Coddenham,	E. W.
Lavenham,	S. of Chancel.
Stowmarket,	2 N. and 1 S. of Chancel.
Witnesham,	E. of S. Aisle.
Surrey—Betchworth,	E.

Surrey—G. Bookham,	E.
Clandon,	E.
Shiere,	E. and W. of S. Aisle.
Sussex—Beddingham,	E.
Chailey,	E.
Ditchelling,	E.
Wiston,	E. W.
Warwickshire—Kingstone,	N. Chapel.
Merevale,	S. of Chancel.
Wishaw,	S. Aisle.
Wiltshire—Malmesbury,	N. and S. Aisles.
York—All Saints, Micklegate,	E. and W. of N. Aisle.
S. Denis,	N. of N. Aisle.
S. John,	E.
S. Margaret,	E.
S. Mary, Bishop Hill, Junior,	E. and W. of S. Aisle.
S. Maurice,	E.
S. Trinity, Goodramgate,	N. of N. Aisle.

Of four lights :

Bedfordshire—Dunton,	E. S. Aisle.
Luton,	W.
Berkshire—Faringdon,	N. of N. Transept.
Cambridgeshire—Fordham,	E. and E. of the Ladye Chapel.
Hertfordshire—Standon,	W.
Huntingdonshire—Elton,	E.
Kingston-upon-Hull—Holy Trinity,	N. S. of Chancel.
Northamptonshire—Corby,	E.
Brigstock,	E.
Staffordshire—Tamworth,	N. Chapels.
Suffolk—Stowmarket,	S. of Chancel.
Sussex—Denton,	E.

Of five lights :

Cambridgeshire—Balsham,	E.
Long Stanton,	E.
Flintshire—Caerwys,	E.
Gloucestershire—Minchin Hampton,	S. of S. Transept.
Hertfordshire—Much Hadham,	E.
London—S. Etheldreda's Chapel,	E.
Northamptonshire—Barnack,	E.
Blissworth,	E.
Castor,	E.
Geddington,	E.
Northborough,	S. of S. Chapel.
Wellingborough,	E.

Suffolk—Buxhall,	E.
Lavenham,	E.
Starham Aspal,	E.
Stowmarket,	E.
Stratford S. Mary,	E.
Sussex—Lindfield,	E.
Buxted,	E.
York—S. Denis,	E. of N. Aisle.

PERPENDICULAR:

Of two lights:

Cambridgeshire—Burrough Green,	W.
Cambridge—S. Michael,	W. of N. Aisle.
Dry Drayton,	W.
Eltisley,	S. of Chancel.
Stapleford,	E. of S. Aisle.
Whittlesford,	1 N. of N. Aisle.
Essex—Gosfield,	N. and S. of Nave.
Marks Tey,	Nave.
Northamptonshire—Irchester,	Clerestory.
Suffolk—Baylham,	N. of Nave.
Blithburgh,	Clerestory.
Bury S. Mary,	Clerestory.
Coddenham,	Clerestory.
Hemingstone,	1 S. of Chancel.
Stoke by Nayland,	Tower.
Witnesham,	1 S. of S. Aisle.
Sussex—Angmering,	N. of Chancel.
Barcombe,	W.
Chiltington,	S. of Chancel.
Clapham,	E. N. Aisle.
Coombes,	N. S. of Chancel.
Ifield,	N. of N. Aisle.
Isfield,	1 N. Aisle.
Lyominster,	1 S. of Chancel.
Poynings,	N. S. of Chancel.
Pulborough,	N. of N. Aisle.

Of three lights:

Bedfordshire—Dean,	E. and N. of Chapel.
Goldington,	E. and W.
Knotting,	E.
Potton,	1 N. of Chancel.
Tillbrook,	N. Chapel.
Willington,	N. of Chancel.

Cambridgeshire—Balsham,	N. and S. Aisles.
Cambridge—G. S. Mary,	Clerestory.
Eltisley,	S. of S. Aisle.
Guilden Morden,	W.
Stapleford,	E.
Triplow,	N. and S. of Chancel.
Whittlesford,	E.
Essex—G. Bardfield,	N. of N. Aisle.
Colchester—All Saints,	N. Aisle.
Heydon,	1 N. of N. Aisle.
Holy Trinity,	S. Aisle.
Saffron Walden,	Clerestory.
Weathersfield,	N. Aisle.
Hertfordshire—King's Walden,	E.
Huntingdonshire—Caldecot,	E.
Elton,	S. Aisle.
Hamerton,	S. Aisle.
Kimbolton,	N. of N. Aisle.
G. Stukeley,	W.
Northamptonshire—L. Billing,	E.
Blissworth,	N. and S. of Chancel.
Kettering,	N. and S. Aisles.
Maxey,	E.
Stamford—S. Martin,	N. and S. Aisles.
Rutlandshire—Egleton,	1 N. of Chancel.
Oakham,	N. and S. Transepts.
Ryhall,	E.
Tinwell,	E.
Suffolk—Barham,	N. of Chancel.
Baylham,	2 S. of Chancel.
E. Bergholt,	S. of S. Aisle.
Blithburgh,	S. of S. Aisle.
Bury, S. James,	S. of S. Aisle.
—— S. Mary,	S. of S. Aisle.
Clare,	Chancel.
Coddenham,	2 N. of Chancel.
Copdock,	S. of Chancel.
Hemingstone,	W.
Lavenham,	Clerestory.
Needham Market,	S. of Nave.
Rattlesden,	S. of S. Aisle.
Rougham,	S. of S. Aisle.
Sproughton,	N. S. of Chancel.
Stoke by Nayland,	N. of Chancel.
Stowmarket,	W. of S. Nave.
Washbrook,	S. of Nave.
Surrey—Clandon,	W.
Effingham,	E.

2

Surrey—Shiere,	2 S. Aisle and W.
Sussex—Angmering,	E. and S. of Chancel.
Coombes,	E.
Ditchelling,	S. of S. Transept.
Eastergate,	1 in S. Aisle and W.
W. Ferring,	E.
W. Hampnet,	2 in N. Aisle.
Hamsey,	E.
Lindfield,	E. of N. and S. Aisles.
Lyominster,	E.
Poynings,	N. Transept.
Rodmell,	E.
Tillington,	E.
Yorkshire—Kirk Ella,	W. and N. and S. Aisles.
Rowley,	E.
York—S. Helen,	W. of N. Aisle.
S. John,	1 N. Aisle.

Of four lights :

Bedfordshire—Bedford—S. Paul's,	2 and 3 N. of Chancel.
Willington,	E. and S. of Nave.
Cambridgeshire—Burwell,	N. and S. of Chancel.
Triplow,	W.
Essex—Gosfield,	E.
Thaxted,	N. and S. of Chancel.
Huntingdonshire—Caldecot,	W.
Lincolnshire—Uffington,	E. of N. Chantry.
Northamptonshire—Irchester,	E. of S. Aisle.
Northampton—S. Giles,	E. of N. Aisle.
Old,	E.
Wellingborough,	W. of N. Aisle.
Suffolk—Barham,	E.
Bury—S. Mary,	W. of S. Aisle.
Copdock,	E.
Lavenham,	W.
Sussex—W. Tarring,	E.
York—S. Michael Spurriergate,	E. and W.

Of five lights :

Bedfordshire—Luton,	N. of N. Transept.
Bedford—S. Paul,	E. and W.
Sandy,	E.
Berkshire—Faringdon,	W.
Caernarvonshire—Aber-erch,	E.
Bangor Cathedral,	E.
Conwy,	E.

Cambridgeshire—Burwell,	E.
Orwell,	E.
Denbighshire—Llanrhaiadr in Kinmerch,	E.
Derbyshire—Tideswell,	W.
Gloucestershire—Fairford,	E.
Hertfordshire—Hitchin,	E.
Lincolnshire—Uffington,	E.
London—S. Catherine Cree,	E.
Northamptonshire—Irchester,	E.
Scaldwell,	E.
Stamford—S. Martin,	W.
Wellingborough,	E. of S. Aisle.
Stepney—S. Dunstan,	E.
Suffolk—Blithburgh,	E.
Bury—S. Mary,	W. of S. Aisle.
Lavenham,	N. and S. Chancel.
Needham Market,	E.
Pakenham,	W.
Sproughton,	E.
Stoke by Nayland,	E.
Surrey—Guildford—S. Mary,	E.
Lambeth—S. Mary,	W.
Sussex—Poynings,	E.
York—All Saints, Pavement,	W.
S. Denis,	E.
S. Michael le Belfry,	E. W.
S. Olave,	E.
S. Trinity, Goodramgate,	E.
Hull—Holy Trinity,	N. and S. Aisles.

APPENDIX B.

EXAMPLES OF FONTS.

NORMAN:

1. Isfield, Sussex. Square basin, massy square stem.

   Potton, Beds. Circular basin and stem, octagonal base, massy.

   Great Casterton, Rutland. Massy, square, sides fretty.

   Essendine, Rutland. An octagon, on square base.

5. Stoke Dry, Rutland. A plain octagon.

   Denton, Sussex. Cylindrical, exterior of intertwined cable work.

   Lewes, S. Anne. The same, and probably by the same workman.

   Rodmell, Sussex. Square basin, panelled in three circular headed lights, circular central shaft, four massy square angular shafts.

   Kirk Hallam, Yorkshire. A cylinder, arcaded with intersecting arches.

10. Canterbury, S. Martin. A cylinder, arcaded with circular headed arches.

    Tideswell, Derbyshire. Octagonal, with square kneeling-stone.

    L. Chesterford, Essex. The same, the kneeling-stone being octagonal.

    Elmdon, Essex. An octagon, on square base.

    Blissworth, Northampt. Cylinder, on octagonal base.

15. York, S. Helen's. Bell-shaped, arcaded in circular headed arches, base circular.

    York, S. Denis. Basin octagonal, stem circular, base square.

    Wansford, Northampt. A cylinder, arcaded of five circular headed arches, with square abaci, the figure of a saint under each.

    Helpstone, Northampt. Octagonal, octagonal stem.

    Castor, Northampt. The same.

20. Glinton, Northampt. Much as 1.

    Bourne, Camb. As 19.

    Edith Weston, Rutland. Cubical, on massy square base.

    Woking, Surrey. Square basin, on central cylinder, and smaller cylinders at the angles.

L. Wilne, Derbyshire. A massy cylinder.

25. Yapton, Sussex. A cylinder, on square base, horizontal chevron round the top, under it eight plain circular headed arches, beneath each a tall cross pattée fitchée.

Chithurst, Sussex. A low cylinder, on octagonal base, and square plinth.

Fletching, Sussex. Nearly as 1.

Sawley, Derbyshire. A massy octagon, on two octagonal steps.

Melbourne, Derbyshire. Circular basin, four circular shafts, circular base.

30. Melbourne, Camb. Octagonal basin, on one side panelled in two circular headed arches, octagonal stem and base.

Hessle, Yorkshire. Nearly as 30.

Hauxton, Camb. Basin octagonal, five circular shafts.

Bishop's Castle, Salop. Circular basin and base.

Worcester, S. Andrew's. As the last.

35. Clunbury, Salop. A cylinder, panelled in grooves.

Shiere, Surrey. Square basin on circular central stem, four slender circular shafts at angles, capitals flowered, base square.

New Shoreham, Sussex. As the last.

Ramsey, Hunts. Hexagonal, circular stem at centre, with circular base and capital, six circular shafts at angles, without capital or base.

Pen-y-gos, Montgomeryshire. Octagonal basin, octagonal stem chevronée, octagonal base.

40. Coton, Cambridgeshire. [Restored and modelled by the C. C. S., Nov. 1839.] Square basin, two sides chevronées, two arcaded with circular headed arches.

Ancaster, Lincolnshire. A cylinder, arcaded with plain intersecting arches, circular base. [Modelled by the C. C. S.]

Lydiard-Millicent, Wiltshire. A cylinder, arcaded with plain intersecting arches, circular stem, and irregular base, with kneeling stone.

Up Waltham, Sussex. Large cylindrical basin, circular base on square plinth.

Bignor, Sussex. Circular basin, no stem, semi-circular base, large square plinth.

45. Coates, Sussex. Low square basin, panelled in four circular headed lights, circular central, and four small circular angular shafts, without capitals, circular base, square plinth.

Barlavington, Sussex. Reversed cone, circular base.

Thorney, Isle of Thorney, Sussex. Reversed cone, panelled for about three quarters of the circumference in twelve circular headed lights, the rest chevronée.

Bosham, Sussex. Basin octagonal, panelled in two plain lights, cylindrical central, and four octagonal angular shafts, square plinth.

Stoughton, Sussex. Square basin, panelled on three sides in four circular headed lights, cylindrical stem, four shafts just marked out.

50. E. Marden, Sussex. Cylinder on square base.

E. Wittering, Sussex. Plain cylinder.

Selsey, Sussex. Square basin, panelled in four circular headed lights, large cylindrical stem, four angular circular shafts, square base.

Earnley, Sussex. Octagonal basin, built into the wall, sloping off to a point.

Henley-in-Arden, Warwickshire. An octagon.

55. Llanfihangel, Merionethshire. Square basin; circular stem with reeded capital; square plinth.

EARLY ENGLISH:

1. West Ferring, Sussex. Basin circular, circular central shaft without base or capital, four circular shafts, at angles, with circular base and capital.

Whittlesford, Camb. Square basin, circular central stem without base or capital, four shafts at angles, as in 1.

Finden, Sussex. Basin octagonal, circular massy central stem, four angular shafts, as before.

W. Hoathly, Sussex. As 2.

5. Tarring Neville, Sussex. The same.

Ifield, Sussex. The same.

Cuckfield, Sussex. Circular basin, stem octagonal, and panelled in trefoiled lights, base circular. Execution very good.

Iford, Sussex. [Restored under the direction of the C. C. S., August 1841.] As 1.

Street, Sussex. Basin square and massy, four circular shafts at angles, with circular capital and base.

10. Lyominster, Sussex. As 2. Square base.

Rowley, Yorkshire. Basin square, and arcaded in equilateral arches; four shafts at angles, circular, with circular capitals and bases, base circular.

Guilden Morden, Cambridgeshire. As 1. With beaded wreath round the top of the basin.

Corby, Northampt. Basin circular, panelled in seven equilateral arches, toothed, rising from the centre of the basin, stem and base circular.

Barnack, Northampt. Octagonal, a very rich and good model.

15. Scaldwell, Northampt. Circular basin, central stem circular, without capital and base, round and adjacent to it five slender circular shafts, with circular bases and bell capital, the space between each two panelled in two quatrefoiled arches, one above the other.

Wittering, Northampt. Circular basin, stem and base.

Thornhaugh, Northampt. The same.

Horningsea, Camb. Octagonal basin, central stem octagonal, without capital or base, four angular shafts, octagonal, with octagonal capitals and bases.

Oakington, Camb. Basin square, panelled in three equilateral arches, four octagonal angular shafts, with octagonal bases and capitals, square base.

20. Shepreth, Camb. Basin octagonal, five octagonal shafts, with octagonal bases and capitals.

Wistow, Hunts. Octagonal basin on four shafts, alternately circular and octagonal, with similar bases and capitals, central shaft circular, without capital or base.

Amberley, Sussex. The same as 2.

Poling, Sussex. Circular basin and shaft, octagonal base.

Henfield, Sussex. As 2, central shaft octagonal.

25. W. Tarring, Sussex. Basin octagonal, central circular stem, without capital or base, eight circular slender shafts, with circular capitals and bases.

Warboys, Hunts. As 2, but central shaft has base.

Foxton, Camb. [Restored by the C. C. S., June 1, 1841.] Octagonal basin, as 25, only shafts and stem octagonal.

Sutton, Sussex. Octagonal basin, panelled in two plain lancets octagonal stem and base, large irregular plinth.

Cold Waltham, Sussex. Circular basin, octagonal stem, square base.

30. W. Wittering, Sussex. Circular basin, circular stem, square base.

Duncton, Sussex. Circular basin, cylindrical stem.

Irchester, Northamptonshire. Square basin, panelled on each side in trefoil, containing a figure and a flower alternately, four angular octagonal shafts, with similar capitals and bases, and central octagonal stems, without capitals or bases.

L. Bookham, Surrey. High circular basin, circular and deeply banded shaft, square base.

Witcham, Cambridgeshire. Basin octagonal, panelled in angels swinging censers, four slender circular shafts, with circular capitals and bases, round a plain circular stem.

35. Newton, Cambridgeshire. Basin octagonal, with angular volutes, on alternate sides, five shafts circular, the central having capital and base.

Sandon, Hertfordshire. Square basin, octagonal stem, four angular octagonal shafts.

Old Hurst, Huntingdonshire. Basin octagonal, panelled in three trefoiled lights, with eight octagonal shafts.

York, All Saints, Micklegate. Basin octagonal, circular stem, square base.

Polsworth, Warwickshire. Octagonal basin, each side panelled in a trefoiled light, crocketed and finialled.

40. Yarnton, Oxfordshire. Basin octagonal, elaborately carved, stem octagonal, panelled in a trefoiled light.

Hemingstone, Suffolk. Octagonal basin, panelled in cinqfoiled lights, with triangular canopy, crocketed and finialled, stem octagonal, buttresses to both that and basin.

DECORATED:

[It is impossible to fix with any degree of certainty the exact date of the first seven of the following list; the mouldings are however good, and the fonts may well serve as models.]

1. Eastergate, Sussex. Octagonal, octagonal stem and base.

Horsted Keynes, Sussex. The same.

Welton, Yorkshire. The same.

York, S. Olave. The same, but no base.

5. Steeple Morden, Camb. As 1.

York, S. Mary, Bishop Hill, Senior. The same, square base.

Northborough, Northampt. As 1.

Goldington, Beds. Base and stem circular, between the two a hollow moulding with ball flowers.

Hull, Holy Trinity. Basin octagonal, central shaft circular, eight four-clustered angular shafts. A fine model.

10. York, S. John. Chalice-shaped, octagonal basin, stem, and base.

Stamford, S. Martin. As 1, but sides of basin filled with rich tracery. A good model.

Houghton, Sussex. As 1.

Cowfold, Sussex. Much the same.

Effingham, Surrey. Octagonal basin and stem, square base.

15. Llanfair-next-Harlech, Merion. The same; very good.

Llanendwyn, Merion. As 1; good.

Stanion, Northampt. An excellent model, basin octagonal, each side panelled in a quatrefoiled lozenge, stem in niches, with buttresses of two stages between.

Broughton, Northampt. Octagonal, very rich, with projecting niches. A good model.

Northampton, St Peter's. Octagonal, each side panelled in two cinqfoiled lights, with a quatrefoil in head, under a triangular canopy, crocketed and finialled.

20. Rusper, Sussex. As 1.

Luton, Beds. Fine octagonal, on five shafts, with an elaborate Decorated Baptistery.

PERPENDICULAR:

1. Llanfwrog, Merion. An octagon, on square base.

Chester, S. John. Octagonal basin, each side of stem panelled in an ogee trefoiled light, angular buttresses of two stages.

Llanaber, Merion. Octagonal basin, panelled in quatrefoiled circles, Tudor roses, and the like, octagonal stem and base.

Mildenhall, Suffolk. [Much mutilated.] Octagonal basin, panelled in quatrefoiled circles, containing shields; octagonal capital and base.

5. Clymping, Sussex. Octagonal basin, panelled in quatrefoils, containing flowers, stem octagonal, panelled in trefoiled lights.

L. Chishall, Essex. As the preceding, stem not panelled.

Patching, Sussex. As 5, but mouldings bolder.

Lolworth, Camb. Octagonal basin, panelled in quatrefoils, stem octagonal, panelled in two plain lights.

Northampton, S. Giles. Basin octagonal, panelled in various devices, each side of the stem in two trefoiled lights, with a quatrefoil in head.

10. Abington, Northampt. Much as the preceding.

Fittleworth, Sussex. Basin octagonal, panelled in quatrefoils, containing shields, stem as in the preceding.

Poynings, Sussex. An octagon, each side of the lower part panelled in a trefoiled ogee light, large circular base.

Castle Acre, Norfolk. Octagonal. A very excellent and rich model.

Fen Stanton, Hunts. Octagonal basin and stem, the former panelled in two trefoiled lights, the latter in one.

15. Bassingbourne, Camb. Basin octagonal, stem octagonal, having each side panelled in two trefoiled lights, each containing a shield.

Whaddon, Camb. Octagonal basin, each side panelled in a quatre-foiled square, that on the S. has a shield in the square, stem and base octagonal.

Meldreth, Camb. The same, but basin panelled in quatrefoiled circles.

Telscombe, Sussex. Basin square, each side panelled in three equi-lateral lights, stem a little smaller, and panelled in two similar lights with mullions, base square and plain.

Dunton, Beds. Basin octagonal, panelled in two cinqfoiled lights, stem and base octagonal and plain.

20. Stamford, S. Mary. Octagonal basin, each side panelled in two trefoiled lights, stem octagonal, panelled in one ditto.

Stamford, S. John. Octagonal. A good model.

Geddington, Northampt. Basin octagonal, stem circular.

Foulmire, Camb. Basin octagonal, panelled in quatrefoiled circles, stem and base octagonal and plain.

25. Weybridge, Surrey. Basin octagonal, panelled in quatrefoiled circles, containing square flowers, stem and base octagonal and plain.

Byfleet, Surrey. Basin octagonal, panelled in quatrefoiled circles, containing heads and flowers, stem in two trefoiled lights.

York, S. Lawrence. Basin octagonal and embattled, round the slope and base a moulding of flowers and monsters' heads. A very good model.

Broadwater, Sussex. Basin octagonal, .panelled in quatrefoiled circles, in the slope a monster's head and flower alternately, stem panelled in trefoiled lights.

Llandanwg, Merion. Basin octagonal, panelled in quatrefoiled circles, slope and stem in two trefoiled lights, base in trefoils, with the apex downwards.

30. West Dean, Sussex. Good octagonal basin, panelled in quatre-foils with shields, receding flower moulding, octagonal stem tre-foiled, octagonal base on square plinth.

Thakeham, Sussex. Very good octagonal basin, a quatrefoiled circle and trefoiled light in each panel, stem and base plain octagonal.

Washington, Sussex. Octagonal basin, panelled in two lights tre-foiled, octagonal stem, panelled in a cinqfoiled light, base octagonal, panelled in two square quatrefoils.

Hamsey, Sussex. Octagonal basin, panelled in two plain lights, mullions not running through them, stems in one light, all trefoiled.

Minster-Lovel, Oxfordshire. Octagonal basin, stem, and base, elaborately panelled.

Faringdon, Berkshire. Octagonal, panelled in various figures.

Llanbedr, Merion. Octagonal basin, octagonal stem, square base.

35. Lindfield, Sussex. Late, octagonal basin, sides alternately plain and panelled in three trefoiled ogee lights, stem octagonal, base square.

Conwy, Caernarvonshire. Very fine; basin octagonal, each side panelled in a quatrefoiled circle, stem octagonal, panelled in trefoils.

Ysceifiog, Flints. Basin octagonal, panelled in quatrefoiled circles, stem and base plain octagonal.

Copdock, Suffolk. Basin octagonal, panelled in angels holding shields and flowers alternately, stem square, supported by four lions.

Washbrook, Suffolk. The same.

40. Baylham, Suffolk. Nearly the same, lions alternating with angels on basin.

Witnesham, Suffolk. Basin octagonal, panelled in angels alternately with and without shields, flowers in border of panels, stem octagonal, panelled in very large flowers, lions at angles, base octagonal.

Lavenham, Suffolk. Hexagonal.

Bangor Cathedral. Basin octagonal, panelled in quatrefoils, stem octagonal with shields of arms in trefoiled lights, base octagonal.

Hunsdon, Herts. Octagonal basin, panelled in quatrefoiled circles charged with roses, octagonal stem, square base.

45. Burwell, Camb. Octagonal basin panelled in quatrefoiled circles, octagonal stem in trefoiled lights, raised upon three steps.

Tottenham, Middlesex. Octagonal, panelled in quatrefoils charged with roses and heads alternately, octagonal panelled stem.

APPENDIX C.

LIST OF ROODSCREENS.

1. Bedford, S. Paul's. A good Perpendicular model, of two compartments; above is a series of trefoiled lights.

Dunton, Beds. Slight remains, Perpendicular.

Higham Ferrers, Northampt. Decorated; three compartments, each of two cinqfoiled lights, crocketed and finialled; door ogee, over it five trefoiled lights; embattled.

Wrestlingworth, Beds. Perpendicular.

5. West Wickham, Camb. Perpendicular, two compartments; embattled.

Goldington, Beds. Late Perpendicular, two divisions ; both screen and door extremely perfect and elegant.

Irchester, Northamptonshire. Parclose, at E. end of S. Aisle, date 1540, but good.

Cambridge, S. Botolph. Of three divisions, Perpendicular, with rich tracery.

Lavenham, Suffolk. Perpendicular, four divisions, very rich.

10. Southwold, Suffolk. Perpendicular, very fine.

Woking, Surrey. Perpendicular.

Thirsk, Yorkshire. A good Perpendicular parclose to N. Aisle.

Ketton, Rutland. Perpendicular parclose to S. Aisle.

Skipton, Holy Trinity, Yorkshire. Perpendicular. Very fine.

15. Barnack, Northampt. A good Perpendicular parclose.

Stamford, S. John, Lincoln. Very fine Perpendicular; three divisions of four ogee cinqfoiled lights; embattled. Also a fine parclose.

Egleton, Rutland. Excellent Perpendicular ; two divisions, each of three ogee trefoiled lights, with fleur-de-lys for cusps. Over door five trefoiled lights. A band of heads and flowers alternate runs on each side of the upper beam.

Caldecot, Rutland. Three trefoiled lights; door Tudor.

Brigstock, Northampt. Fine Perpendicular parclose; three grand divisions, each of six trefoiled lights, double-feathered with roses for cusps; very rich; above, a series of sixteen ogee trefoiled lights.

20. Stoke Dry, Rutland. Three divisions, each of three trefoiled lights; vine-leaf round top.

Brixworth, Northampt. Late Perpendicular; three divisions, sept-foiled.

Foulmire, Camb. Decorated; very plain; embattled.

Ashwell, Herts. Perpendicular ; one division, of three ogee cinq-foiled lights.

King's Walden, Herts. Two divisions of two ogee cinqfoiled lights ; buttresses and pinnacles between.

25. Sandon, Herts. Perpendicular; two side lights, trefoiled and ogee. Tudor flower in head.

Ovingdean, Sussex. Very small and perfect; one cinqfoiled ogee each side entrance, with quatrefoiled circles in head.

Brighton, Sussex. Perpendicular; three compartments, each ogee, trefoiled, crocketed, and pinnacled.

Old Hurst, Hunts. Perpendicular.

Bury, Hunts. Perpendicular; two divisions, ogee, cinqfoiled, double-feathered.

30. Ramsey, Hunts. Perpendicular; two parcloses of the same date.

Luton, Beds. Very rich Perpendicular parclose to N. Aisle.

Clynnog, Caernarvonshire. Good Perpendicular: one cinqfoiled side light; vine leaf at top.

Cymmes, Montgomeryshire. Excellent Perpendicular remains, removed to W. end.

Whitchurch, Denbighshire. Good Perpendicular; vine leaf round top. Now in belfry arch.

35. Llandanwg, Merionethshire. Three divisions; late Perpendicular.

Manchester, Christ church. Late but good Perpendicular. The head only remains; it has ten cinqfoiled divisions.

Mildenhall, Suffolk. Good Perpendicular; three compartments, each of two lights, cinqfoiled. Spandrells well worked.

Brandon, Suffolk. Good remains of lower part. Two divisions, each of two ogee trefoiled lights; double feathered, over each two quatrefoiled circles, containing painted shields.

Montgomery. Very fine Perpendicular; five divisions, with elaborate tracery.

40. Bassingbourne, Camb. Very fine early Perpendicular.

Old Shoreham, Sussex. Simple but good Early English.

Melbourne, Camb. Perpendicular; five divisions.

Horseheath, Camb. Perpendicular; two divisions.

Ludlow, Salop. Magnificent Perpendicular.

45. Wistow, Hunts. Perpendicular; three divisions.

Castle Acre, Norfolk. Lower part remains; three divisions; curious paintings of the Apostles.

Balsham, Camb. Very fine Perpendicular.

Weathersfield, Essex. Fine Perpendicular; painted and gilt.

Irchester, Northampt. Remains of fine Perpendicular screen; now made into banisters for pulpit stairs.

50. Fletching, Sussex. Good Perpendicular.

Elvaston, Derby. Very fine Perpendicular.

Lolworth, Camb. Good Perpendicular; five divisions, each of two lights, cinqfoiled.

Chaddesden, Derby. An excellent model of a fine Perpendicular screen.

Ufford, Northampt. A plain, but good model; nine compartments.

55. Barton, Camb. Perpendicular; five ogee cinqfoiled divisions, crocketed and finialled.

Whaddon, Camb. Good Perpendicular.

Blissworth, Northampt. An elegant Perpendicular model, of five divisions; each ogee double feathered, crocketed, and finialled, with rich tracery above, and rood-beam carved beautifully.

Glinton, Northampt. Perpendicular.

Kirk Ella, Yorkshire. Decorated; of singular character, but good.

60. L. Chesterford, Essex. Perpendicular.

Triplow, Camb. Decorated; very light and good; of three cinqfoiled double feathered compartments.

Erith, Kent. Perpendicular with some arabesqued imitation.

Northfleet, Kent. Early English. Very fine and perfect.

Stanton, Harcourt, Oxon. Early English. Good.

65. Much Hadham, Hertfordshire, Perpendicular. Good.

Baldock, Herts. Parclose.

South Carlton, Lincolnshire.

Scrivelsby, Lincolnshire, (much damaged.)

L. Wilne, Derby. Perpendicular.

70. Dry Drayton, Camb. Good Perpendicular. Now in belfry.

Deane, Beds. Very good Perpendicular parclose; five cinqfoiled divisions; crocketed and finialled.

Tillbrook, Beds. Good Perpendicular, of three divisions.

Wellington, Beds. Late Perpendicular.

Sawley, Derby. Fine light Perpendicular.

75. Wellingborough, Northampt. Perpendicular; four divisions; cinqfoiled, double feathered, crocketed, and finialled. A good model.

Elmdon, Essex. Good plain perpendicular.

Steeple Gidding, Hunts. Good Perpendicular.

Combe Martin, Devonshire. Decorated, very rich.

Conwy, Caenarvons.
80. Newtown, Montgomery, } Perpendicular, of four divisions, very rich.
Llanrwst, Denbigh.

In addition to these, as specimens of magnificent roodlofts may be mentioned.

Llanegryn, Merionethshire.
Balsham, Cambridgeshire.
Montgomery, Montgomeryshire.
Guilden Morden, Cambridgeshire.
Clynog, Caernarvonshire.
Conwy, Caernarvonshire.
Llanrwst, Denbighshire.

N.B. In the foregoing list, by the words, one, two, or three compartments, is meant, one, two or three compartments on each side the door.

ERRATA.

PAGE	LINE	FOR	READ
14	14	dark	double
17	27	shape	slope
22	19	6633	1633

A Few Words to Churchwardens on Churches and Church Ornaments No 1 Suited to Country Parishes, first published in 1841. The edition reproduced here is the eighth of 1841

The pamphlet has two main themes. Firstly, it reminds the wardens of their duties as well as the privilege of office, and it encourages them to consider themselves as something rather more devout than as mere guardians of the building. Secondly, it is concerned with practical advice aimed at keeping the church sound, guarding against inappropriate change and encouraging the reversal of earlier unsympathetic alterations. The greater part of the pamphlet deals with the second of these. Throughout, the language is basic and the tone conciliatory without being patronising. Terms that might be unfamiliar or interpreted by readers as arrogantly erudite are avoided. Thus, when pointing out the 'mistake' of boarding over the 'three seats in the wall' to the 'right hand, as you stand facing the altar … one higher than another … [where] priests and deacons used to sit' (p. 8) the writer avoids the term sedilia. The pamphlet contains a short and simple, but remarkably comprehensive account of why medieval churches were designed as they were and how they would have been used before the Reformation; there is, predictably, no mention of the term 'Reformation' or hint of the church's original Roman Catholic use.

The 'hints' on maintenance are largely unremarkable. Wardens are advised of the best ways of avoiding damp, 'The great cause of almost all the ruin and unhealthiness that are found in our Parish churches may be told in one word,

31. Walmer Parish Church, Kent, an engraving from the *Illustrated London News* of 25 Sept. 1852, showing a service in progress in a church yet to be 'restored'. One assumes that the chancel is through the arch on the left hand side. *(Geoff Brandwood collection)*

DAMP.' (p. 6). Interestingly, the benefits of cure are not seen solely in terms of the fabric, but also 'because of the poor' who may be tempted to 'betake themselves to the next meeting-house, where they will at least be sure of being comfortably seated' (p. 6). The need to protect old monuments, copy the design of original windows when repairs are needed, maintain steep pitches if roof repairs become necessary, are all stressed. The church yard must not be used as a place where washing is hung or hen coops kept, and gates need to be kept closed 'so as not to allow pigs or cattle to stray in' (p.15).

'But there is another evil to which a church is liable, which arises from the wish of the churchwardens to "beautify" as it is called … Indeed you cannot be too much on your guard against every kind of change if you would not have your church spoilt.' (pp. 7–8). There follows advice about the dangers of altering the ancient fabric in the name of modernisation. As one might expect, there is much justification for the removal of box pews and galleries which 'have spoilt more churches than perhaps any other thing whatever' (p. 11). However, and interestingly in the light of other Camdenian dicta,[1] while it stresses that 'galleries are altogether bad', it does concede that, if there is not enough room, 'it is better to build a gallery than to pew the chancel' (p. 12). The pamphlet also stresses the importance of keeping in good repair the boards on which are written the Commandments, objects now normally associated with Georgian innovations and usually removed in Camdenian-inspired 'restorations'.

The pamphlet was written by Neale and the first edition was published in 1841. It was priced at 3d. per copy. Within months of its appearance, it was claimed that its 'success … has gone beyond [the Society's] warmest hopes. There is scarcely a diocese from which accounts of its usefulness have not been received; and it has been distributed by more than one Archdeacon to the Churchwardens at his visitation.'[2] Further editions of the pamphlet followed quickly; by the end of 1841 a tenth edition had already been needed, the eleventh and twelfth appeared in 1842 and a fourteenth and final one in 1846.

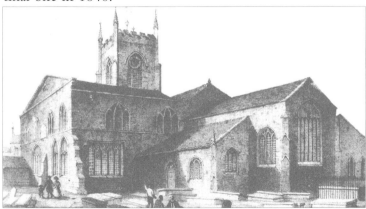

32. Huddersfield Parish Church, West Yorkshire, medieval with several later additions, from an early-nineteenth century engraving, view from the southeast. The 'transept' to the left of the illustration was a substantial post-Reformation extension to increase accommodation including a huge gallery. The transept windows, despite their loosely Gothic style, are obviously not medieval, and their arrangement denotes the two storeys within.

Notes

[1] Cambridge Camden Society, *A Few Words to Church Builders* (University Press, Cambridge, 1841) published at almost exactly the same time, and also written by Neale, states 'THE ABSOLUTE INADMISSIBILITY OF … GALLERIES in any shape whatever'.

[2] Ibid, p. 30.

A FEW WORDS

TO

CHURCHWARDENS

ON

CHURCHES

AND

CHURCH ORNAMENTS

No. I. SUITED TO COUNTRY PARISHES

Published by the Cambridge Camden Society

"In that it was in thine heart to build an house to My Name thou didst
well that it was in thine heart"

EIGHTH EDITION
WITH CORRECTIONS AND ADDITIONS

CAMBRIDGE
AT THE UNIVERSITY PRESS
T STEVENSON CAMBRIDGE
RIVINGTONS LONDON PARKER OXFORD
M DCCC XLI

Price 3d.; or, 25 Copies for 5s.; 50 for 8s.; 100 for 10s.

CAMBRIDGE CAMDEN SOCIETY.

Instituted May, 1839.

PATRONS.

His Grace the LORD ARCHBISHOP of CANTERBURY.
His Grace the DUKE of NORTHUMBERLAND, Chancellor of the
University of Cambridge.

His Grace the LORD ARCHBISHOP of ARMAGH.
The Right Hon. and Right Rev. the LORD BISHOP of LONDON.
The Right Rev. the LORD BISHOP of WINCHESTER.
The Right Rev. the LORD BISHOP of BATH and WELLS.
The Right Rev. the LORD BISHOP of LINCOLN.
The Right Rev. the LORD BISHOP of CHESTER.
The Right Rev. the. LORD BISHOP of GLOUCESTER and BRISTOL.
The Right Rev. the LORD BISHOP of ELY.
The Right Rev. the LORD BISHOP of HEREFORD.
The Right Rev. the LORD BISHOP of WORCESTER.
The Right Rev. the BISHOP of EDINBURGH.
The Right Rev. the BISHOP of NOVA SCOTIA.
The Right Rev. the BISHOP of NEW JERSEY.
The Right Honourable the LORD LYNDHURST, High Steward of the
University of Cambridge.
The Hon. and Rev. the MASTER of MAGDALENE COLLEGE.
The Rev. the MASTER of CLARE HALL.
The Rev. the PROVOST of KING'S COLLEGE.
The Rev. the MASTER of DOWNING COLLEGE.
The Very Rev. the DEAN of PETERBOROUGH, Regius Professor of
Divinity.

PRESIDENT.

The Venerable THOMAS THORP, Archdeacon of Bristol,
Tutor of Trinity College.

OFFICERS.

CHAIRMAN OF COMMITTEES.
JOHN MASON NEALE, Esq., Downing College.

TREASURER.
ARTHUR SHELLY EDDIS, Esq., Trinity College.

HONORARY SECRETARIES.
BENJAMIN WEBB, Esq., Trinity College.
JAMES GAVIN YOUNG, Esq., Trinity College.

A FEW WORDS TO CHURCHWARDENS.

In the following remarks I am going to speak only of that part of your duties which has to do with the Parish church. About your other duties, though they are weighty enough, I shall say nothing just now; but if you will spare half an hour to read what I am going to tell you about these, you may perhaps gain a few hints that may be of use to yourselves, and to others after you.

But you will say, I know that the care of a church is a thing not to be slighted; but the Archdeacon at his Visitation seldom ends his charge without a few words to us Churchwardens, and I do not see what need we have of any advice besides.

It is indeed true, I am glad it is so, that the Archdeacon often gives you some share of his address; and you may be sure that nothing I say will interfere with his authority, or that of the Rural Dean; first, because I take for granted your Clergyman will put you on your guard against doing any thing without their consent, which in any but the commonest matters is altogether necessary; and next because, as you must see from what I do say, my only purpose is to lighten their work by giving you some insight into the right and wrong of things they may order, as well as some directions suited to save both them and you trouble in matters belonging to your every day duties. So that if it should happen,—as happen it may, for what in this world is perfect?—that in any thing here said I differ from either the Ordinary or the Clergyman, you will at once make up your minds that they are right, and I am wrong. For I do not pretend to speak, as they do, with authority, being but a way-faring man that go about visiting churches for the love of Him that is worshipped in them, nor to pass for an oracle just because nobody knows who I am. I hope I am better acquainted with these things than I was a few years ago, and am happier for it, if not better too: yet some of them are matters about which people's minds may differ, and some things I recommend may be right in themselves without being wise or practicable, and some that are wrong perhaps cannot be got rid of without more harm than will come of letting them be as they are; besides that their being so is something in their favour, for it is a good rule, as we all know, to "let well

1—2

alone": and, above all, it is easy for me to say "this is right", and "that is wrong", who have nothing to do with it, and can come by no blame or discredit by my advice, when very likely, if it rested with me, I should find, after weighing every thing, that the balance turned the other way; and that what I may *talk* about very safely as Nobody knows who, I should be very sorry to *do* if I happened to be an Archdeacon. So now I hope you will find nothing in these pages but what will make the business of Visitations easier, and your share in it greater than you have been used to think it, as well as more to your liking: and indeed at all seasons of that kind there is so much to be said, and so little room in which to say it, that whatever you then hear about churches must needs be very short; so that you may still find some further remarks will help you better to know what you have to do. And if I should happen to tell you, as it is not unlikely I may, something that you knew well before, you will forgive this when you remember that it may be of use to some Churchwardens who know less about such affairs than yourselves. And before I quit this matter, let me pray you to make a point of attending the daily service when the Bishop or Archdeacon holds his Visitation, that you and the Church may have the blessing of your prayers along with those of the Clergy at a business of so much importance, instead of dropping in at the end, as is too often the case, only to answer to your names and make your Presentments, as if you did not belong to the Church, but were heathens or heretics. And if I should only have brought you to take this view of your duties, I rather look to be thanked than to be called a busy body, as well by you as the Bishop or the Archdeacon.

I cannot begin better than by reminding you of your privilege in being allowed to watch over God's earthly dwelling-place. Little as we may think of it now-a-days, it was not so thought of by wiser and better men than ourselves in former times; and the "Homily of repairing and keeping clean and comely adorning of churches" has given us some very good advice on this point, as well as warned us of our sin if through our fault we let them run to decay. Many people who have not troubled themselves about the subject seem to believe that, so long as a church is in such repair as will keep it from tumbling down, so long as its windows give light enough, and the doors turn on their hinges, it matters not how much the building has been spoilt, how much of its beauty it has lost, how damp and unhealthy it has become. But do you think it befitting the Majesty of Him Whose House this is, that things should be done in it which the poorest peasant would not do in his cottage? Do you think that it is,—I will not say right, but even decent,—that the church windows should be blocked up with brick or boarded over with wood, the roof patched and plaistered till it can hardly be called the same, and the floor made up of bricks and stones and tiles, and these the cheapest of their kind? Let me ask you a plain question. You have a house, good and comfortable, which you let to a tenant on the understanding that he should keep it so. You stay away for some years; and when you come back, you lose no time in going to your house to see after it. You are shocked to find many of the panes broken, and the holes stuffed with paper, or straw, or rags; instead of the handsome door you had left, a piece of coarse unpainted deal; the cieling wretchedly damp, with here and there the laths peeping out wherever the plaister has fallen down; and the whole house so changed that you hardly know it again. Would you think it enough if your tenant were to say, " Why, sir, the house is in no danger; I did indeed block up some of your windows, but I don't think we much wanted the light; as to the door, I forget how it got off the hinges, but plain deal is much cheaper than oak, and I thought it would answer as well; and the rain used to come in at the windows, so I made the best shift I could to stop up the holes." You will find there is as much reason in such an answer, as there would be in that of a churchwarden who lets his church go to decay.

But you may ask me,—if all this be true, why have we not heard more about it from the clergyman, whose business it is to tell us of it? In the first place I will venture to say that you *have* heard something from him on the duty of keeping your church in order; but in the next place, you must remember that to look after this is more your business than his; and besides all, he has hindrances of his own, which a stranger like myself whose name you do not know, and who does not know yours, cannot have. For example: a clergyman comes into a new parish, and finds that the church has been shamefully used. He calls on Mr A. the churchwarden, and points out the alterations that are wanted; here something ought to be pulled down, and there a door altered. Now both these things were made as they are by Mr C. the late churchwarden, who rather prides himself on what he has done. Do you not see that, if Mr A. does as the clergyman advises him, Mr C. will bear them both a grudge for their pains?

I am not fond of quoting Scripture, but there is a passage which has so much to do with what I am saying, that I shall quote it whole.

" Thus speaketh the LORD of hosts, saying, This people say, The time is not come, the time that the LORD'S house should be built. Then came the word of the LORD by Haggai the prophet, saying, Is it time for you, O ye, to dwell in your cieled houses, and this house lie waste? Now therefore thus saith the LORD of hosts; Consider your ways. Ye looked for much, and lo! it came to little; and when ye brought it home, I did blow upon it. Why? saith the LORD of hosts? Because of mine house that is waste, and ye run every man unto his own house." Haggai i. 3.

But there is another reason why you should look well after your church. It is because of the poor. If the building they meet in on the Sunday is not opened from week's end to week's end; if the walls are allowed, as is too often the case, to be covered with green mould, and the water to stand in little pools on the cold damp stones; can you wonder if they betake themselves to the next meeting house, where they will at least be sure of being comfortably seated, rather than stay away from public worship altogether? I am not speaking of what they ought to do, but of what they will do. Is it not very sad to think of, and will it not be a sin laid to your charge, if through your neglect in not keeping the church dry and healthy any of your poorer brethren should take themselves away, not only from the earthly building, but from that spiritual Church of which it is a type and shadow?

The great cause of almost all the ruin and unhealthiness that are found in our Parish churches may be told in one word, DAMP. And, as matters commonly stand, how can it be otherwise? In the first place there is a mass of wet soil always rotting in the churchyard: this is mostly heaped up to some height against the walls: the mound so raised every week becomes higher by sweepings from the church, pieces of old matting, and all the odds and ends that the sexton carries out on the Monday morning: and on this pile, damp and decaying of itself, the eaves of the roof are every now and then discharging fresh water, and the sun can shine but little upon it. Our forefathers made their foundations very strong; but it is not in stone and cement to stand for ever against wet, and above all wet earth. It follows of course that the outside walls crumble away by degrees, and in the inside long tracks of green slime shew themselves one after another. If they make any one's seat uncomfortable, and it is agreed to get rid of them, there are two ways used for this purpose. The one is, to board over the piece of wall so diseased: and thus the wall, being now shut out from the drying of the air, cracks all the quicker. The other is to whitewash the place: and when the mould comes again, to whitewash it again, and so on; unless sometimes by way of change lamp-black is used instead. But you may try these plans for ever without getting rid of the enemy you want to destroy. Your plan must be rather more troublesome, but it will be both sure and speedy. You must begin by clearing away all the earth from the walls of the church, about three or four feet broad. If unhappily any graves have been made close to the wall, they must be moved further back. This advice may seem at first hard-hearted; but it is not so. To leave them where they are is cruelty to the living: and you will not, I think, suspect me of wantonly disturbing the remains of the dead. You will next have to make a gutter of drain-tiles all round the building, and carry it off at a slope from the churchyard. I need not remind you that, unless your eave-drains and water-spouts are good, and so contrived that all their water may run into the drain-tiles, your pains will have been altogether in vain. When you have done this, however green the inside walls may have been, in a very short time you will find that they are beginning to dry: and you may drive away the stains all the faster by mixing equal quantities of water and sulphuric acid, or (which you will get still cheaper at any chemist's) corrosive sublimate, and mopping the wall lightly with the mixture.

You will find the following plan also very useful in making the church drier. The door and some of the windows should be left open for a thorough draft during the whole day, and in all weathers: to prevent mischief, there should be wire over the open windows, and a lattice door, which may be kept locked; and which should exactly fit the whole opening, to hinder birds from getting in.

But there is another evil to which a church is liable, which arises from a wish on the part of the churchwardens to "beautify" as it is called; whereas, through unskilfulness in setting about their work, they often do a great deal to spoil the building. And here I must say a few words to explain one or two hard names which I have to use, in order that you may understand me with the greater ease.

There is no one but knows that every old church is built East and West, and has at least two parts, which are mostly divided from each other by an arch; the part to the East being called the Chancel, from a Latin word *Cancelli*, which means *rails*, because it always used to be railed off, as it sometimes is now; and the part to the West the Nave, in French *Nef*, though some have thought the name comes from a Latin word meaning *a ship*, to teach us that the Church of God may be likened to a vessel tossed up and down upon the waves of this troublesome world. Very often the Nave is divided by two rows of pillars from the Aisles, or *wings:* and, in churches built like a Cross, the cross arms that go off to the North and South are called the Transepts. The Chancel, as I have said, used to be parted from the Nave by rails, or a *screen*, as it is called; the old name was the *rood-screen*, that is, *Cross-screen*, because a Cross with certain figures used to stand over it. You will often find a little round staircase left in one of the pillars of the Chancel arch, (that is, the arch between the Chancel and the Nave), which led up to this Cross. You will also commonly see on your right hand, as you stand facing the altar, a recess in the wall, with a hole leading to a water-drain: this was used to pour away the water in which the clergyman rinsed the sacred vessels, which he always did after the Holy Communion. By the side of this it is not unlikely that there may be three seats in the wall, one higher than another: it was here that the priest and deacons used to sit. All these things you will sometimes find in like manner near the East end of the South Aisle. The reason I speak of them is because in many churches they have been boarded over, either to hide the damp, as I said before, or from a fancy that it made the church warmer. But this is altogether a mistake; and the things so hidden are at any rate great ornaments, and so is the rood-screen, which is often taken away out of a notion that it hinders the clergyman ·from being heard when reading the Communion service.

The Chancel Arch itself is too often knocked about to make room for pews: you ought to remember that the beauty of a church, when you look up it from the West, is entirely spoilt wherever this arch has been allowed to be hurt. There is also almost always a door either on the North or South of the Chancel, which has been blocked up. Let me ask you to open it as soon as you can: it will cost but little, and be a great improvement.

A word or two as to the windows. Perhaps you are not aware that any one used to such matters can tell how old a window is by only looking at it; and, if they have to be repaired, the old form ought not to be lost. This is a matter in which you never can trust a country mason: you must take it into your own hands. What I would advise is this, and the rather if the window you are going to repair be a large or fine one, and if your clergyman cannot help you, though that is not very likely. Send an account of the window (if you can get a drawing done, so much the better) to the CAMDEN SOCIETY at Cambridge, or to the ARCHITECTURAL SOCIETY at Oxford (which have both been formed for the purpose of preserving ancient churches, and teaching others how to preserve them), and they will tell you all you want to know. But if for some reason or other you should not be able to do this, then I can tell you no better way than the following:—you must get a piece of lead, two or three feet long, about half-an-inch broad, and as thin as you can: with this let your mason take the shapes of the *mullions, tracery,* and *labels* (he will understand these words, if you do not) by pressing it tight round them; and when he has got them, he can take them off upon paper, and must make his new work just like the old. And this will do for the doors and pillars of the church, as well as for its windows.

Indeed you cannot be too much on your guard against every kind of change if you would not have your church spoilt. What may seem to you an improvement may be, and most likely will be, the very contrary. Perhaps it might seem to you an improvement to move the Font away from its place by the door, and to put it (as is now often done) just before the Altar. Now they who do so make two great mistakes. The Font was not put near the door by chance, for it was meant to shew by this that Baptism is the door by which a child is brought into the Church. They first lose sight of that meaning; and then they make another and a worse mistake, by carrying the Font into the Chancel. For the Chancel is that part of the church which is set apart for the holiest services: and yet they would bring a child into it for the purpose of being admitted to the very first privilege it can have as a Christian.

Now this reminds me to say something about your altar. It is a sin and a shame to see, in many Parish churches, a shabby table used for this purpose, only because it is good for nothing else. The table, if of wood, in the first place should be made of either mahogany or oak, and covered with the best cloth or velvet; in many places they have the letters I H S, (more properly I H C,) worked into the covering, and it is a becoming mark of remembrance of Him whose Body was broken and whose Blood was shed: for these letters stand in Greek for the name of JESUS.* A piece of thick carpet should be spread over the floor within the altar-rails. And do not treat the holy sacraments so lightly as to let the vessels employed in them be so cheap and poor, or so ill used, as one often finds them. If we cannot now spare our gold and silver for the holy table, as they did of old, let us at least have vessels set apart for this purpose alone, and which are not disgraceful from their meanness.

In the same way the Font should be taken care of: it should have the water-drain and plug in good order, and should itself be filled when wanted with fresh water; for those small basons which sometimes stand in it are against the orders of the Church. I need not say how painful it is, on lifting up the cover of the Font, to find it used as a box to hold rubbish, torn books, ends of tallow candles, and the like.

You are required by the 82d Canon to have the Commandments put up on the East wall of the church or chapel: they are often seen in other parts of the church. Whenever they want renewing, if renewed at all, they should be painted in large black letters, with the first letter of every sentence red: this is called *rubricating*, and it gives them a handsome look. By the same Canon it is ordered that certain chosen sentences should be painted up in several parts of the church. This is a very beautiful custom, and one that it is a pity to see every day more and more disused.

* See the List of Publications, p. 16.

It may not be amiss now to say something about the roof. There are few churches which have not lost much of their beauty from their roofs being of a much lower pitch than they used to be. If you look at the East side of your tower, you may see what is called the *weather-moulding* of the old roof remaining; and from thence you will be able to judge how much lower the roof is than it was once. Now the reason is very plain. In this figure

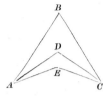

ABC shews how the roof stood at first: in time the ends *A*, *C*, which are fixed in the wall, become decayed, and instead of getting new rafters the parish vestry think it enough to cut off a foot or so of the old wood, and thus the rafters being much shorter can of course reach only to *D*. At this slope they stand till the lower ends decay again; which happens much sooner this time, because they were most likely not very sound at first; and then another piece is cut off, and the roof sinks down to *E*. Now, besides the ugliness of a flat cieling, there is more harm done here. Suppose that in this church there was a window which reached nearly as far as *B*. What is to be done with it when the roof gets down to *D* and to *E*? Why of course it must be blocked up: and many of the finest windows in the country have been spoilt in this very way. Besides, a high pitch is best for the roof, whatever the roof may be made of; the higher the pitch, the quicker the drainage, and the smaller the thrust on the walls. If you have a lead roof, keep it: I hope you will never think of that shameful way of raising money, when you want it for the church, to sell the lead, and put tiles in its place.

I now come to speak of the monuments in your church. It is a very sad thing that these should have been treated as they often have been. Those of brass, inlaid in the floor of the church, have been stolen and sold for the sake of the paltry sum they would fetch; the alabaster figures have sometimes been broken up from mere wantonness, and sometimes ground into powder for cattle medicines. I pass over the great use such monuments are of in the study of history, and the beauty they give to the building where they are put up. What I think most of is the hard-heartedness of allowing such havock. It is true that they whom they were meant to remind us of are far beyond our reach either for good or ill: "they rest from their labours, and their works do follow them." But what would be your own feelings, if you could foresee that the monument you had raised to a father, or a wife, or a child, was to be pulled down to please some idle whim of those who ought to take care of it, and the only re-membrance left of them on earth to be lost for ever?

Brasses are of all things most likely to be hurt. They may be quite worn out by the many feet that pass over them. You must hinder this as well as you can. If the nails which fasten them to the stone come out, the holes should be filled with pitch, and the nails driven in again. And if you have any loose brasses kept in the parish chest, or elsewhere, you should try to find the stone where they were imbedded, and put them down in it again: but if you cannot find it, it will be easy to have another stone cut so as to hold them, always remembering that their feet should be turned towards the East. If you can do nothing else, you may fix them in a safe place upright against the wall. But never allow a brass to be boarded over: if you should find one that has been boarded over before your time, it ought to be uncovered. If that cannot be, the place where it lies, and a copy of the legend, (that is the *reading*,) should be entered in the Parish Register. And do not let such brasses be rubbed, like a brass kettle, to keep them bright: for you thus wear away all the marks in them, and make them worth nothing. As to those who take alabaster monuments to serve their own purposes, they are guilty of sacrilege as well as the thief who steals the communion plate: I do not say that their guilt is as great as his, because I hope they do it thoughtlessly; still, thoughtlessness is a poor excuse to those who might know better if they would.

One word more about brasses. There is a way of taking copies of them by laying thin paper upon them, and rubbing it over with black lead; and some that are curious in these matters may find their way to your church for the purpose: you will of course give them all the help you can. To hinder them is no proof of any care for the brass, because what they do may save it from being forgotten, and cannot in the least hurt it.

About pews and galleries it is hard to speak; we are so accustomed to see them in churches, that we do not rightly judge of the harm they have done, and still do, both to the buildings themselves, and to the people assembled in them. They have spoilt more churches than perhaps any other thing whatever; and as to the congregations, it surely looks like selfishness to make one man shut himself up in a comfortable pew, while many can find no room at all. The fashion of pews was brought into general use by those who endeavoured to overthrow, and for a time did overthrow, our Church and State, and martyred their anointed sovereign, Blessed King Charles the First. But these are not the men we should like to follow.

But there is something more to be said against these wooden boxes. In ancient times it was the custom for all to kneel to the East; whether because, as the Sun rises in the East, that part of the sky seemed to remind them of Christ, the Sun of Righteousness, or because they thus turned in their prayers, like Daniel, to the Holy Land. But now in our huge square pews people, if they kneel at all, often kneel face to face, whether they look into their own or their neighbour's pew, as if they were worshipping each other rather than God; and the wandering of thought that must arise from this is very mischievous and painful. If there must be pews, let them be without doors; but open benches with backs to them are what befit a church best; and every bench should have a place to kneel on, and perhaps a ledge for the books. There is scarcely any country church but has some of these, and they may be copied when others are made. Pews have been well called eyesores and heartsores; but I hardly think you will be able to get rid of them all at once; still if you can do away with one or two this year, the next churchwarden may do the same next year, and so on; and if you should have to repew the church in your year, and are able to bring in benches, you will have done no little good both to church and people. At any rate, whether pews or benches, they should look the same way, and that should be to the East.

Galleries are altogether bad. But, you may ask, what is to be done where the people are too many for the church? must not a gallery be built then? I will tell you a case of this kind that happened in a parish I know. The church, pewed as it then was, held 280; room was needed for 350. The churchwarden called on the clergyman, and wanted to have a gallery at the West end made to hold 50. I have a great dislike to galleries, said the rector; and besides you still will want 20 seats. May be, sir, answered the churchwarden; but the gallery will not hold more, and we must do the best we can. I think, if you will leave it to me, said the other, I can shew you a better way. And so it turned out; the pews were all taken away and open benches were put in their stead; and then there was found room for 400 people. In this case, 5 feet were left for the passage midway down the Nave, 36 inches by 18 being given to each seat; and less than that will not allow of a man's kneeling.

However, if this does not make room enough, it is better to build a gallery than to pew the chancel: at least that is my opinion. For the Altar ought to be seen from all parts of the church; and to put the pulpit just before it is unreverent and ugly. If the gallery must be built, let it be built where it will hide least; and let it be plain. A tawdry, flaunting gallery is the most hideous of all hideous things. And never let it rest on the pillars of the church, but on wooden uprights behind them.

If you have new windows to put in, let the glass be in lozenges, as in the old casements, with their dim chequered light making the quiet church feel so calm and holy, and not in staring square panes such as we often see now. And never let a broken pane remain a day unmended: to do so lets in the birds and the rain, and leads to the breaking of more. Remember the old saying, "a stitch in time saves nine." If the old windows have any stained glass, you should fence them outside with wire. And if you happen to find any scattered bits of stained glass that have been left here and there by the church-destroyers of other days, you may gather them together, and put them up in such a way as, though not to be like the beauty of the former house, may still make them an ornament to the latter house; and will at any rate shew respect to those who once spent of their wealth to adorn it, as well as be an encouragement to others to do the like hereafter. Sometimes in repairing a church the remains of old paintings are found on the wall. I would earnestly advise you, if this should happen, to send to one of the two Societies I told you of before, as the cleaning these paintings is a very difficult thing, and they are so curious that they ought to be looked to with great care.

Take care too that those parts of a church which are not wanted to hold people, such as the Tower and the West ends of the Aisles, are kept clean and not used as lumber places; one is often shocked to find coals kept in them. And if you must have a stove, be sure that it does not stand near a brass or a tombstone; and let the smoke be carried through a flue under the floor and wall of the church to a chimney outside, with a fire-place at the bottom to make the air draw,—and not through the roof or window. Very often too the arch leading to the Belfry is blocked up to make the church warm; by all means, if you can, pull this screen down, and if your Tower is kept as it ought to be, the church will be none the colder for it. The tower is too often looked upon as if it did not belong to the church; people put on their hats when they go into it. You should teach the ringers to treat it as a holy place: they should not be allowed to send for beer to drink there. Do you not remember what St Paul says—"What, have ye not houses to eat and to drink in? or despise ye the church of God?"

The scores of *triple bob majors*, and the like, should not be written up in white or red chalk on the tower walls; you may get a smooth board, on which they will show plainer. And take care that the candles used by the ringers have good stands, otherwise the Tower is made untidy by the drippings of grease. The more you encourage ringing, I mean good ringing, the better; but I hope you will never let the bells be rung at an election, or any thing of that kind. The church is in all countries what it is called in some, The House of Peace; do not make any dislike the sound of its sweet bells, by hearing them rung because their own side is beaten; no, not even though they should be wrong and you right. And therefore a flag on a church tower during a contested election is what ought never to be seen. You are told

in the Canon the fit time for the bells to be rung, namely, on
Saints' days and their eves. They should not be rung in Lent.
I hope, if any money happen to be left for the keeping up that
good old custom the curfew, you take care it *is* kept up, and
that the money is not spent otherwise.

The Bells, you must know, are often very curious, and well
worth seeing. Keep them in good order; and let your ladders,
and bell frames, and belfry-floor be good and safe. Let the Belfry
be kept always clean; and, if you do not like to banish the birds,
at least remove the sticks and rubbish they bring in and leave
there. I know of one cathedral where there were found whole
stacks, I might say, of such rubbish, brought together by the jackdaws or caddows; and you know that this is supposed to have had
something to do with the dreadful destruction of York Minster.

The pavement of the church must be well looked to; take
care of any painted tiles you may happen to have; and lay them
down in front of the Altar or in the Chancel. Stones of course are
best for the floor; tiles next, as we make them now; then bricks;
and wood worst of all.

Do not, if you can help it, let the school be taught in the
church; at any rate not in the Chancel. The children break the
windows, wear out the brasses, and the like; and, what is worse,
they get to look on the church as a common place. Hence it
comes that one often finds hatpegs stuck all over the church:
by all means take them away. And let there be, as the Canon
orders, a poor box; I would put it near the door and write over
it some such text as " He that giveth to the poor lendeth to the
Lord."

I must also ask you to look well to the care of your churchyard. It pains and grieves one to see the place where our forefathers are laid, and where we are to lie, cut to pieces by paths
that have been made from time to time for passers by, who are
in too great a hurry about their worldly business to let the dead
rest in peace. You should stop up these paths wherever you
can do so with the good will of the parishioners; they will often
be persuaded by you, when they might not by the clergyman, to
give up such encroachments. And at any rate you should not allow
children or idle people to play there, defacing the gravestones, and
learning to think lightly of hallowed places, where, if an angel
were to meet us, he would say, " Take off thy shoe from off thy
foot, for the place whereon thou standest is holy ground." And,
talking of gravestones, you will often have some that have fallen
down, lying along, whole or in pieces, for want of one to set
them up again. If there be any of the family of the deceased
to be found in the parish or elsewhere, it will be your duty to
seek them out, and theirs to repair their family monuments; but

if not, then I advise you to have the stones carefully moved to the side of the churchyard wall, where a number of them standing side by side will be an ornament instead of an eye-sore, and will leave room for smoothing and clearing the ground, instead of being in every body's way. And if you can by degrees bring about a tidier look of the churchyard ground, which may be done by little at a time, by clearing away rubbish and useless earth, you will, I am sure, make your parishioners take a pride in it, though they may not have liked all your doings at first; and all the more if you will now and then plant a few evergreens, yews, cypresses, or such like shrubs, where the ground allows of it, to shew that it is a place to be held in reverence. And you will of course take care that it be surrounded by a stout fence of a proper height, to guard it from inroads of cattle and children, without shutting it out from sight; and above all you must keep the entrances closed, as much as may be, so as not to allow pigs or cattle to stray in, which is a grievous wrong to the dead. The larger cattle, at any rate, ought never to come into a churchyard; and even sheep, which from their harmlessness are favourites, and mow the grass cleaner than a scythe, nevertheless often do mischief to the gravestones by rubbing their backs against and dislodging them. But this is rather a matter belonging to the clergyman, who will I am sure always set you herein a good example.

You should be careful not to let ivy grow so as to do harm to the walls of your church. It often spreads and then winds in through the mortar and between the stones of the building, so that I have even seen it make its way through the wall into the church, or through the panes of the windows: after which, as it begins to swell, it pushes against the stones on each side of it, and forces them asunder, to the ruin (in the end) of the whole building. Not that I would wish you to banish it altogether, as it is a great beauty to the church, and is said to keep the walls dry.

I hope the minister, to whom the custody of the church key belongs, will take care that one is kept near the church. It is a very tiresome thing, when one has come a long way to see a church, to find that the clerk lives a mile off: and when you get to his cottage hot and tired, to hear that he is gone out, and has taken the key with him.

It is my wish to be as short as may be; and therefore though I have not said the tenth part that I might have said, I shall only make one or two remarks before I end, on the use of paint and whitewash, which are with most churchwardens very favourite means of beautifying a church. Paint should never be used unless for the texts I spoke of before; and whitewash, at least over stone, never at all. The finest ornaments of a church are often so clogged with one coat of it after another, as to be scarcely seen. Doors, windows, pillars, monuments, all alike are spoilt by it. Far from adding to the mischief you ought, to the best of your power, to remove whitewash where it has been already laid on. This may be most easily done by means of a brush, and two parts of sulphuric acid with one part of water. In doing this, you must take care not to hurt the stone itself, either by putting too much acid at first, or forgetting to wash it off with water afterwards. Paint is harder to get rid of; it is sometimes done with soft soap; or with spirits of wine; but this plan costs so much that it can only be used where the thing to be cleaned is very small. Or you may try this way: get a quarter of a pound of pearl-ash: boil it with a little soap in three pints of water, till it becomes like paste : then lay it on what you want to clean, pretty thick : two days after, lay it on again, without washing the old away : do this four times, and then scrub the whole off: the paint will come off too. This does either for stone or wood.

You must be quite aware that I can have had no other reason for speaking to you thus, than the wish to help you to understand and to be fit for your duties, which are becoming every day more weighty and important on account of that zeal for the Church both as to its buildings and its worship, which is now spreading through the country. You may, or you may not, do what I have been telling you ; if you do not, you will at least have been told your duty; if you do, it will not be your church alone that will be the better for your pains; the blessing of Him who is the Lord of that church will rest upon yourselves.

NOTE. *Since I wrote these few words it has been told me that there are some now who go about to churches, and try to buy the old armour, or helms, or spurs, which are still to be found on many an old tomb. I hope that no one who has the charge of a church will ever let these, or any other things, however small, be taken away by visitors; for they are all hallowed by having been placed in the House of God.*

PUBLICATIONS OF THE CAMBRIDGE CAMDEN SOCIETY.

The Report for 1841, *with the President's Anniversary Addresses, Lists of Laws, Members, &c.* 1s. 6d.
Hints on the Practical Study of Ecclesiastical Antiquities, 2nd. Edit. 1s. 6d.
Church Schemes, 4to. 2s. 6d. per score.
Illustrations of Monumental Brasses. Parts I. and II. 5s., Part III. 8s.
Transactions of the Cambridge Camden Society. Imperial 4to. Part I. 5s. 6d.
An Argument for the Greek origin of the Monogram IHC. 1s. 6d.

A Few Words to Churchwardens on Churches and Church Ornaments No II Suited to Town and Manufacturing Parishes, first published in 1841. The edition reproduced here is the second of 1841.

The 'words' to churchwardens was always intended to be divided into two parts with those addressed to the wardens in 'towns or in manufacturing counties' coming 'many weeks' (p. 3) after those aimed at the country

33. Huddersfield Parish Church, West Yorkshire, medieval with later additions. This is typical of the changes likely to take place in a medieval church during the Georgian period. Such alterations were particularly prevalent in urban centres where accommodation was at a premium. The entire church, including the big southern extension seen through the arches to the left of the view, appears to be taken up with private pews and there is no identifiable space for free seats. The high box pews, seemingly higher with their curtains, afford almost total privacy to their owners.

parishes. Neale acknowledged that this was 'the hardest half of my work', but having been 'heard … kindly' (p. 3) in the first part, nerved himself for the task. One perceives that Neale was more comfortable writing about country churches than their town equivalent, and while he acknowledges that wardens in towns are more likely to 'be richer and more learned', the faults in their churches are likely to be 'more weight and harder to be mended.' (p. 3). Problems arise not from an absence of funds for maintenance but 'wealth and show and comfort … had crept in and changed the House of GOD into places meant only for the ease and comfort of man.' (p. 4). In addressing the 'evils' Neale identified in town churches, he confines his discussion almost entirely to medieval structures; although we know from his other writings he despised the Georgian churches, which were much more likely to be found in the expanding cities and industrial towns rather than in the country, here he says little about them.

While we may conclude that the problems facing the wardens of town churches in the 1840s had much in common with those encountered by their country colleagues – at least from a Camdenian perspective – this pamphlet differs considerably from that aimed at the latter, not least in its language – which is more sophisticated – and its tone – which is more forthright. The 'town' version is also considerably longer. Nevertheless, the two publications share a number of common issues: the inappropriateness of box pews and galleries; the necessity of having a stone font in the nave, near the door; the importance of treating the altar decently; the need to remedy damp etc. There is much concern for the preservation of ancient physical features, 'nor should you … let slip any old parish-customs' (p. 15). And Neale exhorts the town wardens to discourage the congregation from wearing hats in church, 'even on weekdays.' (p. 16).

34. A Victorian caricature of a service in an unrestored church. Note the size of the pulpit, the height of the box pews hiding their owners, the poor on benches at the back, including a woman denied sight of either the pulpit or altar. The family arriving late are being shown to their pew by a pew-opener. These paid officials served the pew owners, but not those in the free seats who, of course, had no pew doors to open. The social division they represented was much criticized by the Camdenians. *(Geoff Brandwood collection)*

The pamphlet says less than that addressed to the country parishes about symbolism in medieval church planning and about the features associated with pre-Reformation ritual, but says much about the problems which arise from the demands of comfort and privilege. Neale rehearses his objection to big unsightly pews, not simply because they are ugly modern innovations, but in this publication he adds the further objection that they take up valuable space that should be available to the poor or to visitors. Furthermore, the owners are too concerned with their own status and comfort, particularly when their pews are 'fitted up like a drawing room, with fire-place and chimney, and a separate

35. Skelton Church, North Yorkshire, 1785, the private pew of the Stevenson family from nearby Skelton Castle. The 'pew' is really a self-contained room – rather like a small transept – extending from the north wall of the church. It is raised above the level of the nave and has its own fireplace, apparently the only source of heat in the entire church. It is directly opposite the pulpit, from where this photograph was taken.

entrance.' (p. 6). Additionally, Neale has much to say about the evils of stoves and their concomitant flue-pipes, 'true emblem[s] of the age which puts its ease and comfort higher than the pains and crosses which should be our teachers here!' (p. 11).

After this litany of potential 'evils', Neale offers some optimism. 'Perhaps after reading such a list many will think that it is too late to try to stop such a flood of change and evil: but I could give a list almost as long of such faults lately amended, and therefore believe that the zeal for the LORD'S HOUSE which has so lately sprung up will work widely enough to set right all.' (p. 20). As a reward for your endeavours, 'I cannot promise you fame … [but] I can promise you the love of all who are working in the same good cause' (p. 23).

The *Few Words …No II …*were written by J. M. Neale

and first appeared in 1841, price 3d. Interestingly, this pamphlet ran to far fewer editions than its sister publication aimed at the country parishes: a second and third editions also appeared in 1841, the fourth and fifth in 1842, a sixth in 1843 and the seventh and final one in 1851. Meanwhile, the *Country Parishes* pamphlet had reached its fourteenth edition in 1846.

A FEW WORDS

TO

CHURCHWARDENS

ON

CHURCHES

AND

CHURCH ORNAMENTS

No. II.

SUITED TO TOWN AND MANUFACTURING PARISHES

𝔓𝔲𝔟𝔩𝔦𝔰𝔥𝔢𝔡 𝔟𝔶 𝔱𝔥𝔢 𝔠𝔞𝔪𝔟𝔯𝔦𝔡𝔤𝔢 𝔠𝔞𝔪𝔡𝔢𝔫 𝔖𝔬𝔠𝔦𝔢𝔱𝔶

SECOND EDITION.

"Is it time for you O ye to dwell in your cieled houses and this house lie waste?"

CAMBRIDGE

PRINTED AT THE UNIVERSITY PRESS
STEVENSON CAMBRIDGE PARKER OXFORD
RIVINGTONS LONDON
M DCCC XLI

Price 3d; or, 25 copies for 5s; 50 for 8s; 100 for 10s.

CAMBRIDGE CAMDEN SOCIETY.

Instituted May, 1839.

PATRONS.

His Grace the LORD ARCHBISHOP of CANTERBURY.

His Grace the DUKE of NORTHUMBERLAND, Chancellor of the University.

The Right Honourable the LORD HIGH CHANCELLOR OF ENGLAND, High Steward of the University.

His Grace the LORD ARCHBISHOP of ARMAGH.

The Right Hon. and Right Rev. the LORD BISHOP of LONDON.

The Right Rev. the LORD BISHOP of WINCHESTER.

The Right Rev. the LORD BISHOP of BATH and WELLS.

The Right Rev. the LORD BISHOP of LINCOLN.

The Right Rev. the LORD BISHOP of CHESTER.

The Right Rev. the LORD BISHOP of GLOUCESTER and BRISTOL.

The Right Rev. the LORD BISHOP of ELY.

The Right Rev. the LORD BISHOP of HEREFORD.

The Right Rev. the LORD BISHOP of WORCESTER.

The Right Rev. the LORD BISHOP of NOVA SCOTIA.

The Right Rev. the LORD BISHOP of NEW ZEALAND (Elect.)

The Right Rev. the BISHOP of ROSS and ARGYLL.

The Right Rev. the BISHOP of EDINBURGH.

The Right Rev. the BISHOP of NEW JERSEY. U. S.

The Hon. and Rev. the MASTER of MAGDALENE COLLEGE.

The Rev. the MASTER of CLARE HALL.

The Rev. the PROVOST of KING'S COLLEGE.

The Rev. the MASTER of DOWNING COLLEGE.

The Very Rev. the DEAN of PETERBOROUGH, Regius Professor of Divinity.

PRESIDENT.

The Venerable THOMAS THORP, Archdeacon of Bristol,
Tutor of Trinity College.

OFFICERS.

CHAIRMAN OF COMMITTEES.

The Rev. JOHN MASON NEALE, Downing College.

TREASURER.

ARTHUR SHELLY EDDIS, Esq., Trinity College.

HONORARY SECRETARIES.

BENJAMIN WEBB, Esq., Trinity College.

James Gavin Young, Esq., Trinity College.

FREDERICK APTHORP PALEY, Esq., St John's College.

A FEW WORDS TO CHURCHWARDENS.

I⊤ is now many weeks since I wrote my first Few Words to the Churchwardens of Country Parishes: and thus I have had time to hear what has been thought of them by those to whom I wrote. And right glad am I to find that they have not scorned my homely English, but have seen how my plain speaking only betokened my own earnestness and wish to do good, and not any pride in my own knowledge, nor any belief that other people did not know all these things as well as I. Thus, since those who have heard me kindly and even taken my advice are already more than those who have found fault, I am emboldened to keep on my old way, when I take up my pen to write a few words to the Churchwardens of large parishes, whether in towns or in manufacturing counties.

But I must own that I feel some fear in beginning this the hardest half of my work; for while those to whom I now write are often richer and more learned than my former hearers, so the things about which I wish to speak to them are often more weighty and harder to be mended. It is not only, as in country parishes, that churches have for the most part been left to run to decay, their roofs to fall in, their mouldings to be broken, and their windows to be blocked up: here, besides all these, there are yet greater evils. For many town-churches have been so spoilt by having misshapen additions made to them to hold more people, and had sometimes so little of the true plan of a church at first, that now unless you were told it you would often scarcely know you were in a church. You can neither make out a Chancel and Nave and Aisles, nor yet a goodly cross church with its Transepts; but perhaps you may find yourself in a large square room with a pulpit against the south wall, and pews ranging one above the other all the way to the north: and if you ask for the Altar, you are shewn it in a little Chancel quite out of the way on the East, or it may be some other side. Again, when town-churches are rebuilt, it is generally without a thought of the old pattern of a church; so that what with new churches, and what with old churches made new, I have no easy task in trying to bring them back to the old ways.

It may be as well to say at the outset that all the faults I shall speak of are somewhere or other really to be found: and I could give the names of the churches, but I will not do so, lest it should be thought that I had any bitterness or unkindness even against those who have used their churches so ill. Yet it has cost me much grief to see these faults so many, and much trouble when I went about to look for them. I have been through counties where there were far more tall chimneys piercing the sky, than spires leading to heaven:

and many more factories and costly mansions, than Houses of God. And when I passed through such places, or through crowded streets, amid the crash of hammers and engines, with smoke and dust around me, I longed for the peaceful country churches I had so lately seen; where the only noise was the birds' sweet note, and where above my head was the open sky, below me the flowered turf.

And when, through such dismal scenes, I reached the parish-churches, peaceful and holy even there, I found that in them another enemy had been at work. It was no longer poverty, which had brought about coldness and neglect and decay: but wealth and show and comfort which had crept in, and changed the Houses of God into places meant only for the ease and comfort of man. But while every thing which touches man is so carefully thought of, there is seldom any care for the church itself and its proper ornaments. A showy Altar-cloth may hide a shabby Table, and a few handsome things be put where they can be most seen. In the mean while the building may be going fast to decay for want of timely help: and so it has proved of late years, when some unhappy parishes have begun to withstand the church-rates, and have thus not only defrauded God of His due, but scorned the earthly laws under which they live. In such parishes the church has been found to be in so bad a state, that when the yearly cobbling could no longer be given to it, it threatened daily to fall, and has had in some places to be shut up.

I do not know whether those who may read this will have read what I have lately written about country parishes; I should much wish them to do so, because there is much there which suits just as well for town-churches: particularly what is said about the holiness of a church, and about the sin of ill-using God's chosen abode. There is also a great deal which cannot well be said over again, though it is fit for the churches of manufacturing parishes, which stand as it were half way between town and country-churches. But as I have to speak of these as well as of town-parishes, I must try to make what I say suit both as well as I can; and if I must now and then say again what has been said before, I hope it will not be taken amiss.

Now perhaps the very first thing which strikes one in going into a town-church is the pewing. The pews are almost always higher than in country-churches, and take up much more room. Indeed there are sometimes not left any free sittings, as they are named, (as if we had not at least as much to do with kneeling as with sitting in the House of Prayer,) except in the very narrow alleys which run between large plats (as they may be called) of pews. Is not this a sad thing, when we remember that the poor cannot have any places whether for sitting or kneeling unless they be free? Sometimes all the pews are of different height, and shape, and kind, and colour, having been built as every man thought best: not indeed that the case is much better when the church has been 'repewed' all on a level, for then there is less chance of seeing a change. Perhaps it is too much to hope as yet to bring back the old plan of open seats in town-churches; but still it is our duty to lift up our voice against the present plan, so fraught as it is with ill. Besides, a Churchwarden may always lessen the evil by making the pews very low and all level with each other; by making them all look one way, and that towards the East; by getting rid of all *square* pews, and by giving to each person a place to kneel.

This last thing is very needful : for to oblige men to sit down or to stand at the Church's prayers, when all are bidden to kneel, is very wrong. Who would think that men were in the House of GOD, and beseeching His aid, when one sees some of them sitting, some standing, and only a few, if any, kneeling? Now many of our prayers are common to the whole of Christendom : and when the Holy Church throughout all the world is at the same time uttering the same ancient words, shall there be members of it who are too proud or too idle to kneel down?

Again, it will be easy to get rid of pews which range one higher than the other, like the seats in a lecture-room or theatre. Some churches indeed,—or rather sermon-houses, for they are not fit for prayer,—remind one rather of auction or assembly-rooms : the inside being full of comfortable boxes, and the outside having a fine portico for the company whose carriages roll up with pride and bustle and strife.

Give me leave to say yet more about pews. There can never be enough said; for after seeing very many churches, and trying to find out the reason of such falling off from the old ways of Church-worship, and thereby of Church-feeling, I fully believe that most of the mischief comes of pews. I might speak of the jealousy and heart-burnings likely to flow from such an allotment of room to the wealthier parishioners, as leaves no suitable provision for their poorer neighbours, and so drives them from the House of GOD, which by the law of the land, as well as by GOD's will, is their own : but this I will not do, because there are every day more tokens of a desire on the part of the rich to make sacrifice of their own convenience in order to extend the opportunities of worship to the poor, and to shew that, though both reason and law make allowance for those distinctions which come by GOD's appointment, yet *they* at least are bound to recollect that all men are equal in the House of Prayer. But this principle, which the rich man ought ever humbly to cherish and the poor man to respect, has been sadly lost sight of in the times that have gone by, when (to say nothing of large pews in the Aisles railed off for particular families, and inherited by them from ancestors who built and endowed the Chapels which these pews now cover, and whose right the Law allows) we not seldom see pews, even in the Nave, half-roofed like country villas, and sometimes even *embattled*, as if it were necessary to set up a warlike fence betwixt neighbours and brethren! To give up a whole Aisle, or

1

Transept, or, much more, the greater part of the Chancel for a pew, is bad enough : but it is still worse when this great pew is fitted up like a drawing-room, with fire-place and chimney, and a separate entrance.

I cannot say that I like the setting aside of a great pew for the Corporation, often with seats of a different height, like the Bench in a Court of Justice. Churchmen always love to pay reverence to magistrates, since they are taught in their Catechism "to honour and obey the Queen, and all that are put in authority under Her:" but surely they need not do this at God's cost. Yet I have seen this pew placed where it interferes with the respect due to the Altar itself: and the whole church so arranged that the people may look towards that pew and the pulpit instead of the East. Indeed all pews must more or less hide the Altar, even where a middle passage is left leading to it. But men are beginning to fill even this passage with pews, which are the more valuable as having so good a view of the preacher. I have told you that the several parts of a church have generally a symbolical meaning, just as the Jewish Tabernacle was figurative and typical. Now if the open passage from the door to the Altar typifies the whole Christian course and the straight way to Heaven, when that passage is so blocked up it seems to mean that this way is now closed. Do not let such a blot as this remain in your church. Indeed pews have nearly made us quite forget the meaning of the parts of a church. Thus, because there is mostly a passage left between the rows of pews up the Nave and each of the Aisles, people think no more of the Nave and the Aisles themselves, (in which they might find an emblem of the Most Holy Trinity), but only of these passages within them, which they call the 'middle aisle' and 'side aisles.' Now 'aisles' mean 'wings' or 'sides:' so that we talk of 'middle side' and 'side sides.' It were greatly to be wished that this way of speaking were dropped.

Once more, think of the strange practice of having pew-openers, without whom one cannot go into one's own seat; and sometimes, which is worse, without a fee a stranger cannot get room anywhere. Now though all good Churchmen go to their own parish-church, yet there may always be strangers and travellers, who have a right to look for room in any church they may come to without paying for it. But perhaps it is not quite in my place to speak of these things.

A word next about galleries, which spoil a church as much as pews. If they cannot be got rid of, they may often be at least made less frightful by being painted some modest colour: dark oak is perhaps the best. As I said before, "a tawdry flaunting gallery is the most hideous of all hideous things." You would think with me if you had seen, as I have, a bright green bow-gallery thrown out between two piers, with a red curtain round it, or a sky blue gallery with gilt panelling. To see in great staring gold letters on the faces of these galleries the names of the Churchwardens who built or 'beautified' them is very painful: and I am quite sure that all these, when they came to think about it, would allow with me that it is a most selfish and irreverent custom. Let us remember that all record of those who built the old church itself is gone: *they* indeed left no such vaunting record; they built only for God's honour, without one thought of themselves. Strange that now-a-days we should take pride to ourselves in putting up what is nothing but a tasteless deformity! Again, would any one wish that his name should stare where the Canon bids that holy texts should be for wandering eyes to rest on? Surely not.

Another evil, which is now becoming more common, and reaching even to country parishes, is the use of double or even triple galleries, one above the other. The upper tier is often given to the charity-children or national schools: or sometimes these are put behind the organ. Neither of these places is a good one for the children, and the first quite spoils a church besides. If they could be arranged on either side of the Nave, like the two half-choirs in a Cathedral, they might be made very useful in the performance of Divine Service, by chanting the Psalms verse by verse in the *antiphonal* or answering way, which from the first ages the Church has always loved. And they would thus not only be more in sight, but would be well placed for the ancient and reviving practice of catechising.

There is another practice, very common in some parts of the country, against which I cannot speak too strongly: I mean the having separate doors to the galleries, either through a window, or a hole cut purposely in the wall. By this the outside of a church is as much spoilt as the inside: for there are great flights of steps all round to these new doors, beautiful windows are stopped up, and shapeless openings made where once all was order and evenness. Besides this, there is good reason why the doors of the church should all be towards the west end, (excepting one in the Chancel for the Priest alone), to bear their part in the general symbolism of the building. For as the Altar stands at the east end of the Chancel representing the full Communion of the Christian, and the end of the Christian life in Heaven, so the entrance ought to be at or towards the west end of the Nave, *and the Font by it*, to show that thus the entrance into the earthly building typifies our initiation by Holy Baptism into the spiritual Church[*]. Thus beautifully does the plan of a church hang together! But this is quite lost when doors are placed without any regard to it. If any one doubts this, I would ask him to explain how it comes to pass that he never saw an ancient church with any doors (except the one I have just described) that were not further from the east than the west end. These doors always put one in mind of what is said about entering into the sheepfold by the wrong way. It is a strange thing that new entrances are now mostly made nearer the east end than the west. I know of a church where a fine old door-way and porch near

[*] See A Few Hints on the practical study of Ecclesiastical Antiquities, p. 25. 2nd Edition.

1—2

the west end are stopped up, and a new staring door opened in the Chancel. Indeed, some new churches, and some old churches that have been restored, have their only entrances at the east end itself, one on each side of the Altar: so that those who come into the church cannot help turning their backs at once upon that part of it, which in other days no one ever passed or looked at without reverence; a custom indeed in some places still kept up amongst ourselves.

Though I have spoken before about the Font, I must say something more now, both because it is of so much concern, and because in this matter town-parishes are much more in fault than country-parishes.

You know then why the Font is to be placed near the door, and that by the eighty-first Canon you are bound to have one " of stone; the same to be set in the *ancient usual places :* in which only Font the Minister shall baptize publickly." How wrong then must those wooden stems be which we now so often see with earthen or tin basons set upon them! You may say perhaps that it is not for you to see that the Minister shall baptize publickly only at the Font; but it is at least your bounden duty to see that the Font is a proper one, clean and in good repair, and in every way fit for the Clergyman's use. Few will baptize from a bason in the vestry or at the Altar, if the Font is where and what it should be. But sometimes there is not a Font in the church! and sometimes—one of my instances of this is from an archiepiscopal city—the Font has been very lately put out of the church to catch the rain from a water-spout. This is too painful a thing to dwell upon. Should you ever be able to rescue a Font from such desecration, you will have done GOD a service. Again, what do you think of old Fonts being used as horse-troughs, or as ornaments to a publick teagarden? And when they are allowed to remain in the church, they are often little better used. Sometimes their tops are cut off because they are too high; sometimes a gas-pipe is made to branch out of them; sometimes they are blocked up with rubbish and plaister, or filled with candles and brushes; sometimes built into the wall; sometimes cut over with the names of former Churchwardens; sometimes cased with wood; sometimes made to serve as a singing-desk for the clerk; sometimes used instead of tressels for coffins to lie on. To paint them all sorts of colours, however ugly and unmeaning, is, after this, but a small evil.

Let me warn you against buying those cheap ' Composition' Fonts of which we hear now-a-days, if ever you should want one; (which may be the case, for, as I said, I know of several churches without Fonts altogether.) The patterns in which they are made are both poor and faulty; and a plain stone Font is not only much better than so worthless though perhaps gaudy a thing, but it is in obedience to the Canon. One cannot speak too strongly against this new-fangled plan of buying *cheap* Fonts, or crockets or other ornaments in ' artificial stone': and the cast-iron ugly Altar-rails are just as bad.

Thus much about the Font. Nor has the Holy Altar fared better.

This also is most spoilt in town-churches, whether from neglect on the one hand, or ill-judged ornament on the other. For if, as is often the case, the Chancel has been quite shut out from the Nave by a boarded screen up to the roof, or by an overgrown pew, that holy part of the church is sure to be given up to dirt and decay. In other churches where there is no Chancel at all, or at best a little alcove for the Altar, there is much room for fault. I have seen some Tables which would not be thought good enough for a kitchen, and some which also serve as cupboards for books and cushions: nay the church-chest itself is in one place used for the Altar, and in another the same thing serves both for an Altar and a stove! and though these be covered with showy Altar-cloths, their meanness, though hidden, is just as much to be blamed. A fault, on the other hand, is to have a Table on one or two legs with large claws, like a drawing-room table. But this is at least well-meant. I wonder men are not ashamed to use the holy Altar for a tool-box or work-bench while repairs are going on: and it is nearly as bad to make it the place for hats and shawls to be thrown on by school-children and others, or a desk for the registering of Marriages or Baptisms.

And, as I said before, the way of decking an Altar, though well meant, is often in bad taste. To let it be overtopped by large monuments at its back is shocking. Then, again, the Altar-screens mostly found are very bad pieces of wood-work, not only not in the style of the church, but in no style whatever: and the emblems often used are poor, and not nearly so good as the older sort. Thus the Hebrew letters for JEHOVAH in a triangle are not so good a symbol as IHS. Very often there is a space left in the screen for some text or sentence: perhaps the best words to put up in it are "Lift up your hearts," from the Communion Service. In the Altar-cloth also and other hangings none but proper emblems should be admitted. Above all things, I would shun such as are not of a religious cast, such as the rose, thistle, and shamrock. Nor would I put angels and cherubs in such places.

Sometimes in larger churches the two candlesticks (which with so beautiful a meaning the Church bids us place on the Altar*) are still to be found. But I know at least one Parish church in which these have been moved from the Table to the rails, and the wax-candles replaced by gas-pipes, to give more light to the church. You should not let this be done. If the old Altar-stone remains in your church (you may know it by the five little Crosses cut in it) you should take care of it. Its having been once used for such holy purposes should secure it from contempt.

Where there is a niche on each side of the Altar, it ought to be kept up, and re-opened, if already blocked. These are often hidden by ugly paintings, so bad as to be unworthy of admission into a church. Nor is there any good reason that I can find for placing pictures of Moses and Aaron in this part. A picture of the Holy

* See what I have said in my "Few Words to Churchbuilders." p. 24.

Person in whose name the church is dedicated to God would be much more appropriate, and might suggest a holy example to ourselves.

You should provide two seats at the Altar, and let the space before it be well carpeted. I do not like to see cushions on the Table, as if it were a mere kneeling place: modern Altars are generally too low. By all means let the coverings be taken away during the weekday services, even though the Communion Service be not used. To hide the Altar in any and every way seems to be what people now desire most. I have seen the pews nearest to it fitted up with a curtain on brass rods, as if they were not high enough in themselves. For this not even fear of draughts is a sufficient excuse.

The best place for the pulpit is on the north or south of the Nave, or against one of the piers of the Chancel or Nave-arch. If ever in an old church it is found elsewhere, be sure it has been moved. Perhaps the worst of the modern places for it is in front of the Altar: sometimes it bestrides the passage which separates two rows of pews: sometimes it has a huge sounding-board over it. Almost equally wrong is it to put the pulpit at the west end facing the East: for in such cases almost all must turn their backs to the East. Parishes in which such things are done are often remarkable for their irreverence and bad taste: thus in one of them, which I have now in mind, there is a plan on foot to build galleries, "because the church is too light." The next worst arrangement is when there are two pulpits of equal height, one on each side, the one for the prayers, the other for the sermon; and worst of all when there are three pulpits, one for the Priest, another for the clerk, and a still higher one between the two for the sermon; all of course with their backs to the Altar. In the same church, as if a witness against the innovation, there still remains an old stone pulpit against a pier: this is now the seat for the Minister's wife! Nor is it better when the pulpit, reading-pew, and clerk's pew, are put together one under the other. How can the Priest lead the people in prayer or in the Creed, turning as of old to the East, when the pulpit soars just behind him? The Church never wished to exalt preaching thus above prayer: indeed, the sermon is only a part of the Communion Service, and not a separate office: for which reason the Priest still preaches in a surplice in Cathedrals, which may be considered as patterns for parish churches.

Almost all these newfangled ways arose at that unhappy time when the Church of England was trampled upon by rebels and puritans: and they became more, as it were, inbred after the revolution in 1688. For after that men were for pruning every thing old and hallowed just because it was so: but we have learnt better now, and know that we can never be quite safe when we begin to stray from the old paths.

I have already spoken of gas. I for one do not love to see gas-pipes all over a church: but much less when the pipes are made showy and gay, and in the shape of snakes and other things unfit for a church, instead of being as plain and humble as may be. At any rate you should take care that the smoke, particularly from oil-lamps, does not soil the church: I know one church made quite black by it. Wax candles are by far the best for lighting a church, but they should not be put in a large chandelier. Nothing can be uglier than the chandeliers for the most part; and yet they are often kept when the church is fitted up anew with oil or gas.

Next about the stoves, another new thing which we are told we cannot do without. Yet our fathers did not want such comfort, though they had not warm cushioned pews and greenbaized doors as we have. If the church be kept well aired and dry, and, above all, if it be filled twice every day by a large congregation, it will never be very cold. At least let the stove be some easily managed thing, without any cumbrous pipes or heated flues, which have destroyed so many churches by fire. I have seen a great pipe carried nearly the whole length of a church upon iron hoops, which spring from pew to pew over the middle passage: and this sometimes passes over the Clergyman's head, and is made zigzag and up and down, that it may throw out more heat from its greater length. Instead of this, it should be put as much out of sight as may be, behind a pier for instance: and the chimney should be moveable, that in the summer it may be taken away; and never let the pipe be carried out of the church through a window, or through a piscina, or through a niche: nor let the chimney end at the gable where the Cross used once to stand, or, what is worse even than this, make the chimney in the shape of a Cross. I have seen two chimneys like huge caterpillars, climbing each up a pinnacle: and a chimney from a new vestry thrown like a flying buttress to the east end of an Aisle, and then, blocking in its way a beautiful old window, carried up as before to take the room of the Cross;—true emblem of the age which puts its ease and comfort higher than the pains and crosses which should be our teachers here!

It is very hard indeed to say much that I wish to say to you, without trenching upon what concerns the Clergyman more than you. But it must be so, that your high office will often bring you and him together. You must work hand in hand: and while a friendly Churchwarden is one of the greatest blessings a Clergyman can have, so one who fails in his duty is just as much the other way. There is no saying how many plans for furthering GOD's honour and His people's welfare have been thwarted by the ill-will of the Churchwardens. But this is an unnatural and wrongful state of things. You may for instance do much for the more solemn and reverent performance of Divine Service, by encouraging the organist to teach the children to sing: and very often your countenance will make it easier for the Clergyman to get rid of those unauthorized hymn-books which have been so much used of late years, and which are often only kept because they have taken such hold on the minds of the congregation.

I hope your organ is in the right place, that is at the west end: to have it over the Altar itself, or between the Chancel and Nave so as to block off the one from the other, is not to be borne. You should move it at any cost. It is often in this place in Cathedrals, and even in them it would be better at the west end, though it does not block up the Chancel-arch there as it does in small churches. The Transept-arch is not a good place for it, if as it often does it destroys the effect of the four arms of the Cross. You will not, I dare say, be of those who would let the organ go to decay or remain out of tune, because some evil-minded people may say that it does not fall under the *necessary* repairs of the church; nor of those who would let the bells go without ropes on the like grounds. Necessary repairs! as if these only ought to be thought of for His House Who gave us all we have! and this when we are but called upon to repair what our fathers built for us, and not to build anew for ourselves! We are indeed unworthy of our fathers, who will not be at the cost even of keeping up what they left for us;—the holy monuments at once of their piety towards God and love for us, and no less monuments (in their decay) of our coldness in religion and our contempt for those that have gone before us.

You should be proud of your bells, particularly if you have a good peal: and it is well to have a lock on the belfry-door to keep out such bad people as would purposely crack them: (for this has been done before now). If a bell is cracked, I would not let it hang so, or lie about in the church, but get it recast, and that in the right tone. You will see in the 88th Canon, about "Churches not to be profaned," what power the Minister and you have over the bell-ringers, and you are bound to support him in this matter. In some churches the conduct of these men is shameful. Sometimes there are rival companies who think they may go into the belfry whenever they wish, and who drink and quarrel there, and will for a fee ring the bells on any occasion, however profane or even wicked. It may be a hard task to withstand an abuse thus sanctioned by custom, but I hope you will not shrink from doing your part in the work.

One sometimes sees in large churches tables of fees for different things, even (I shudder to say it) for the Holy Sacrament of Baptism. If this is required by the Law in any case, and done or even approved of by the Clergyman, I have nothing to say: but if it has been done unwittingly by yourself or by a former Church-warden, I do earnestly entreat you to undo the evil as quickly as you can. Besides the selling a rite, so holy and so 'necessary for salvation,' think of our poor and ignorant people being driven to those who will not come back to the Church, and who are in some places but too happy to give what they call baptism at a lower rate.

Again, tables of fees for burials, from the vault down to the churchyard grave, are grievous eyesores. It is good indeed to be reminded of death: but every thing about us in church teaches us of this; and one does not like to have death brought before one only by what it would cost to bury us. It is distressing also to see tables of the cost of pews, though this is much worse abroad. Money should never come into our thoughts at church, save when we think of what we can give for His sake Who became poor for us. We know what He thought of buying and selling in the Temple, and may therefore well grieve to see books sold in churches, whether hymn-books, or descriptions and guide-books of the church if it be a fine one. I have shrunk from hearing money ring upon the cold tombs of the dead, money for guide-books or for viewing the church. If the advice of one who has seen many churches in his time be worth anything, you should have, besides the alms-box for the poor which you are bound to have, another box for the repairs of the building and payment of the servants: and these should have a fixed salary, unless you think a varying one more likely to ensure courtesy from them to strangers. Indeed you would have no reason for regretting the change: for the rich would give more largely than what is usually expected as a fee, and the poor would be able to see for nothing the mighty piles which former ages have raised; though they too would often give their grateful mite.

But I have been led away from speaking about what concerns the dead. If you are able to hinder burials beneath the church itself, you should do so, as it causes great unhealthiness. Sometimes when a long-closed vault is opened, the air has to be made pure by burning fires for several days together. But this, though no great hinderance now-a-days, when we have only service on Sundays, would have been, and will, I hope, again be too crying an evil to be borne, when keeping people from the Daily Service of the Church. Besides, many churches have been ruined by vaults undermining the piers or walls. If but one pier gives way, the whole building almost always follows.

I have spoken before at much length about burials in churchyards: but I wish to say a word upon monuments. Nothing can be more unsightly than most of these, not to say irreverent and profane. You may often persuade your fellow-parishioners to give up the ugly headstones, with their vulgar doggrel rhymes, and make them choose proper emblems instead of those which are now most common. What can be worse than poppies and broken columns, which typify everlasting sleep and thwarted hopes, instead of the peaceful and hopeful rest of the Christian? But of all things shun urns: they are heathen and silly emblems, though more used perhaps than anything else. Nor are they put on monuments only: I know of more than one East end stuck about with urns and pots of different sizes and colours; of a beautiful porch groaning under the weight of a shapeless modern urn; and even of a Chancel-arch removed altogether to make way for an urn on the top of each pier. At any rate you can hinder the mutilation of the church itself for urns and monuments. It is a shame to cut away piers and carvings and mouldings, and to block up arches and windows for such things as these. It is a shame also to use monumental stones over again, and thus destroy the record of one man's life to make room for that of another. And again, it is worse than dishonest to take gravestones for one's own purposes, and even to give them away to others for doorsteps and lintels, or the like uses.

Nothing is more strange than the modern taste in monuments: the same people who would gladly get rid of the few statues of Saints and Martyrs of old which have been saved for us, will themselves put up images to modern preachers, and perhaps even to wicked men, and this over or close to the very Altar itself!

A word about the register, which is often now-a-days under your charge, though it belongs properly to the Clergyman. Great care should be taken of it; and there should not be a high fee required for 'searching' it or getting a certificate from it. Neither as is sometimes done, should all access to the register be denied except on Sundays. Those who must search registers have something better to do on that day than to wander about and buy certificates. The parish-clerk ought not to be trusted with the register. Sometimes he takes no care of it at all: sometimes he is very uncivil about it. Neither should this person be allowed to hinder strangers from looking at monuments and the like unless they give him a fee. Uncourteousness on his part throws much of the blame upon you, who might in many ways put a stop to it.

It is a very good plan to enter in the Register an account of all that is done for the repair or adornment of the church: such records are really valuable, and are very easily made.

It is very hard to speak about vestries, as we have very few of the old sacristies left as patterns. Sometimes the *parvise,* or room over the porch, where there is one, is used as the vestry: but it is seldom large enough, and is not easy of access, besides being often kept as a room for deeds and records. I know of one case where this room is used as a lawyer's office, and where business is managed least of all fitted for a church. In another place it is made into a town-hall; in a third, into a drinking-room. If you must build a new vestry, never put it, as is sometimes done, at the East end behind the Altar: you may make it like a chapel or chapter-house, north or south of the Chancel, if you like. Never block up a Transept for this, or a porch: nor should the tower be so used. If you must have a place railed off within the church, you should make it as little seen as may be, and should have a good parclose or carved screen around it.

Take care also to hinder parish-meetings from being held either in the vestry or in the church itself. The way in which the holy buildings are sometimes profaned by those who never go into them at other times, is enough to make the very stones cry out.

You ought to have a loose board on which to fasten the notices for these parish-meetings, and for election and game-law papers. I have seen many fine old panelled doors quite spoilt by broken nails and wafers and paste.

You are bound by the 58th Canon to 'provide a decent and comely surplice with sleeves, at the charge of the parish': one too often finds the surplice dirty and ragged and covered with *iron-mould*: which is disgraceful to a parish.

In parishes such as yours there are often endowed services which ought always to be kept up: for they sprang from a good motive, although we may well grieve that the Church's daily voice had been stopped so as to make such bequests needful. Nor should you ever let slip any old parish-customs, such as giving out bread to the poor at Christmas, putting up holly at Christmas, and yew at Easter, or the like. Yet in this also there is room for care as to the way of recording these benefactions. The tables on which they are painted ought to be put where they will not interfere with any thing else: but never on gallery-fronts, or in any too conspicuous place.

Some of the things about which I have spoken may be harder to mend, and some easier: but let it be remembered that all are possible with patience and zeal. Let every one do a little ; and as formerly almost every Churchwarden made his name known by defacing some old ornament, or bringing in some evil, so henceforth let each in his year endear himself to the parish by getting rid of some barbarism, or bringing back some old custom. And if any one should be persuaded even by these lowly words so to work for GOD's Church, let me tell him he is not alone in his good deeds. I could tell of earnest and painful labours by Churchwardens who are not so rich as most of those to whom I now write. I could tell of sacrifices of time and money and self which would startle many in these lazy days. And there are others who have done their little ; who have brought back Fonts to their old places, and saved them from defilement, or the like. It is not for me to thank these ; for there is ONE for Whose sake they did these things, Who will not forget their labours. Such men, worthy of a better age, do not look for praise or name: and I may pain them perhaps by having said even thus much. But they will forgive me this wrong if they think how their example may lead others to do the like. Shall I compare these with the greater part of those who were Churchwardens before them ? It is even now a scorn and reproach with those who have left our communion that our Churchwardens have so often made a gain of their high office ; have done towards GOD what an honest man would not do towards his fellow. I have seen, for instance, a good old stone church faced throughout with brick, most needlessly and wrongly, by a churchwarden builder; another wainscoted within and repewed by a carpenter ; or painted all over by a painter, or plaistered all over by a plaisterer. But such things I hope will no longer be seen amongst us.

And besides the sin of such conduct, think also how much it spoils a church. What need has a stone church of brick facing and paint and roughcast; and beautiful carved wood of paint and whitening? It is a good thing to pick out the clogged-up mouldings, and bring to light long-hidden beauties, by scraping off the many coats of whitewash: and I have before shown how this may best be done. The Chancel is often spoilt by a Grecian screenwork quite unsuited to the church. I would always get rid of this, even if there be only a plain stone wall behind it: this is much better than so poor and tawdry a covering. I have seen the whole of an East end painted to look like marble: it would have been much better left plain. For in a church every thing should be real and good, and with no false show. Where a parish is really poor, a simple and reverent plainness is much better than tinsel and trumpery ornaments, and is much more suited to the majesty of GOD. But this is no excuse, it is clear, for niggardliness, or for an outlay lower than our means would allow.

It is a sad feature in modern church-building to put all ornament outside and where it can be seen, leaving all the rest mean and bare: for what is this but to take thought only of ourselves, instead of GOD's glory? But I hope people are now beginning again to look upon the church as a holy place; and you may greatly help forward this better feeling by enforcing, as you can do, the uncovering of the head in church even on week days. I have seen even Churchwardens, unwittingly I am sure, keep their own hats on: and there is no telling how much ill springs from such bad examples. For then the sexton and clerk and bell-ringers all think fit to do the same; and idle boys in turn copy these. On the other hand, the greatest good may come from setting a pattern of due reverence. Even workmen will take their caps off, and will stop their thoughtless whistle, when they see every one else giving such honour to GOD. Why should we uncover our heads on Sundays, and not on other days? Surely the presence of a congregation cannot make the place holy: but HE is always present, in Whose sight even angels hide their faces. The good old feeling of awe however is in most breasts hidden only, not quenched: I have seen many, when the question was put to them, pull their hats off with hearty shame and confession of their unmeant fault. This bad habit is much encouraged by the custom of screening off in town churches a large place under the western gallery as a *vestibule*, in which people think they have a right to put their hats on. You should always have a Porch instead of allowing a thing like this: but do not let it be a poor shabby building of brick, or as I have even seen it, of mud. Let it be of stone, suitable to the church, and it should have two seats.

Your duty often becomes most trying when any alteration in your church is mooted. It becomes you then to watch the scheme very earnestly. If you have not studied Church Architecture enough yourself, (as is very likely, for who has time for all things?) you should, after consulting the Clergyman, call in the aid of some one who has:

otherwise things may be, and often are, put up, which are quite unsuited to the style of the building. Thus it is dangerous to put up a
new screen unless it be copied from some old work in the church. But
when an enlargement of the church is set on foot, it is then not only
advisable, but quite necessary, to get assistance from such as are skilled
in these matters. However, as a broad rule, never build a Transept
when the church was not meant for one: for thus you cannot help
spoiling the whole proportion. In a small church with only a Nave,
it is well to build an Aisle; and often double Aisles may be made,
(as in the beautiful new church of S. Peter, Leeds,) the windows of the
old Aisles being kept in the outer wall of the new. I would never
lengthen the church without due advice: as you may thus mar the
fair proportion which all parts of a church should have to each other.
The one thing to be remembered in meddling with a church is this:
that we are not enlarging a house, or fitting up a hall, but have to do
with a building hallowed in itself, and so well devised that there is
probably not a single point in it but has its own and deep meaning.

Your duties indeed are now becoming every day more weighty:
for as we grew more civilized we seem to have grown more sacrilegious,
and to have learnt a new lesson, that every thing, however holy, must
give way before what we call "publick convenience." At one time,
we were quite shocked to hear of a porch made away with to improve
a road. But now you may be, as so many of your body of late years
have been, called upon to get rid of your church altogether, to make way
for a new or enlarged street, or for a new insurance-office, or the
like: or to cut off a corner from the church, or the tower, or even to
shave off the east end, as was done in an archiepiscopal city. In such
cases you must act as becomes those who are allowed to watch over
the earthly House of God; manfully, temperately, and guilelessly.
You may or may not meet with success: if not, you will have done
at least your part, and made your protest; and it will remain
only to make the evil as light as may be. But you must withstand
to the last any attempt to pull down your church only because it
is in people's way, and when, if rebuilt at all, it must be rebuilt in any
corner the street-commissioners may give. Thus in London, no great
while since, an old church was pulled down, and a new one, octagonal
in shape, built on one side: each of the eight sides except that to the
north having two galleries. The Altar is put in the northern alcove,
although the eastern would have done at least as well. So one wrong
step is almost always followed by another. If however you must remove,
insist on having such a plat of ground as may do for the only allowable plans for a church, a cross or an oblong. For now that our towns
are no longer walled, there is so far less reason than there was
formerly for cramping a church: and if no cost is spared to get a spot
good enough for a secular building, how much less should it be spared
for a church!

But now to go back to smaller things. I need not again ask you to take care of what stained glass has been left. You should pick all the pieces out and fill some one window with them, placing them in a pattern. Leave a border of plain ground glass round the edge, if you have not enough to fill the whole light. Above all things avoid having windows, as we now sometimes see them, of plain glass with a streak of red, or yellow, or green all round. Nothing can be more frightful than such a glare. In old glass sometimes the pattern is spoilt because some of the pieces have been unskilfully put in wrong side outwards : now this it would be very easy to put right. Sometimes fancy coats of arms are made up without any regard to the laws of heraldry : but heraldry is an old science, and one full of meaning to those who know it, so that to them a sham shield is worse than foolish. Indeed it is as bad as to see an unmeaning and silly inscription purposely set up in a church. If any one wishes to give a modern stained glass window to a church, you should withhold your consent till some fit person has looked carefully at the design, so that no wrong emblems may be admitted, and above all that no piece of the mullions, or tracery, or cusps of the window be cut away for it. Lastly, it is bad to have the royal arms in stained glass in the east window : for though no one loves the Crown more than I do, yet I do not like to see its mark where some higher and holier symbol ought to be. And for the same reasons I would not renew the royal arms painted on board, and put up over the Chancel-arch. There is no authority for this, and surely it is at least an unseemly successor of the holy Rood or Cross which used to stand there.

But why need I speak of what used to be over the Chancel-arch, when that arch itself is so shamefully maltreated ? Besides the deep meaning to be found in its position between the Chancel and the Nave, typifying the faithful death of the Christian as the soul passes the barrier between Earth and Heaven, it is often one of the most beautiful ornaments of the church. I will tell you from real examples what is sometimes done to it. I have known a fine old Norman arch, which had stood some seven hundred years, and had outlived every other part of the church, taken down at last to give, as was said, more room. I have known Chancel-arches enlarged, or the sides pared down and got rid of, for the same purpose. With strange inconsistency this arch is at other times blocked up to the very cieling, thus cutting off the Nave from the Chancel, and hindering the Communion Service from being ever read in the right place. Nor has the arch into the Tower fared better. Nothing is easier, and nothing will make the church look better, than to open these at once. Here also I may speak of the fault of boarding up a Transept, whether for a school, or a vestry, or any other purpose ; and of putting a wooden screen across the Nave for the sake of warmth.

The Roodscreen which used to stand under the Chancel-arch should be carefully kept up wherever it remains. Sometimes it has been moved to the belfry-arch, and there set up with the carved work inside: sometimes it is turned to the use of a great pew, or when left standing is cut through, that the pews in the Chancel may have a fair view of the pulpit. Sometimes the beautiful carving is made into rails for the steps of the pulpit, or worked into gallery fronts or pew-sides. Wherever this has been done, you should gather the pieces to-gether, and put them back into a screen. When there are but very few of them you may work them on to a door, and so give a very good effect. Very often the Roodscreen has been cut down just above the lowest panels, and these have been boarded or baised up to make com-fortable pew-backs. If you can strip these you will often find very curious carvings and paintings.

The Nave-arches sometimes have fared no better than that at the Chancel. Sometimes the pier is quite taken away and two arches thrown into one, to give perhaps a better view of the pulpit, and thus a most shapeless and ugly arch produced. Sometimes the piers are jagged and notched for a gallery to rest upon. As I said before, if you *must* have a gallery, let it rest upon uprights behind the pillars, not upon the pillars themselves. But sometimes to give more room the pillars are quite taken away, and thin posts put up instead: and even where the gallery was at first laid upon posts these have been kept, while the gallery was brought forward to the piers themselves. There is, I hope, only one case in England where the pinnacle of a tomb is used as a gallery-post, and this, I grieve to say, was allowed by a Society which, when it shall be at liberty to consider what is due to taste and reverence in proportion to its means and good will, will be, even still more than it has been, one of the Church's best and ablest handmaids. As it is, that body itself probably little knows how many churches have to rue in this respect ever having come under the hands of the 'Incorporated Society for building and repairing churches and chapels.' Never have anything to do with *fluting* piers by way of beautifying them; nor with painting them yellow, perhaps with the capitals and architrave black for contrast. Neither ought the obelisks on old monuments to be tipped with lamp-black for effect.

There is however one thing worse than all this: to take away the capitals and arches, " because they are of no use," and hold the roof up by wooden props! This was done, and this the reason given for it, in a village of Worcestershire: and in the same county's Cathedral city, no longer ago than last year, a church was pulled down because it was in the way of another. After this, to block off a north Aisle because the church is too large, and then to build a gallery because it is too small, will seem trifling. I know also of a north Aisle which was pulled down, that the sale of the materials might pay for beau-tifying a door: and (though this is a less matter) of poppy heads being sawn off, because they were in the way!

After all I have said you will see for yourselves how great an advantage it would be, if you could ever repair any damaged windows, or open them if they are blocked up: or raise a roof which hides the top of a window; or move houses or sheds which interfere with the church on the outside. I need not remind you how good a work it would be if you could ever rescue from desecration any ruined or disused church. There are more such to be found in our country than would be readily believed: but they are often in a very bad state. I know a beautiful chapel that has been used as a dwelling house, its Chancel as a kitchen, with the Altar fitted up as a fire-place with a brick chimney! These might very often be restored so as to become district chapels, and would be much better than a new cheap room.

Perhaps after reading such a list many will think that it is too late to try to stop such a flood of change and evil: but I could give a list almost as long of such faults lately amended, and therefore believe that the zeal for the LORD's House which has so lately sprung up will work widely enough to set right all.

I have put off till now speaking of DAMP, though, as I said before, I think it perhaps the greatest ill that can befall a church. There can be no doubt but that the graves close to the church-walls, clogging up the drains and making the heap of earth against them higher and higher, are the chief causes of damp. In how many churches is there a flight of several steps down to the door from the heaped-up church-yard! In one case the outside level is that of the top of the pews, and those high pews too, within. About this I may mention one place by name, though against my general plan, since it is not a parish-church; I mean the ancient and beautiful church of the Hospital of S. Cross, near Winchester. Here,—though this is by no means the worst case I could bring forward,—the earth in the close is now a good deal higher than the floor of the church: so that last winter when the thaw took place a great body of water forced itself through the west door, and could scarcely be kept out of the Choir, which I am sorry to say is pewed off to the great damage of the building. In the north Aisle to the Chancel also this beautiful church is much hurt by damp. Now no one can deny that such a state of things as this should at once be mended: and how can this be done but by clearing away the earth which has become piled up round the foundations? And here I may say, that I am sorry a Review which deserves all our thanks for what it has so ably done for Church Architecture among us, has, while most kindly praising my former 'Few Words,' partly mis-understood my meaning in what I said about damp *. I never meant that the earth should be cleared away lower than the blocking-course or break in the masonry, which almost always marks the proper earth-line. So far down as this may safely be cleared, and then a trench should be made deep enough to carry off the water which may fall from the eaves: and this trench should be lined or

* British Critic, July 1841, p. 252.

paved with brick or stone, and made to deliver the water out of the church-yard, and at any rate clear away from the foundations of the walls. If this be done with judgment it will seldom if ever be followed by the 'spreading of the walls': and even if it should be, this would be because the wall had been weakened by the pile of wet earth which had been left to lie against it, rather than because the wall had never stood without so hurtful a prop. However you should always watch the wall so cleared, and, whenever you can, get the advice of an architect.

The loathsome smells which taint some churches often arise from damp, as well as do those green stains which so hurt the eye. When you find this you should keep the church as open and airy as possible; and make drains and clear away the earth, as well as forbid the burying of any more bodies near the church or within it. Indeed this should be stopped at any risk, and in every case. I shall not soon forget seeing a church in which a vault had just given way. It was deep and full of broken coffins, but had no smell; for this had long ago escaped through cracks in the roof. How unclean is this for the House of GOD, and how unspeakably hurtful for those who worship in it! You should, among the first things, see that the pavement is good and well cemented. Nothing is more needful than a free passage of air over the floor: but this is much hindered by pews. I remember once taking up the bottom of a pew to reach a brass, and being almost overcome by the stench. You should therefore, if you have pews, have holes made in the skirting-boards for a free passage of air.

One thing more. All old churches were dedicated to GOD in honour of some Saint. Now, in some places not a soul in the whole parish knows the name of the Patron Saint of the church. This is a sad contrast to some little villages in Wales, where this is known by all even the poorest. But, to be sure, comfort and civilization have not made so much way there as with us. There is however something worse than this: in one church there is in the vestry a long puritanical inscription scoffing at the Blessed Saint, S. Alkmund, to whom the church is dedicated. And this is allowed to remain!

In some few churches there are old libraries which have been bequeathed for the parishioners' use. These should be kept up, as there are often very valuable books in them. I have seen where the books have been torn to pieces, it would seem on purpose.

Wherever also there is a lettern with a large Bible or other book chained to it, you should take much care of it. And even if the books are gone the lettern should be saved: and not left to lie about in some dark place. One would scarcely believe that any one would think a brass eagle-desk a piece of lumber: yet such is sometimes the case. This is the place also to remind you of having the Bible, Prayer-Book, and Office-Books of the church in good repair. And there ought to be ribands to point out the Lessons, the Psalms, and other parts of the service: for the untidy plan of allowing the clerk to turn down one or more leaves for the Clergyman not only fills the Books with 'dog-ears', but wears them out in a very short time. The parish should never be niggardly in what is necessary for divine service: and I would strongly advise you (when you want new books) to get the beautiful edition published at the Cambridge University Press, with the Rubricks properly printed in red.

Sun-dials should be kept up, unless where they have been put on the stem of the old Cross. You should care for this old Cross, and keep it clean: for none but wicked men would have broken that emblem of all our hopes. Clocks, which have now supplanted that old sun-dials, often spoil a church; their very shape is unsuited to pointed architecture. Do not seek to make them suit a Tower by blocking a window or cutting away a moulding for them: for you cannot succeed, and you will perhaps spoil the building in the attempt. Let them remain, if they must remain, in their ugliness.

And now I have done. And though I know how feebly I have raised my voice, yet it has been raised with the one view of trying to recall some of my brethren of the laity of England to a sense of what GOD claims from those who are entrusted here with the overcharge of His House; and of giving what little aid to them a life devoted to Church-antiquities may have enabled me to give. If I have had much fault to find, it is not from a love of finding fault, far from that, but from a hope of amending. And if many have been persuaded by my former Words to do something for GOD's Church, although with such scanty means, it is not much to hope that some of those to whom I now write, who mostly are so much better able to afford such cost, will also do their part. You to whom I have now been speaking are often men of wealth and influence: you have fair houses and costly furniture, and all comforts you can wish for. I earnestly call upon you to think of the claims which the church, which you are allowed to watch and guard, has upon your aid: the church, within which you were by Holy Baptism made members of the spiritual Church; in which it may be you knelt before the Bishop in Confirmation, and in Holy Matrimony plighted your troth in the dearest earthly tie; the church which you have perhaps daily entered for prayer and praise, and how often for Holy Communion! around which your fathers and brethren who have departed in faith are resting in the sleep of peace; in which lastly the solemn Funeral Service will ere long be heard over your bier. It is no slight band which ties you to your Parish-church: it is no far-off call which is rousing you to do your duty. Your oaths, your honour, your manliness, must force you, one would think, to fill the office which you have taken as a good man should: a happy office surely, to watch that church round which all your hopes are or ought to be centered ; and a high office, (it cannot be said too often) to care for the holy House where GOD Himself deigns to dwell.

Join then for your Church's sake the zealous band who are now on all sides working, each in his way, for GOD's glory. I cannot promise you fame, but you will not desire that. I can promise you the love of all who are working in the same good cause ; and, what is more, a lasting record of your labours by Him in Whose name and for Whose sake you labour.

A Few Words to the Parish Clerks and Sextons of Country Parishes, first edition, 1843

Of the four *A Few Words* … pamphlets, it is, perhaps, not surprising that that addressed to the Parish Clerks and Sextons – the least influential group of Neale's comprehensive readership – should be the last to be written. Perhaps he was encouraged by the success of the two earlier documents intended for churchwardens and felt that clerks and their assistants too should be enlisted in the Camdenian cause. Neale's stated purpose here was 'to lead people to behave themselves reverently in God's House' (p. 3), but in practice this is only one of a number of topics encompassed.

Predictably, there is advice about routine cleaning, airing and avoiding damp. This is dealt with partly in the context of practical maintenance and partly as a means of keeping God's house decently. Both are heavily over-laid with Camdenian proselytising. Thus clerks and sextons are advised to scrape away layers of old whitewash from pillars, fonts and old monuments, not just because they are unsightly but also because they could reveal historically interesting material. Similarly, they are encouraged to take just as much care of 'the old fashioned open seats … of oak' as they do of 'those wicked things called pews or pues' with which your church might be 'infested'. (p. 5). Interestingly, Neale doesn't attempt to explain his damning opinion of them.

Neale also touches on the issue of ritual – without making any explicit reference to it – by reminding clerks of the important contribution they can make to the 'decency and order' of services. At the funeral service he points out the importance of providing 'a place for the Clergyman at the west end of the grave, so that in reading the prayers, he may turn to the east.' (p. 7).

There is also advice about dealing with animals, birds and insects. Neale is concerned that jackdaws are not able to enter the tower although he discourages sextons from shooting them, both because it is an 'unseemly' habit and because it endangers the old windows. In a rare moment of sentimentality, he advises that the nests of swallows and martins ought not to be taken from the church eaves, not only because they 'do no great harm' but also 'from having chosen the church as their home, seem to have a kind of claim to be taken care of.' (p. 8). Quite why jackdaws are not the recipients of the same benevolence is not made clear!

A Few Words to the Parish Clerks and Sextons was written by J. M. Neale and first published in 1843. A second edition followed later that year and a third and final one appeared in 1846.

A FEW WORDS

TO THE

PARISH CLERKS

AND

SEXTONS

OF COUNTRY PARISHES

𝔓𝔲𝔟𝔩𝔦𝔰𝔥𝔢𝔡 𝔟𝔶 𝔱𝔥𝔢 ℭ𝔞𝔪𝔟𝔯𝔦𝔡𝔤𝔢 ℭ𝔞𝔪𝔡𝔢𝔫 𝔖𝔬𝔠𝔦𝔢𝔱𝔶

"He that despiseth small things shall fall by little and little"

CAMBRIDGE

AT THE UNIVERSITY PRESS

STEVENSON CAMBRIDGE   PARKER OXFORD

RIVINGTONS LONDON

M DCCC XLIII

[*Price Twopence*]

A FEW WORDS

TO

PARISH CLERKS AND SEXTONS.

Introduction. I DO not know whether those who may read this little book will have seen or heard of a Tract called *A Few Words to Churchwardens.* If they have not, I wish they would read it, should it ever come in their way: if they have, they will not wonder at my taking up my pen to write *a Few Words to Parish Clerks and Sextons.* My reason for writing advice to Churchwardens was my wish to lead people to behave themselves reverently in GOD's House: and I have the same reason for writing to Clerks and Sextons now.

What a Clerk's business is. 2. You, to whom I am speaking, have no power to order that the church shall be taken good care of, but, in your way, you may do a great deal of good; and if you do not take care, will certainly do a great deal of harm. You cannot, it is true, have things your own way; you must take them as you find them: and it will often happen that you will have to make the best of a bad thing. Still, do your best; take pleasure in your office; do what you can to serve GOD in it: and you will find that you can do a great deal more than perhaps you now think. I hope that what I am going to say may help you to know your duty, and stir you up to do it.

The necessity of doing all little things in the best way. 3. Now never give way to the thought that it can be no matter how you get through your business, so it is done sufficiently well to give you a claim to your year's salary. None but an idle man would say this: for in every thing there is a right and a wrong; and why should you do it wrong, when you may do it right? "If a thing," says the proverb, "is worth doing at all, it is worth doing well." It was once said by a good and a very great man, "If I had been born a street-sweeper, my crossing should have been the cleanest in London." And it was the spirit that led him to say this, which made him a great man.

1

4. Now all this is very true, even in the case of those who are only engaged in common business: but how much more with respect to those, who like you are allowed to be employed in the service of God! The meanest office in His House is a great honour; and if you do not do your very best to serve Him you are altogether unworthy of your place.

And much more when they concern the church.

5. The first thing which it is your business to do, or to see done, is the keeping the church clean. And here I hope that you will never give in to any of those untidy ways of which so many Clerks are guilty: such as sweeping up odds and ends into dark out-of-the-way corners, where no one can see them,—or strewing them in the churchyard. They often get put into just the very worst place possible, namely, the drain which runs round the church: this hinders the water from flowing off, and the rubbish thrown in soaks it up, and decays: then the wall against which it is thrown begins to decay: then more rubbish is thrown in, which takes away the only chance of the wall drying: and soon the whole side of the church becomes ruinous; and all because the Clerk would not take the trouble of walking a few yards further to throw his odds and ends away. If you really, as you ought to do, take a pride in your church; you will not grudge the trouble of now and then cleaning out this drain, if there is one: if unfortunately there is not a drain, you can at all events cut down the nettles and other tall weeds which are sure to grow against the wall, and to remove loose earth and rubbish from it. And indeed it would be a good thing to cut down weeds wherever they spring up in the churchyard, more especially about tombstones; for they very soon hide, and then destroy, the letters engraven on them.

The church to be kept clean:

rubbish carried out of the churchyard:

nettles cut down.

6. There is a proverb which says, ' Let your house be kept clean, but no dusting be seen:' and this is very good advice about churches. To see, on going into a church, a broom in one place, a duster in another, and a scoop in a third, is very sad: for it shews that a habit, which no decent persons would allow in their own houses, is thought very allowable in the church of God. And these things generally get put into the very worst places possible: the broom within the Altar rails, the duster in the Font, and the scoop in the Chancel. Another thing, too, which has a very bad look, is to find torn leaves, especially of Bibles and Prayer-books, lying about: and very often filling up the *Piscinæ* or little

Brooms not to be left about:

torn leaves burnt.

recesses in the wall. These leaves, if you cannot find the books to which they belong, you should burn.

Pues,

7. I suppose that your church is infested with some of those* very ugly and wicked things called pews or pues. If it be so, it is of course your duty to keep them clean and decent; to beat out their cushions, and brush or dust their sides. But when you do this, you should take just as much, or more, care to keep tidy the old-fashioned open seats where the poor people sit. These seats, carved in hearty four-inch old English

and open seats, oak, not built of miserable half-inch pieces of deal, are a great deal worthier of your care than the pues. Therefore you should not leave them, as I have too often seen, dirty or greasy. They are always good in their way: and often very handsome indeed. By-and-bye, when the fashion of pues goes out, as it has begun to do with all sensible people, if any of those old-fashioned seats with their dogs, and lions, and flowers, should have been hurt by your carelessness, people will owe you very little thanks for it. Some old churches have a kind of stalls, where the

and stalls. bottom lifts up, or shuts down, and either way makes a very good seat: these are often, for no possible reason, nailed down. You should get the Churchwarden's leave, which he will be sure to give you, to knock out the nails which fasten them down; you will often find some beautiful carving for your pains.

Whitewash.

8. Indeed you may often get leave from the Clergyman or Churchwardens to do what they would not perhaps *order*, but will nevertheless be very glad to see done. I mean such things as scraping whitewash off the pillars, or off the Font, or, it may be, from some fine old monument. I know of a Clerk, who took a great deal of pains to clear a monument which was quite clogged up with whitewash and paint, and who thought himself well repaid for his pains (as indeed he was) when the letters of the inscription came as sharply and clearly out as if they had only been cut a day, instead of being in such a state that no one could make out what they were.

Matting and hassocks.

9. You ought not to let matting, or trusses, or hassocks, lie on the damp floor of the church: not only because it destroys *them*, but, much more, because it hinders the floor from drying. You should do every thing you can to

Dryness of the make it drier; and, (unless you live a long way off)
Church. you do not take proper care of your church if you are

---

* Every body, I suppose, thinks them ugly: why they are wicked you may see in a little tract, called *Twenty-three Reasons for getting rid of Church Pues.*

not there at least once every day, to see that the windows are kept properly open. If the casements are wired on the outside, as they always ought to be, there are very few seasons of the year in which they may not be left open all day, except when the rain sets directly upon them. And in the fine summer nights you need not shut them. And the more you can safely leave the door open the better. There ought, by rights, to be a wicket to the outer gate of the porch, not only that the inner doors may be set open, but that sheep, and other animals, may not get into the porch itself. If the casements are not wired, you will have to be out and in all the oftener, to drive out any birds which may have come in. I have some times seen the whole church, and the holy Altar itself, in a vile state by means of these birds. In like manner, it is disgraceful to see slugs, or moths, or spiders in the corners of the walls.

10. If jackdaws are allowed to come into the *Rubbish brought in by birds.* Tower (which should never be) you should often be up there to scrape the bells, to which otherwise they do a great deal of harm, and to carry away the stacks of rubbish which they bring in, and leave about. I have sometimes seen the Tower stairs so choked up with this rubbish, that I could hardly make my way up them. I knew one church where the Clerk was allowed by the Churchwarden to have for his own use all that the caddows had brought into the Tower: and he took home, at one time, two cart-loads of good firewood, besides a great quantity of rubbish which he threw away. Birds also often leave sticks under the eaves of a church, and behind the cornice. This you should watch your time and take away as you can.

Morning's business before service. 11. The first thing you have to do on the Sunday Morning, and whenever else there is service in the church, is to make, if you can, a thorough draft from one end of it to the other. Then in uncovering the Altar, and the Pulpit or desk, do not go to work as some Clerks do, treating holy places and holy things with great irreverence. If old customs were kept up as they ought to be, you would never be allowed to go within the Altar-rails: and this, I hope, may some day be the case again. In the mean time, I would not go there needlessly: and when there, would behave so as to shew that I knew myself to be on very holy ground. If you have an assistant *General reverence in church.* in getting ready the church for service, do not allow him to talk, or talk yourself, loudly or irreverently. In some countries the people always speak in a whisper at church, at whatever time they may happen to go in:

and it is a good and a wise custom. You will of course take care that the places are found properly in the Bible and Prayer-book, and if the Church-books are any the worse for wear, as they too often are, (a sin and a shame it is!) you should look through the Lessons to see that nothing is missing, from a leaf being lost or torn. While the congregation is assembling, you may do much good by keeping order, in making boys take off their hats, and so forth. I surely need not tell you to be careful in taking off your own.

Font: how to be filled.
12. I take it for granted that your Font has a drain and plug, as our Church orders. In this case it will be your duty to see that, when wanted, it is *filled* with *pure* water: the best thing in which to bring it in (if your church has not a worthier vessel for that purpose) is, I think, a plain stone pitcher, which should be used for nothing else, and should be kept in the church. As during the Service of Baptism the Clergyman does not kneel down till after the child is baptised, you had better not put a hassock before him till then: else it is apt to be in the way. And you will put it on the *West* side of the Font.

Funerals.
13. In burials you will have much to do with the decency and order of the arrangements: and if you are also Sexton, almost every thing depends on you. It is shameful to see a Clerk, while waiting for a funeral, laughing and talking with the Bellringer. You should be careful to make every one in the churchyard at the time take off their hats, and behave soberly and reverently. You ought also to spare the feelings of the mourners as much as possible. Therefore the sides of the grave ought to be well and evenly cut, lest (as I have sometimes seen) stones should be knocked out when the coffin is let down, and fall in upon it. And the grave should be a little larger than is quite necessary, to prevent that scraping and rubbing against the sides which it is so very painful to hear. Your ropes, too, should be long enough to be kept at the top: they are too often so short, that the ends have to be let down into the grave. Above all, remember that as it is in the church, so it is in the churchyard; " the rich and the poor meet together" as equals: and you should be as careful in ordering and managing the funeral of a pauper child from the Union in his plain deal shell, as you would be in that of the first nobleman in the land, with his pall and plumes and escutcheon and silver coffin-plates. You should provide a place for the Clergyman at the West end of the grave, so that in reading the Prayers, he may turn to the East.

14. So much of your time must be passed in the church or the churchyard, that you will be able pretty well to tell how people behave in coming into them or passing through them. It was once the custom, as it still is in some parts of England, to take off the hat on coming into the churchyard; but though this has now-a-days gone out of fashion, there are many ways in which you may lead people to look at it as holy ground. You should with the Churchwarden's help put a stop at once to all shouting and playing in the churchyard, jumping over the tombstones, or playing at hide-and-seek behind them: and should give in the names of those who do so to the Clergyman.

Churchyard.

15. Also, though I much wish that daws, as I said before, could be banished from the Tower, I do not mean that they should be shot in the churchyard. Besides the danger of breaking the church-windows, there is something very unseemly in this. And as to shooting swallows or martins as they fly round the Tower, it is a cruel and barbarous custom: neither ought their nests to be taken away from the eaves, for they do no great harm; and, from having chosen the church as their home, seem to have a kind of claim to be taken care of.

Birds not to be shot there.

16. At Christmas you will take care that the church is adorned handsomely with holly, laurel, and yew. (Mistletoe is not a proper plant.) Do not put very little twigs in every hole and corner: but let there be here and there, and especially round the Altar, a large handsome bunch. In some churches they take them down at Twelfth Night: in others, they let them stay till Septuagesima Sunday: beyond which they should never be kept. In some parts of the country they also put up flowers at Easter and Whitsuntide; and a very good custom it is. There is generally a yew-tree in the churchyard, which was planted for the very purpose of having boughs and branches cut from it for the church; and therefore it is a very foolish thing, when, as I have sometimes known, the parish does not like any of its branches to be taken. One word more I must say about yews: many people now-a-days look on it as a sad and melancholy tree, because they often see it in churchyards. But this is quite a mistake: the reason it used to be planted there is this, that being an evergreen, and bearing fruit in the winter, it seemed to be a good type, or figure, of Immortality. Therefore it is very fit to be used at joyful times.

Dressing the church at Christmas with holly.

The yew not a melancholy tree.

Church key.   17. Lastly, although the church ought to be always open (as it once used to be) for persons to pray and meditate within its holy walls, yet, till this custom is restored, it becomes necessary to speak about the key. The Clergyman and Church-wardens ought always to have a key: but if you are entrusted with it, you should take care to be at hand when wanted. Never take it in your pocket when you go out, but let it always be left at home. And if your house is ever shut up, leave the key with one of your near neighbours. And when you are sent for to shew the church to

Visitors to the church.   any visitor, you will often spare yourself trouble, if you bring the key of the Tower too, as they may very likely want to see the bells. You will of course take care that no harm is done to the church: but you should be as civil as you can, and shew every thing in your power, and tell every thing that you know about the church.

Visitors not to be allowed to take anything away.   18. And here I wish to add a few words on a very important subject. You must on no account allow visitors to take away from your church any fragments of stained glass, encaustic tiles, pieces of carved wood or stone, or of monumental Brasses, which may be lying loose and unemployed about the church. It is grievous to find so often portions of the most beautiful and ancient pavements torn up and thrown loose into a corner, or into a chest, or into that common but ⚊ improper receptacle for all disused church furniture, the bottom of the Tower, when they might be laid down again in the Chancel with very little trouble or expense, and very greatly to the ornament of the church. Again, fragments of stained glass often lie about in the *piscina*, or the church chest; and it is a very common but very scandalous practice of parish clerks to let visitors carry away any number of pieces they please for a small sum of money. Now if there should be any remains of this kind in your church, if possible have all the fragments carefully cleaned and replaced; but if this cannot be done at present, you must keep them under lock and key till an opportunity may occur. To sell the smallest portion of what has been in ancient days solemnly devoted to God's service by pious men, is very wicked; for you are not only selling what does not belong to you, but you are at least implicated in an act of sacrilege, and are shamefully betraying the trust that is reposed in you as the guardian of such things. Therefore I say very earnestly, that you must religiously preserve, and if possible restore to its proper place, every fragment of this sort that you may find. For the value of tiles and stained glass, and such relics, is often in itself very great; and as belonging to the church they ought to be held doubly precious and sacred.

Conclusion.   19. And now I have done : and I hope that what I have said may both lead you to take greater delight in your office, and shew you what you ought to do if you wish to act like a good man and an honest Clerk; and, by your care of God's House, to bring down His blessing upon your own.

———————

Church Enlargement and Church Arrangement, **published in 1843**

A lthough the title of this pamphlet does not begin with 'A Few Words to ... ', it is very much on the model of its four predecessors that do. It is addressed to the constituency neglected by the others: clergymen. More specifically, 'Clergymen as find themselves ... compelled ... to increase the size of ... their church: as well as those who are prompted by their zeal for the honour of GOD'S HOUSE to take steps towards its restoration to its original beauty' (p. 3), but find themselves ill-equipped for the task. The two topics of enlargement and restoration are treated separately, although inevitably there is some overlap of subject matter. There is also much duplication between the material in this publication and that to be found in *A Few Words to Church Builders.* However, whereas the latter is concerned with the design of new churches, this one is restricted to existing pre-Reformation buildings, and essentially those in country parishes. Nevertheless, there is much in *Church Enlargement* that is applicable to the design of new churches and there are several topics in the work – for instance discussion about the location of choirs and organs – that are not addressed in ...*Church Builders.* Taken together, the two volumes encapsulate the Camdenian manifesto of church design in its early years.

In the section dealing with enlargement, an early point is that if pues are removed, sufficient room may be created to render an addition to the structure unnecessary. Generally, Neale discourages extending the church, unless such a course was anticipated by 'the founder', for instance if the church is without one or both aisles. However, if further space is needed for worshippers, the pamphlet discusses the merits of the various options. Lengthening

36 & 37. St Denys, Ibstock, Leicestershire, before and after the two late-nineteenth century restorations. Plate 35 is from a watercolour by Mary Maden of 1836, viewed from the west gallery. Note the flat chancel ceiling and the plaster chancel arch of the earlier view. *(Geoff Brandwood collection)*

naves or chancels is not sanctioned since either would destroy the original proportions of the building; a transept is appropriate where there is a central tower but is 'unadvisable' in other cases (p. 9). Neale favours the addition of chancel aisles, although he doesn't address the obvious issue of which way worshippers in such places would face.

The other half of the pamphlet is concerned with restoration. It points out the frequency and absurdity of undertaking 'ornamental' work while the structure remains in need of repair but, having made this point, goes on to list all the items which should be contained in a church 'as it should be' (p. 12). There is discussion about stained glass, encaustic tiles and, following the question 'what is necessary for decency in a Chancel', there is a useful check-list of essentials (p. 14).

The pamphlet was written by J. M. Neale and published in 1843. It was not reprinted.

CHURCH ENLARGEMENT

AND

CHURCH ARRANGEMENT

"The palace is not for man but for the LORD GOD"

𝕻ublished by the Cambridge Camden Society

CAMBRIDGE

AT THE UNIVERSITY PRESS
STEVENSON CAMBRIDGE   PARKER OXFORD
RIVINGTONS LONDON
M DCCC XLIII.

[*Price Sixpence.*]

CHURCH ENLARGEMENT, &c.

1. THE present Tract may, it is hoped, be useful **Design of the present Tract.** to such Clergymen as find themselves, without any previous knowledge of church architecture, compelled, by the increase of population, to increase the size of, or at least the *room* in, their church: as well as to those who are prompted by their zeal for the honour of GOD's House to take steps towards its restoration to its original beauty, but who feel nevertheless that they are incompetent to direct the work without assistance. I propose first to speak of church enlargement; and then of church reparation. And if I **Method.** shall be able to simplify any difficulties arising from the present real or supposed wants of congregations, and thereby to prevent any desecration of, or needless alterations in, one of GOD's Holy Temples, most amply shall I feel myself rewarded. The very nature of my subject may perhaps sometimes make me appear to speak in an utilitarian way, and as if churches were to be built "grudgingly or of necessity:" but they who are acquainted with the principles by which the CAMBRIDGE CAMDEN SOCIETY **Not written on utilitarian principles.** is actuated, and on which it was founded, will feel sure that nothing which I shall say about making the most of room, or loss of 'available space,' is intended to teach people how to make small churches hold many worshippers, or to encourage the idea that a House builded to the GOD of Heaven should not be "exceeding magnifical." It will also be well to observe that I am principally writing for the use of country parishes, where advice is generally of more avail, as well as less accessible.

2. When it is proposed to enlarge a church on **Previous enquiry necessary, whether enlargement is requisite.** the ground of its incapacity to hold a sufficient number of parishoners, (and by a sufficient number, I mean, *under the* most *unfavourable circumstances,* two-fifths,) the question should first of all be asked, Is such enlargement really necessary? This enquiry need not, indeed, be instituted in a case which we shall mention presently, where the design of the founder has never yet fully been carried out: for in this case, to give the church the full proportion which he intended, will be an actual improvement to the fabrick. In other cases, since however correctly the additions may be designed, and however well executed, the proportions of the church, as a whole, must more or less suffer, the greatest

1—2

care is necessary that an enlargement be not undertaken when a re-arrangement would amply suffice. This rule is of course intended to forbid all additions, which it is intended to appropriate to a particular house or family, and which sometimes make their appearance in the shape of transeptal excrescences.

3. In order to answer the question, Does a given *Arrangement of a Church.* church hold as many worshippers as it ought to do,—that is, as it would hold if arranged in a catholick manner,—we must first, (though we thereby in a measure go over old ground,) say a few words on the proper arrangement of a church. And this is the more necessary because, though it is the characteristic of this economical age to make the most of every inch of ground, it is certain that few churches do contain as many worshippers as they might, and ought to, accommodate. We will take a cross church, of given size, and use it as an example.

4. *We assume that there are no pues in the church:* *Ejection of Pues.* for till their ejection has been effected, a necessary loss of *twenty*, a probable loss of from *thirty* to *fifty* per cent. will be the consequence. There must be a passage down the Nave of *Passages.* five feet width *at least:* down each Aisle, *next to the piers*, of three feet six inches *at least:* down the middle of each Transept, of four feet *at least.* There must be a cross passage from the south-west to the north-west door, of six feet (this width is necessary for a decent performance of the Funeral service:) and along the East end of the Nave and each Aisle, of three feet. The open seats on each side should not be *higher* than two feet six inches: *Seats.* they *need not* be more than the same distance apart: though an intervening space of three feet will conduce much to a solemn performance of the Divine Offices. Only it must always be borne in mind that THE HIGHER THE SEATS, THE FUR-THER THEY MUST BE APART, or the worshippers will not be able to kneel. The seats in the Nave and Aisles will of course face East: those in the North Transept, South; those in the South, North. The Chancel will have two, or if very large, may have three, rows of stalls or open seats on each side: they will extend eastward as far as the Chancel door, but generally speaking, not further: if however, the *Priest's door* be towards the western part of the Chancel, a break must be left for it in the stalling, which may then continue till within ten feet of the East wall.

5. One of these stalls, on the South side, next to the wall, must be a little elevated, and will be the reading-pue. The other stalls will serve for the choristers, and for the communicants during the celebration of the Holy Eucharist. The litany-stool and eagle

or lettern will stand in the middle of the Chancel: the pulpit at the North or South sides of the Chancel-arch:—the former is the better position.

6. Let us now take a church of average dimensions and arrangements, and enquire into the number of worshippers which it will contain. We will imagine one consisting of Chancel, Nave, North and South Aisles, South Porch, and disengaged Tower: that is, a Tower projecting westward of the Aisles. The Chancel we will suppose twenty-six feet in length by twenty in breadth: the Nave, fifty-one by twenty-three: the Aisles, fifty-one by nine feet six: the Tower, twelve feet six square.—Beginning with the Nave, on the South side of our middle passage of five feet, will be a space of fifty-one feet by nine:—in subtracting the cross passage of six feet, we have forty-five feet by nine. Now, allowing two feet six for the space between each seat, we have eighteen rows of benches; and allowing a breadth of eighteen inches for every sitter, each bench will hold six. The North side of the Nave will only have sixteen rows of seats, because the pulpit at its East end will take up the room of two rows. The Nave, therefore, will contain 204 worshippers. Leaving a passage of three feet six in the South side of the North Aisle, we have a space of fifty-one by six feet: this, for the same reasons as before, must be reduced to forty-five by six feet. Here we have eighteen rows, each holding four persons. The South Aisle will not contain more than fifteen such rows, because the Font will take up the room of three seats at least. Leaving a passage of three feet down the middle of the Tower, we have on each side a space of four feet six by twelve: which would afford ample room for four open seats, each containing three worshippers. The number of worshippers who would thus be provided for, would be,

Actual measurements.

In the Nave	204
North Aisle	72
South Aisle	60
Tower	24
Total	360

7. A practical difficulty would present itself *in limine* in most churches. The Western Arch would probably be blocked up: and the Tower in such a state from damp and cold as to render it impossible that any worshippers could occupy it. And it must be allowed that great care is necessary in rendering a large Tower fit for this pur-

Tower may contain worshippers.

pose; the roof must, of course, be perfectly sound, and the Belfry and western doors fitting tightly. But many Towers were in former times filled with worshippers: and there can therefore be no reason why they may not be so again.

8. We will, however, imagine that notwithstanding the substitution of open seats for pues, the throwing open of the Tower, and every other *fair* advantage which can be taken, room is still wanted. Evidently, in this case, the first step would be to raise a gallery. And it is therefore of importance to shew, at the outset, why this method of enlargement must never be thought of: why GALLERIES UNDER ANY POSSIBLE CIRCUMSTANCES ARE TOTALLY INADMISSIBLE. The greater part are, of course, nothing but raised platforms of pues: and all that has been written about pues is doubly strong against these.

Galleries inadmissible, and why.
9. But we are now considering those galleries which have open free seats: and they, if not quite so bad as the other kind, are a great deal *too* bad to be for a moment endured. *Firstly,* their very position, their proud height, their seclusion, their separation from the rest of the congregation, their allurements to wandering thoughts, their theatrical appearance, are quite inconsistent with true devotion. *Secondly,* they spoil a church more than even pues: a western gallery, by concealing or blocking up that essential feature of a church, the Belfry arch; side galleries by cutting off the capitals of the piers, destroying Windows, and doing away with the beautiful effect and mystical signification of a Nave and two Aisles; and both, by involving the necessity of a lath and plaister coating in the underpart. *Thirdly,* they often loosen the walls, and weaken the piers, not only by the lateral pressure, but by causing large holes to be cut into the cores to support their timbers, and so render the building unsafe. *Fourthly,* they never were admitted into ancient churches, and are therefore an innovation: which alone is enough to condemn them. *Fifthly,* they arise entirely from an indisposition to build a sufficient number of churches, and the consequent necessity of packing too many worshippers in the same building. It is true that all these reasons do not apply to all cases, but are generally arguments against the system: and for particular cases many others might be added. For instance, sometimes they are so low and supported by such clumsy props, that they shut out those who sit below them from a view of the Priest and the Altar; besides being themselves close and unhealthy. Sometimes they are carried across the windows, necessarily obstructing some part of them, and often entirely blocking the lower part; sometimes, when used for children, the incessant moving of their feet on the hollow floor disturbs not

only the occupants of the galleries, but those who are under or near them. The system, in short, is radically bad: and therefore 'handsome Gothic panelling' in front, curiously carved legs, Tudor arches of support, and other like means which have been devised to palliate the evil, do in effect increase it, by shewing how incurable it is.

The little real increase of accommodation in them: how this is.
10. But there is another argument against them; which with some will tell more than any of the preceding. It is this: *the very trifling comparative gain of space* which they bring. Indeed it may safely be asserted that a Church, pued and galleried, does not contain so many as it would do, if supplied with open benches instead of both. A western gallery *is generally a cause of loss of room*: as it hinders the possibility of any worshippers finding a place in the Tower. It might however seem at first sight, that a side gallery, extending over an Aisle, would of necessity hold as many as the Aisle below: but this is a very great mistake. For one passage in an *Aisle* allows every worshipper access to his seat, because the seats are disposed at right angles to the passage: but in the gallery over this Aisle, since the seats are not at right angles to, but parallel with, the main passage, there must be in addition cross-passages (in the jargon of

Gangways.
modern church-builders, *gangways*) leading down from this main passage, between the separate rows of seats. The common practice is to have such a gangway between every five seats. It cannot be well less than two feet six inches in breadth. So that for every five seats, or seven feet six, there is a loss of two feet six, *or one fourth of the whole*. Add also the room occupied by the gallery staircase, the dark corners which it renders useless, the hot corners which it renders insupportable, the room required for its supports, (if it does not rest on the piers) and other drawbacks of a similar kind: and the gain of an open gallery will be very trifling, while that of a pued gallery will be next to nothing. It must be remembered that these remarks do not apply to those wretched proprietary chapels which are built on purpose to have galleries:—for here the staircases and other necessary appurtenances are stowed away in a "lobby," so as not to occupy "available space:" but in a church this is impossible.

Barbarous methods of enlarging a church.
11. It is to be hoped, in the present improving state of Ecclesiastical knowledge, some of the more barbarous ways of church enlargement practised by our fathers, would no longer be thought of. Since the Church Commissioners have not adopted the revised instructions of the Incorporated Society, it is necessary to speak against some of the worst ways of providing church accommodation, which are still sanctioned by their rules.

12. One is, the entire *gutting* of a church, by the removal of Piers and Pier-arches: bracing up the roof with iron, and supporting it, and the galleries, on cast iron pillars: the latter being in some cases turned to a further use, as gaspipes. And sometimes the builder has found it necessary to treat only half a church in this way: thereby leaving part of the sacred building to bear witness against his proceedings: and fearfully contrasting the old and the new methods of serving GOD. I could point to an instance where this has been done without even the miserable excuse of increase of room: but simply for the purpose of enabling the squire to erect a gallery, where he should be seen, and see better than would be the case when pues intervened between him and the congregation. To protest against so atrocious a system is, I would hope, almost needless.

Gutting it.

13. Another method which cannot be too strongly reprobated is the lengthening some particular part of a church, as the Chancel eastward, or the Nave westward. That there is a proportion observed between every part of an ancient church is an unquestionable fact; we feel and know it to be so, though we cannot at present explain its rules, nor analyse its principles. This is of course entirely lost when recourse is had to the last mentioned plan.

Lengthening Chancel or Nave.

14. In now speaking of the manner in which a church is to be enlarged, we must divide all churches into two classes: the one, where future enlargment *was*, the other where it *was not*, intended. The first will comprise those with, 1. Chancel, Nave, with or without a western Tower: 2. Chancel, Nave, one Aisle, 3. Chancel, Nave, Aisles, central Tower. The other will contain all except these.

Divisions into Churches designed and not designed, for enlargment.

15. Churches with Chancel and Nave afford great scope for improvement by enlargement. We have here to measure out an Aisle, on one, or on each side, making the breadth not less than a third, nor more than an half that of the Nave: and placing the new Piers in the line of the old wall. The windows, if ancient, may be removed into the Aisles: the roof of the Nave need not be touched; and the accommodation of the church will nearly be doubled. It may be better to have distinct roofs for each Aisle: though in cases where one only is added, a span-roof is very admissible: the exterior width of the Aisle being of course, very low. As a clerestory is unattainable in this kind of enlargement, the exterior should be plain and simple: pinnacles, pierced battlements, and the like, agreeing

Churches with Chancel and Nave.

better with a. clerestoried building. Where any one Aisle is added, it should be on the South side; and there should, in all cases, be a South Porch, its position being in the Westernmost bay but one. The style of the Piers may safely be left to the Architect, with the proviso that they be not earlier than the rest of the church. Where the founder (as is sometimes the case) has left arches of construction in the wall to become the future Pier-arches, they will of course be carefully followed.

Chancel, Nave, one Aisle.
16. The case is even easier where we have *Chancel, Nave, one Aisle :* for here another Aisle may be thrown out, which may, and perhaps in most cases had better, be an exact copy of the former. But where the original Aisle had massy Norman Piers, and room is of very great consequence, the new Aisle may well have later, and therefore lighter Piers. This also may be the case where it is wished to bestow more of decoration on the addition, than a mere copy of the original would admit. It is surprising how many of such one-aisled churches exist: and how seldom has their enlargement been attempted in this most easy and natural manner.

Chancel, Nave, Central Tower, with or without Aisles.
17. *Chancel, Nave; Central Tower with or without Aisles.* Here it is plain that Transepts were designed by the founder: and Transepts, therefore, should be added, though by no means under ordinary cases, a desirable method of increasing Church accommodation. They not only involve a serious difficulty in the method of arranging seats: but they render it excessively troublesome for the worshippers in them to take part with the rest of the congregation in Divine Worship. I have had occasion to mention this before: and if it be unadvisable to attempt Transepts, or rather what we call by courtesy Transepts, in modern churches, much more is it so in en-

Transepts objectionable.
larging ancient ones. For here the original plan and figure of the church is entirely lost. Modern Transepts are indeed quite different things, and serve a perfectly different end from those of former times. They are used as porticoes, or rather lobbies, and have invariably an entrance at the end, which ought never to be. It is not so much their want of projection, for many fine ancient examples project little, and some not at all, beyond the Aisles : witness S. Mary, Redcliff. But their excessive breadth is one distinguishing feature : and a still more remarkable one is, *that they project from the Aisles, and not from the Nave.*

Churches not designed for enlargement.
18. We will now take the case of a church not designed by its founder for future enlargement: and examine what is to be done in this case. It must be

confessed, that the experiment is a dangerous one: and one which only the most extreme necessity would justify. Wherever it occurs, the most strenuous efforts should be made to provide an additional chapel:—A method which our ancestors would have followed, had they not rather chosen to pull down the whole church, and to build it on a new and more magnificent scale. The latter plan, to which we owe many of our finest buildings, is of course, in these days, the very last which I should recommend. And here it is proper to remember, if it be at all times a solemn thing to have to do with the building or reparation of the House of God, much more is it so, when that House is one which we have received as a rich heir-loom from our ancestors, and which we are bound to transmit, at least *as* we received it, to our posterity. In this case, the unnecessary mutilation of the building is not only an offence against Him, but is an act of base ingratitude to them.

19. If however the dangerous experiment must be tried, I will suggest one or two of the best methods of carrying it into execution. Much must depend on the particular character of the church, much on its size, and something on the nature of the ground as to which it may be best to adopt. It must always be borne in mind that nothing is more deceptive than the appearance of a proposed addition in an architect's drawing: and if implicit reliance be placed on this, great may be the disappointment, when the addition stands forth, joined indeed to the church, but not a part of it, and not only is the difference between ancient and modern work plainly perceptable, but it is evident that the latter never could have been a part of the former.

Enlargement by addition of.

20. One method which may be adopted, is the addition of a North or South chapel, or both, to the Chancel. There are many precedents for this; and three Eastern gables, if well managed, give considerable dignity to a church. Yet in this case, there ought to be a parclose, or carved screen between the Chancel and its Aisles; otherwise the former is but too likely to be made a place of common resort. This plan is peculiarly advisable in a church of considerable length, more especially in one which possesses a central Tower.

1. A North or South chapel to Chancel.

21. Another method, which may be adopted when the church is of considerable length, is the addition of another North and South Aisle to the Nave. This practise, which is of perpetual occurrence abroad, does not want authority in England: and Chichester Cathedral, and Kendal church may be quoted as examples. S. Peter's at Leeds, is a modern instance. It is however attended with great difficulties, more espe-

2. By having double Aisles to the Nave.

cially as respects the roof: and may be considered the last allowable
resource of church enlargers. We have, in another place, hinted
that this method ought to be pursued with respect to Great S. Mary's
at Cambridge.

22. In concluding our remarks on church enlarge-
Reverence in workmen. ment, we may drop a hint on the extreme importance of
instilling reverence into the mind of the workmen who
may be employed therein. The Cambridge Camden Society has published a broad sheet on the subject, one or two copies of which are intended to be pasted up when a church is under repair. It has
published a similar sheet for the same purpose in churches which are
in progress of building. When we remember the usual course of
church restoration, for instance the using the Altar for a drawing-
table or workbench, this caution will not be deemed needless.

23. In speaking of the repairing of a church, where
Church repara-tion. enlargement is not necessary, I assume that the removal
of pues and galleries is felt to be a duty: but that the
clergyman wishes, in the course of the long and protracted battle which
must necessarily precede so happy a victory, to set to work on some
other restoration, easier in itself, and which by its evident beauty,
may win men's minds to go along with him in his more startling
schemes. And it is the more important to speak on this subject,
What to begin with. because the work is so often undertaken at the wrong end.
I have known a large sum of money expended in tawdry
painted glass, while a glorious old door, with exquisite
mouldings, and a fine window with delicate tracery were allowed to go
to ruin, though they might have been preserved at less expence. I have
known a fine window cut away to insert in the vacancy a wretched
transparency, a disgrace to any church. I have known an East window suffered to decay, while some stained deal frippery has been
erected in the shape of an Altar screen. And to mention one instance
by name: what but the taste of the eighteenth century would have
blocked up the Altar window of S. Mary Redcliffe for the purpose of
admitting that large picture of Hogarth's? In all these cases the
donors, doubtless, considered themselves great benefactors to the
church: and in some have considered the deed worthy of record, and
have gloried in setting their names to it. To prevent such fatal mistakes, such a worse than misapplication of money, and to put a stop
to less flagrant, but still crying evils of the kind, is a task well deserving our utmost labour.

24. The first thing to be done is scrupulously to
Restoration of original ar-rangements. restore all the original arrangements of the church, if it
be possible. And by saying, *if it be possible*, I do not
mean to insinuate a doubt of its being eventually in

every Clergyman's power to restore them all: if only he will set perseveringly, and fearlessly, and trustfully, and unflinchingly about it. But what I mean is this: that sometimes he must be content to wait for some of the most desirable changes, such as the removal of pues: and therefore some improvements in themselves of far less importance may fairly be undertaken first, as the means of filling up the time, and smoothing the way. Still the great object must constantly be kept in view: a pue may often be demolished here, or lowered there, a word spoken, a Tract given, against them, all tending to expedite the matter, locks may be taken off: parishioners informed that with the Churchwardens' leave they may worship in any empty, or unfilled pue: Dissenters warned that if they do not occupy (what they are pleased to call) their own pues, others will: and above all, since practice goes further than precept, the Clergyman may lose no time in destroying his own pue, and putting his family into an open seat.

25. There is, I am perfectly aware, great danger in *What distinction is meant by necessary and ornamental restorations.* drawing a distinction between necessary and ornamental repairs: because nothing that gives ornament to the House of God ought ever to be spoken of as unnecessary. I employ the words on the present occasion simply in a comparative sense, meaning thereby to distinguish between restorations more or less essential to the being, not more or less necessary to the well-being, of a church. A church is not as it should be, till *every* window is filled with stained glass, till every inch of floor is covered with encaustic tiles, till there is a Roodscreen glowing with the brightest tints and with gold, nay, if we would arrive at perfection, the roof and walls must be painted and frescoed. For it may safely be asserted that ancient churches in general were so adorned: and these decorations are the more appropriate, because they are chiefly and almost exclusively ecclesiastical. Yet because all these things are necessary to perfection, it does not follow that we may begin our restorations promiscuously with any one that we please. By commencing at the wrong end, we lay ourselves open, *Examples.* not to say it irreverently, to the charge: ' These things ought ye to have done, and not to leave the other undone.' Every one would feel it an absurdity to begin the restoration of a church which had not a Font, by frescoing the walls ; or laying the pavement with encaustic tiles. And is it less really absurd to present the stained glass for an East-window while the roof is cieled, or to present Altar-plate while a miserable deal table serves as the Altar ? And yet how often does one hear of such things, and hear of them too, in terms of approbation.

26. Stained glass is a very favourite gift, in all con-*Stained glass.* ditions of a church. I do not wish to speak harshly of

those who are contributing to the honour of the Sanctuary, but I cannot help fearing that the showiness of the present has something to do with the frequency of its selection. If, for example, a decayed window were carefully restored, or a magnificent door repaired, in a few years all traces of the restoration would be lost, from the softening of the new work into the old; and the name of the restorer would consequently be forgotten by men. The case is different with a present of stained glass, the name of the donor being long held in memory. Far be it from me to say, that there is no piety in church restoration, even when debased by such a motive as this: I only say that it much detracts from the merit of the deed, and that it probably would not be owned, nor it may be, consciously felt, by many who are in reality influenced by it.

27. I entreat therefore such persons as are meditating any benefaction to the House of GOD to make it decent, before they make it comely. The very title of our Homily on that subject reads an excellent lesson. *Of* (1) REPAIRING *and* (2) KEEPING CLEAN, *and* (when all this has been done) (3) *comely adorning of churches*. Imagine the restoration of a ruined cottage commenced by filling the windows with stained glass! And yet—I could almost say it with tears—I have seen churches which for damp, filth, and ruin, are worse off than a habitable English cottage; where there is ingress for birds and loathsome reptiles, and the Altar is defiled by the one, and the corners and pues tenanted by the other: and where abominations are permitted around the walls, and sometimes even in the belfry, which heathens would have trembled to be guilty of in their temples.

Not to be the first thing.

28. I am most willing to allow that a clergyman, by way of shewing what a church ought to be, may fairly proceed to bestow on his Chancel the richest ornament of which it is capable, even should he be unable to induce the Parish to make even necessary repairs, as that part of the church which they are bound to preserve. But few seem to be aware of what is meant by decency in a church. I have often been struck with seeing clergymen, whom I have known to be zealous for GOD's honour, point out some elaborate sedilia, or beautiful tomb, perishing through age, or destroyed through Puritan wickedness, and descant on their beauties in a manner that shewed them possessed of feeling as well as taste, yet apparently never have thought of restoring or renewing them. In effigies more especially, this is the case. Many will execrate the hands that mutilated a figure in brass; yet who thinks of sending for alabaster for the one, or applying to the engraver for the production of the pieces necessary for the restoration

Chancel may be completely restored first.

of the other? How often do we see the hands of some beautiful figure sawn off! and yet I never saw a restoration attempted in this case, though it would be so very easy. How often is the canopy of some magnificent brass imperfect, when a very trifling expense would restore it to its original beauty.

29. The question then arises, What is necessary for decency in a Chancel? And the following questions may help to set the matter in a clearer light.

Is there a proper course of drain-tiles round it, with a correspondence of eaves and gutters above?

• Questions, involving *complete* restoration.
Is the whole of the stone-work in the interior, piers, if there are any, sedilia, piscina, Easter sepulchre, window-sills, jambs, tracery, shafts, chancel-arch, monuments, free from white-wash or paint, stucco, and in good and sound condition?

Is any deficiency supplied with Roman or other cement? (which is almost worse than leaving it unsupplied.)

Is the roof free from all cieling and lath and plaster-work?

Is every beam distinctly visible from below?

Is all the wood employed in it or otherwise, oak or chestnut?

Is any deception practised, (a kind of architectural hypocrisy) by graining deal to look like oak, and the like?

Is the Roodscreen with the doors perfect?

Is the Priest's door perfect, of oak, with well-worked stancheons, and only used for the entrance and egress of the Priest?

Is the Altar, of stone, if not, of costly wood?

Are there Altar-cloths, a napkin, 'fair linen,' and other things necessary for the Holy Mysteries?

Are there suitable vessels for them, of silver at the least, and Altar candlesticks?

Is there a Table of Prothesis or credence in the shape of a bracket, recess, or otherwise?

Is all the exterior work, parapet, pinnacles, pierced battlements, crockets, &c. perfect; the decays resulting from the weather duly restored?

Is there a cross at the East end? and this not, as is too often the case, *plain*, (which involves both an architectural and religious solecism,) but floriated?

Is the roof of some superior material to common slate or red tiles,—such as grey slate, lead, shingles, or Hersham slate? Is the floor laid throughout with encaustic tiles, those towards the East end at least being glazed?

Is there any cement or composition or whitewash on the outside? (The only possible exception to an universal condemnation of these articles is, that *whitewash* may *perhaps* be *allowed* over *rubble* in the *interior*.)

Is any part restored with brick?

30. If all these questions can be answered favourably, then any additional money may be laid out in stained glass: but *till they are,* it should not be thought of. And how few, how very few are the churches in which such an answer could be given! It may be proper to observe, that it is a widely different case where ancient stained glass is in question: here its preservation should be made one of the earliest subjects of anxiety.

Practical diffi-culties.   31. There are several practical difficulties in the arrangement of an ancient church, which,—though I firmly believe that a more self-denying age would think little of them—are nevertheless in the present state of things, real difficulties; and if I may be allowed the expression, *tease* a clergy-man far more than things of much higher moment. So many ap-plications are continually made to us on the subject, that it may be well to devote a few more words to it than it may, in the opinion of some, seem to merit.

Position of organ.   32. The position of the organ is one of the things which is often a great trouble. Nine-tenths of the organs in this kingdom stand in a Western gallery. This, of course, falls under the condemnation we have agreed to pronounce on all galleries: and there are many other objections to this position, whether for organ or singers. In country Not in West-ern gallery : churches, the singing loft, during the performance of the Psalm or Hymn, becomes the cynosure of all eyes: the worshippers, or they who should be such, generally turn to it as to a center of attraction. Messages, too, pass during the time of Divine Service between the "first violin" and the clerk, if that anomolous personage be employed, and the noise on the gallery stairs frequently overpowers every other sound. Then, what can be more ludicrous than the slate suspended in front of the gallery, stamped with the letters AN. or PS.? Nothing, too, can be worse as respects the singers themselves. Removed too great distance from the clergyman's eye, having a separate entrance to their seats, and why. possessed of strong *esprit du corps*, and feeling or thinking themselves indispensable to the performance of a cer-tain part of public worship, and too often, alas! privileged to decide what that part shall be, — what wonder if they generally acquire those feelings of independence and pride, which make the singers some of the worst members of the parish. The radicalism both of singers and of bell-ringers is notorious. And where women-singers are allowed, and part-anthems sung, the notice which they attract from their station in front of the gallery might well enough befit a theatre, but is highly indecorous in the House of God.

33. Add to which that we have here a striking instance of the perverseness of modern times. None ought to be in the Chancel but they who are taking an actual part in the performance of the Divine Office, *and they ought.* Now not only are all kinds of people admitted into, or even stationed in the Chancel, but they who ought to be there, namely the singers, are removed as far as possible from it. That the singing in a church would be materially improved by a separation of the voices from the music is an inferior argument, but with some may have its due weight.

Those who are engaged in the Divine Office should be in the Chancel.

34. In other churches, the organ is in one of the Transepts; which position, though it does not block an arch, as the other does, conceals one, if not more windows, and has all the other objections of the first named plan. And others again have the organ over the vestry: both forming a kind of side chapel to the Chancel. This is a practice recently introduced, and adopted in two churches where great pains have been taken to obtain a Catholic arrangement. But I cannot recommend it. Besides its want of authority, another objection is, that it gives the Sacristy, which if it ever exists, should be very small, a most undue prominence, and makes it open to the Chancel by an arch, whereas it should open by a door. It would be better, if any position of this kind were thought of, to place it in an open parvise over the Porch: though this arrangement would still be liable to the first objection.

Not in the Transepts;

nor over Sacristy.

35. Another position still remains to be noticed: that adopted in most of our Cathedrals, and in some of our large parish churches: namely, between the Chancel and Nave. Now I willingly allow that this position has, in the case of our Cathedrals, been attended with some happy practical results: namely, the preservation of the Roodscreen, and the practical separation of the Choir from the Nave. This distinction, though it may seem, in the present state of things, of little consequence, may yet be of essential service when the separation of the laity from the Clergy is again insisted on. But it has led to lamentable consequences, in

Between Nave and Chancel.

the total uselessness into which the Naves have fallen, and the great disfigurement of the whole effect of the Cathedral, in cutting the vista short by the organ. And the arrangement is never, or very seldom, in use in parish churches, except where, as at Beverley, and Tewkesbury, and Selby, the Choir is the only part used for service.

36. It follows then, that the best place for an organ is on the floor. This is opposed by an inveterate, but foolish prejudice: the sound is not at all affected thereby; and indeed is likely to be superior to that which issues from the confined apartments in which some organs are pent.

Proper position, on the floor.

37. Another point, concerning which enquiry is often made, is the best method of lighting a church. With a protest against the modern practice of evening services, I may proceed to observe, that of all methods, that by gas appears to me the most objectionable. There is an artificialness, and luxury, aud glare about it, ill suiting to the sobriety and solemnity of a Temple of GOD: it involves a necessity of laying pipes in all directions, and pulling about the sacred walls very frequently: it leads to the introduction of hideous gas-holders: it can never be made perfectly safe: it must always be *uncertain*—almost every one has heard of instances where churches have been left in total darkness; the pipes are generally made to run up the piers, concealed in channels cut in the masonry; with all manner of ingenious contrivances for hiding a pipe here, and a meter there: than which nothing is more at variance with the principles of reality which it has always been our great aim to inculcate. Wax lights, disposed in standards are far less objectionable: and in small or poor churches may do well enough. But the proper method is the use of Chandeliers, (*Coronæ lucis* as they used to be called) filled with wax lights, and admitting the most delicate and beautiful carving.

Modes of lighting.

Gas, why inadmissible.

Chandeliers, or Coronæ.

38. The fence for the churchyard should, in towns, be of stone: in the country an oak paling, or even a hedge, may also be employed. But cast iron rails are carefully to be avoided: indeed in the whole furniture of a church, nothing made by casting can possibly be allowed. Metals, even for the meanest uses, such as stancheons, door-plates, &c. should be *carved.*

Churchyard enclosure.

39. We will lastly consider—and it is a very important subject—the best method of warming a church. It may seem regardless of the poor, it may seem a sacrifice of necessity to ornament: it may seem an impossible recommendation, but I still say it, and that with the fullest conviction that I am speaking not more for the church than for the worshippers,—DO WITHOUT A STOVE. For, *firstly*, a stove of whatever shape or kind is a great disfigurement to a church. *Secondly*, it must either stand in the middle of one of the passages, in which case it will block up and incommode the way, or it must occupy a space sufficient to accommodate at least eight or ten people, since none can sit close to a stove without running the risk of being burnt, or suffocated, or both. *Thirdly*, stoves not only diffuse an unequal and an uncertain warmth, but they are unwholesome and unsafe. *Fourthly*, they require either a concealed flue under the floor, or a frightful iron pipe to convey the smoke above. Now the former of these cases is liable to the objections urged against gas, and generally against all concealed and disguised constructions ; in the latter, the funnel must be carried either through the roof, a window, or a wall. In the first case the danger from fire is very great ; in the next, it causes a grievous and unsightly mutilation ; in the last, it weakens and discolours the walls. *Patent chunk* stoves, and the rest of the inventions, happily enough eulogized by the makers as fitted for assembly rooms, dissenting 'chapels,' or churches, are hideous in themselves, and never give much heat, except when they happen to set the building on fire. *Fifthly*, a stove is often a mere excuse to counteract damp, loose doors, decayed windows, and chinks in walls, which ought to be remedied in a very different as well as much more effectual way ; for persons exposed to cold draughts in a hot building, and afterwards coming out suddenly into the cold air, are much more liable to harm than those who have to sit without any fire at all. *Lastly*, 'What man has done, man may do." It is an undeniable fact, that up to the Restoration there were no fires in churches, and the winters were then at least as severe as now.

(margin: Method of warming a church.)

(margin: Stoves, why not to be used.)

40. When the doors and windows of a church are made to fasten tightly, and to shut closely, when pues are removed which prevent a free circulation of air, when the church is kept thoroughly dry. When the air is admitted freely, much will be done towards warming the building. Much more will be done when it is crowded twice a day for Daily Service. A church tolerably well attended is never cold on Monday morning : why need it be on any other morning ? It was by means like these that our ancestors and foreign Catholics were and are enabled to do without fires. The use of incense also tended to dry and warm the

(margin: How to be warmed.)

air: and this, it is matter of fact, was discontinued only in the great rebellion. Finally, our ancestors were more self-denying than we: they did not go to church to be comfortable, but to pray: for that they did occasionally feel the cold is evident from the use of the *pomander*, a vessel in the shape of a silver apple full of hot water, which enabled the officiating priest, in bitter weather to warm his hands, that he might be able to grasp the Chalice securely.

Conclusion. 42. Thus then, I conclude these hints: under the hope, that if they appear trifling to some, they may not be without use in affording advice on the best methods of church enlargement and church arrangements to the parish priest.